First Births In America

STUDIES IN DEMOGRAPHY

General Editors
Eugene A. Hammel
Ronald D. Lee
Kenneth W. Wachter

FIRST BIRTHS IN AMERICA

IN AMERICA

Changes In The Timing of Parenthood

Ronald R. Rindfuss
S. Philip Morgan
Gray Swicegood

University of California Press / *Berkeley, Los Angeles, London*

University of California Press
Berkeley and Los Angeles, California

University of California Press, Ltd.
London, England

Library of Congress Cataloging-in-Publication Data

Rindfuss, Ronald R., 1946–

  First Births in America.

  (Studies in demography)
  Bibliography: p.
  Includes index.
  1. Family demography. 2. Parenthood. I. Morgan,
S. Philip, 1953– II. Swicegood, Gray, 1950–   .
III. Title. IV. Series: Studies in demography
(Berkeley, Calif.)
HQ759.98.R56   1988   306.8'74   87–5073
ISBN 0–520–05907–7 (alk. paper)

Printed in the United States of America

1 2 3 4 5 6 7 8 9

Contents

Preface

When we began the research reported in this book, a *Time* magazine cover story on the "New Baby Bloom" suggested that there was a substantial increase in the number of women in their thirties becoming mothers for the first time. At about the same time, the *Wall Street Journal* featured a front-page article describing the increase in the number of older women becoming mothers, and the article went on with a not very subtle warning about the implications of hiring women for positions of corporate importance.

As we completed this project, *Newsweek* ran a cover story titled "No Baby Aboard," which notes that not since the Depression have so many women remained childless. "More and more couples are painting a new kind of American family portrait—one with just two faces, the husband's and the wife's."

Which is it, a "bloom" or a "bust"? As we show in this book, the answer is both—both cover stories are right. The past 15 years have simultaneously witnessed a "bloom" and a "bust." In brief, more older parents and more childless persons are the twin outcomes of substantial fertility delay at younger ages. There are now many more people at risk of becoming parents in their thirties because so many more women and men postponed fertility while they were in their teens and twenties. Thus an explanation of either the "bloom" or the "bust" hinges on what has happened at younger ages.

We examine the substantial changes in parenthood timing that have occurred in the United States in the twentieth century, and the determinants of such changes. We address such questions as: Are current trends and patterns revolutionary, or do they have historical precedents? Are these patterns and trends similar to those in other developed countries?

What socioeconomic conditions promote early and late parenthood? Are these factors likely to change in a secular or cyclical manner? Have trends in parenthood timing been similar for different socioeconomic, religious, and racial groups?

We view the transition to parenthood as a process that unfolds in conjunction with other aspects of the life course. This life course, in turn, is strongly conditioned by the broader social context in which the individual is embedded. Thus activities that compete with childbearing, such as full-time schooling and work, should promote parenthood delay. Of course the extent to which this is true may depend on the social context, as represented by the time period and by different cultural settings.

Before delving further into our subject, some acknowledgments are in order. Like all research projects, this one has its own distinctive history, with a number of institutions and individuals making important contributions. The project began in early 1981 when Rindfuss and Morgan wrote a proposal to examine the new trend toward delayed childbearing. At that point and during the first year of the project, Morgan was supported by a postdoctoral fellowship with funding from the National Institute of Child Health and Human Development (NICHD). After approximately a nine-month gestation period, NICHD funded the project (NO1-HD-12823). Swicegood joined the project in July 1982 when he came to the Carolina Population Center, University of North Carolina at Chapel Hill, as a postdoctoral fellow supported by NICHD funds. We are extremely grateful to NICHD for its support.

The majority of the research reported here was conducted while all three authors were affiliated with the University of North Carolina at Chapel Hill, and we wish to thank that university and particularly the Carolina Population Center for its support. In addition, Morgan moved to the University of Georgia in 1983 and to the University of Pennsylvania in 1984. Swicegood moved to the University of Illinois in 1984. These three institutions have been supportive of the project as well.

This project also benefited tremendously from the assistance of others. Among these, clearly the most central and important is Erika M. Stone, who was responsible for the complex computer programming and file management that was imperative for a project of this scope. Irma Timberlake joined the staff in the middle of the project and has done an admirable job managing the word-processing aspects. Linda Thompson prepared the final drawings for all the figures. Lynn Igoe did her usual excellent editing of the manuscript. Further, many staff members at the Carolina Population Center have been extremely helpful.

Several other individuals provided valuable assistance at various stages of the project. Allan Parnell is a coauthor for chapter 7, which contrasts first-birth timing in the United States and Japan. David Bloom provided the time series data for many of the European countries used in chapter 4, and Dan Crawford provided extensive assistance in examining these data.

Portions of chapter 5 are based on Ronald R. Rindfuss, S. Philip Morgan, and C. Gray Swicegood, "The Transition to Motherhood: The Intersection of Structural and Temporal Dimensions," *American Sociological Review* 49:359–372, used here with permission of the American Sociological Association. Portions of chapter 7 are based on S. Philip Morgan, Ronald R. Rindfuss, and Allan Parnell, "Modern Fertility Patterns: Contrasts Between the United States and Japan," *Population and Development Review* 10:19–40, used here with permission of the Population Council. Table 15 is borrowed from Finis Welch, "Affirmative Action and Its Enforcement," *American Economic Review* 71:127–133, used here with permission of the American Economic Association. Table 16 is based on table 4.1 in Reynolds Farley, *Blacks and Whites: Narrowing the Gap*, 1984, used here with permission of Harvard University Press.

Numerous colleagues have read all or portions of the manuscript and provided comments. We are grateful for their suggestions—even if we did not always follow them. Judith Blake, Larry Bumpass, Peter Donaldson, Barbara Entwisle, and Dennis Hogan read the entire manuscript and provided valuable comments. In addition, the following gave comments on one or more chapters: Mokata Nohara Atoh, Frank D. Bean, David Bloom, Urie Bronfenbrenner, Glen Elder, David Featherman, Thomas Frijka, Frank Furstenberg, Omer Galle, David Guilkey, Kiyosi Hirosima, Hiroshi Kojima, Diane Lye, Naohiro Ogawa, Shigesata Pakahashi, Samuel Preston, Norman Ryder, Robert Schoen, Elizabeth Hervey Stephen, Gillian Stevens, Stewart Tolnay, J. Richard Udry, Audrey Vanden Heuvel, and Susan Watkins.

1

Introduction

Because a society's survival depends on its members' reproduction, incentives to bear children are ingrained into all surviving societies. In high mortality contexts high fertility is required. But even high levels of fertility are well below the maximum possible levels (see Bongaarts 1975), allowing for a broad range of societal solutions. In preindustrial Europe, for instance, marriage was often quite late and spinsterhood was common (Watkins 1981, 1984). But marital fertility was high, compensating for the fertile years spent outside of marriage. In Asia and Africa, marriage was early and nearly universal, but marital fertility was lower than in Western Europe. Within the broad spectrum of the Third World, the World Fertility Surveys of the past decade document a wide array of societal strategies that produce high fertility (see Bongaarts and Potter 1983).

Similarly under a low-mortality regime, a range of possible fertility patterns exists. All women could become mothers and family size could be universally low. Or, there could be larger numbers of children born to fewer women. Both combinations produce low aggregate fertility. Empirically, large families are becoming increasingly rare. The usual explanation involves the high childbearing and rearing costs which parents assume in modern contexts. Other features of modern fertility show greater variability—specifically, the prevalence, timing, and sequencing of parenthood vary across today's developed nations, across periods or cohorts, and within countries by region, urban-rural residence, education, ethnicity, and other characteristics. In this monograph, we examine the trends in and determinants of the initiation of American childbearing in the twentieth century.

THE TRANSITION TO PARENTHOOD

In modern societies, becoming a parent constitutes one of the most important role transitions of young adulthood. In Western developed nations, parents assume nearly total responsibility for their children with a "paucity of preparation" and a lack of accepted guidelines for successful parenthood (see Rossi 1968). In contrast, the transition to parenthood may have been easier in traditional societies. The obligations of parenthood could be assumed more gradually, often under the watchful eyes of coresident kin. As Kingsley Davis (1955) points out, adolescents in extended families were encouraged to bear children because they were not expected to assume the full economic and child care burden.

Unlike most other role transitions affecting a young person, permanence and continual obligations characterize modern parenthood. While there is clearly variation in the support parents provide children, the permanence of the parent-child relationship prevails. In contrast, individuals often change their job and residence. We typically view military service as temporary. While saying "till death do us part," companionship and personal happiness are replacing permanence and commitment at the core of marriage (Swidler 1983). In fact, marriages are increasingly more likely to end with marital disruption than death of one of the spouses (Preston and McDonald 1979). As Rossi (1968:32) phrases it, parenthood is irrevocable: "We can have ex-spouses and ex-jobs but not ex-children." This situation is more likely to be true for mothers than fathers. Following marital disruption, most children live with their mothers, many see their fathers infrequently, and many do not receive any financial support from their fathers (Furstenberg et al. 1983; Weitzman 1985). Yet, even for men, parenthood is one of the most permanent commitments in modern American society.

To justify further the focus on the timing and prevalence of parenthood, there are a wide range of important consequences at the individual, institutional, and societal level. At the individual level, parenthood has consequences for the other roles one can occupy. In traditional societies where women married early and bore children over much of their lives, bearing and rearing children was the primary adult task of women, their principal adult role, and often their only avenue to status. By contrast, in the typical developed Western society, a woman can occupy numerous adult roles either simultaneously or sequentially. Childbearing and rearing consume only a small proportion of the adult years (see Davis and van den Oever 1982). How individuals time and sequence transitions in adulthood is one of our concerns in this monograph.

The transition to parenthood also affects a range of institutional behavior. Marriage and the family are certainly affected. Later parenthood and nonparenthood are associated with more egalitarian relations and reduced role differentiation between spouses (Gerson 1985; Walter 1986). Marital disruption is more common among couples who delay childbearing (Haggstrom et al. 1984; Morgan and Rindfuss 1985). Delayed parenthood and childlessness affect the workplace by allowing women the opportunity to work and compete for jobs that parenthood might preclude. Finally, parenthood pushes many into community and religious activities, and may influence the type and intensity of political involvement (Haggstrom et al. 1984).

Effects at the societal level exist as well. Change in the timing of parenthood largely determines the level of fertility in any time period, which in turn determines the size of new cohorts. Changing cohort size has implications for a range of age-graded institutions—from educational systems to retirement systems. Moreover, change in the timing and prevalence of parenthood can influence the relative degree of equality between men and women. Swafford (1978) points out that despite a number of policies that should create greater sexual equality, women's wages in the Soviet Union are only 70 percent of men's. Women's family roles, as childbearer and rearer, handicap them in the workplace. Gove and Hughes (1979) claim that women's demanding parental roles and their care of other sick family members lead to their higher morbidity levels and greater absenteeism. Later parenthood allows women to achieve nonfamilial roles heretofore unattainable not just because of overt discrimination, but because of the additional burdens and obligations motherhood entails.

THEORETICAL AND METHODOLOGICAL HERITAGE

The life course or life cycle perspective occupies a central role in our research (Elder 1974, 1985; Hogan 1981; Modell, Furstenberg, and Hershberg 1976; Riley, Johnson, and Foner 1972; Winsborough 1978). As Clausen (1972:459) describes it, this perspective emphasizes the sequence, timing, and ordering of roles and "the personality development, identity and the psychological dynamics" associated with role incumbency and progression. Some roles are linked to others; for instance, one usually cannot enter graduate school without first successfully completing an undergraduate education. The life course consists of several such sets of interlocking roles: student roles, family roles, career roles, community roles. Within a set, roles are likely to be closely linked, but across sets links are more tenuous. Nevertheless, a marked change in one set is likely to affect others. The timing, sequencing, and reversibility of life events and transitions are essential in understanding a single event, such as becoming a parent, and they have important implications for subsequent events in that individual's life. Simply put, the past affects the present, and the present affects the future.

For our study, role succession and role complementarity are important concepts. A given set of roles places one on a life course trajectory that tends to have a momentum of its own. Doing well in high school greatly enhances the chance of attending college, and strong college performance opens the doors to graduate or professional school. As many earlier studies have shown, such a trajectory is associated with late marriage and childbearing since student and spouse-parent roles are time demanding and, therefore, somewhat incompatible (Kasarda, Billy, and West 1986). Poor school performance, however, closes these other options and reduces the opportunity costs of early parenthood. Consistent with this argument, note that poor school performance is strongly associated with early sexual activity and teenage childbearing (Jessor and Jessor 1977). Likewise at older ages, job dissatisfaction can cause women to veer their life course toward domesticity and parenthood (Gerson 1985).

Social science research contains numerous examples of how the unfolding life course is constrained by one's socioeconomic status and individual characteristics, and by the broader social context (see Bronfenbrenner 1979, 1985). The status attainment literature, for instance, makes it clear that educational attainment is dependent on parents' socioeconomic status (see Blau and Duncan 1967; Featherman and Hauser 1978). But independent of this parental influence, individual ability and initiative play a strong role in educational attainment (Jencks 1979). Further, a changed social context can influence the entire process. Featherman and Hauser (1978) argue that reduced discrimination against blacks across the late 1960s and early 1970s not only led to increased education for them but fundamentally altered the status attainment process for blacks. Specifically, the ability of black parents to transfer their socioeconomic gains to sons increased.

Although they have only recently begun to merge, the broader socio-logical life course or life cycle approach shares an intellectually similar framework with recent social demographic analysis, particularly the study of fertility. This demographic work began with the identification of the components of family building (such as trends in parity progression ratios) and with attempts to identify their determinants (e.g., Ryder 1969). Others analyzed the determinants of decision making at different parity transitions (e.g., Namboodiri 1974). This early family-building work made it clear that the importance of different socioeconomic factors changes across parity transitions. Recent work, including our own, makes it clear that the importance of various factors changes within different parities as time elapses. Part of the reason, of course, is that as time elapses, individuals change with respect to other aspects of the life course.

Similarly, we also continue and expand on the social demographic tradition of incorporating macro- and microexplanations in fertility analysis. The twentieth century has seen massive fluctuations in the timing and quantity of fertility. These fluctuations have been pervasive; they are found in every social and economic group (Rindfuss and Sweet 1977; Sweet and Rindfuss 1983). Thus, macrofactors that transcend individuals and the smaller social groups to which they belong must be operating. Yet, simultaneously, differentials across various racial, social, and eco-nomic groups have persisted throughout the twentieth century, under-scoring the importance of individual characteristics and membership in various social groups.

FERTILITY TIMING AND QUANTITY

Much of the original demographic interest in the timing of fertility in general, and specifically the timing of the first birth, stemmed from a desire to explain and predict fertility trends. Demographers of an earlier generation tended to be concerned with the number of children women were having. Aspects of the timing of fertility were treated as a nuisance. In fact, one of the major problems being addressed by demographers during the late 1940s and early 1950s was the separation of timing and number changes so that unambiguous conclusions could be reached re-garding the number of children people were having (e.g., Ryder 1956).

From these efforts to separate timing and number changes in U.S. period fertility trends emerged an important finding: changes in fertility timing played a major role in the fertility fluctuations that have occurred since World War II (e.g., Freedman 1962; Ryder 1969). More recent work by Ryder (1980a) identifies changes in first-birth timing, in particular, as having exerted the major impact on overall fertility trends in the United States. Tsui's (1984) results, based on Current Population Survey data, reinforce this point by documenting relative stability in the timing of later births given that a first birth has occurred. In particular, she shows the remarkable stability of second-birth intervals. Thus, at the aggregate level, interest in parenthood timing was intellectually driven by concern with the demographic determinants of the quantity of fertility.

At the microlevel, the link between timing of the transition to parenthood and quantity of fertility is also well established (Bumpass, Rindfuss, and Janosik 1978; Trussell and Menken 1978). Those who become mothers at a relatively young age have shorter interbirth intervals and ultimately have more children.[1]

ADOLESCENT FERTILITY

Over the last decade, a substantial amount of the demographic work on timing of the transition to parenthood has focused exclusively on adolescent fertility. In fact, this topic has received so much attention that Westoff, Calot, and Foster recently noted that adolescent fertility "bids to become a major subdiscipline of population studies" (1983:105). Justification for this focus lies with the substantial social problems associated with adolescent fertility. Campbell's (1968:238) often quoted passage mentions most of these problems:

The girl who has an illegitimate child at the age of 16 suddenly has 90 percent of her life's script written for her. She will probably drop out of school; even if someone else in her family helps to take care of the baby, she will probably not be able to find a steady job that pays enough to provide for herself and her child; she may feel impelled to marry someone she might not otherwise have chosen. Her life choices are few, and most of them are bad.

Recent work by Furstenberg, Brooks-Gunn, and Morgan (1987), however, shows great variability in the life script of unmarried, adolescent

[1]Some evidence suggests that the link between early childbearing and subsequent fertility is weakening (see Teachman and Heckert 1985), possibly because of greater use of abortion and sterilization among more recent cohorts.

mothers, but the negative correlates of very early childbearing are still apparent. Because it was perceived as a social problem by a very wide constituency, adolescent fertility attracted considerable academic and political attention in the 1970s and early 1980s. Educators were concerned that pregnant teenagers were being forced to drop out of school. The medical and public health communities were concerned about the elevated mortality and morbidity levels experienced by mother and child as a result of teenage parenthood. The professional social work community was alarmed about the high incidence of adolescent mothers on welfare rolls. Child psychologists questioned the ability of teenagers to be effective parents. Finally, although their motivations often differed, politicians from liberal and conservative viewpoints found the "adolescent pregnancy problem" to be a policy issue worth considering.

Overall, adolescent fertility rates are now higher in the United States than virtually all other developed countries (Westoff et al. 1983). Blacks are substantially more likely to become adolescent parents than whites, although the difference has narrowed in recent years. Mexican American and American Indians are also more likely to become adolescent parents than Anglos. Rural teenagers are more likely to become parents than urban teenagers. Women who physically mature earlier are also more likely to become adolescent parents. Finally, no matter how socioeconomic origins are measured, adolescent parenthood is more common among teenagers coming from lower socioeconomic origins.

Not only are these correlates well established but their causal ordering is also clear. These background characteristics are causally prior to adolescent fertility. Less well known are the causal mechanisms underlying these differences. For example, why have blacks consistently had higher rates of adolescent fertility than whites? Some of the intermediate mechanisms are known. Blacks mature physically earlier than whites (Udry and Cliquet 1982). Blacks initiate intercourse earlier than whites. Black teenagers have somewhat higher rates of coital frequency than white teenagers. Black teenagers are more likely to engage in unprotected coitus than white teenagers. However, the social mechanisms that lie behind these intermediate differences are more controversial (see Furstenberg et al. 1987).

Education and educational aspirations provide a good example. High educational levels are associated with low levels of adolescent fertility. One well-established cause of this relationship is that the time commitment required to bring high educational aspirations to fruition is not only extensive but also is widely recognized by teenagers. As a result, teenagers with high educational aspirations are likely to take a variety of actions to ensure that they do not become adolescent parents. It is also possible that causality operates in the opposite direction—and this has been the subject of considerable conjecture and dispute (e.g., Hofferth 1984; Hofferth and Moore 1979; Marini 1984*b*; Rindfuss, Bumpass, and St. John 1980). Basically the argument is that some teenage girls accidentally become pregnant and continue that pregnancy despite their having unmet educational aspirations. As a result of the pregnancy and birth of the child, their educational aspirations remain unfulfilled. Given the widely acknowledged incompatibility of the student role and the mother of young children role, such an explanation has widespread intuitive appeal. Our review of the evidence (Rindfuss, St. John, and Bumpass 1984) suggests that young women exercise more control over their lives than the scenario above implies. Leibowitz, Eisen, and Chow (1985), for instance, show that pregnant teenagers with high educational aspirations are more likely to choose an abortion than those with lower aspirations. Further, Furstenberg, Brooks-Gunn, and Morgan (1987) show that more educationally capable and motivated adolescents are more likely to remain in or return to school following their first birth. In sum, little evidence supports the contention that early parenthood has a major causal effect on educational attainment. We note, however, that the final word on this issue is probably not yet in, because most of the analyses rely on two-stage least squares type approaches which in turn require strong, and often questionable, theoretical assumptions. This issue of causality is one that will arise at numerous places throughout this monograph. In some instances it is not possible to conclude categorically that the relationships we observe are unidirectional. But we are able to deal more precisely with the issue in the longitudinal analyses that make up chapters 8 and 9.

The focus on adolescent fertility by American social demographers in the past decade has been important for our understanding of the determinants of fertility timing. This research has also been valuable to national and local policy discussions. However, the focus on adolescent fertility is somewhat arbitrary. There is nothing magical about one's twentieth birthday. In fact, the sixteenth, eighteenth, and thirtieth birthdays are probably more socially relevant. Relatively little is known about the determinants of the timing of fertility for those who reach age 20 childless. Yet at age 20, most individuals are still maturing socially and intellectually. They are still in the process of setting their adult life course. For certain types of career goals, entering the parent status at age 20 may be every bit as incompatible with the attainment of those goals as entering the parent role at age 16 would be for less demanding career goals. In short, we need to understand the determinants of the timing of the entry into parenthood for the entire age spectrum. Thus, even though many of our results are relevant to the adolescent fertility literature, it occupies only a portion of our concern. Rather, we focus on the entire age range: early, late, and "on time" parenthood.

DELAYED CHILDBEARING

The transition to parenthood at the other end of the age spectrum has also been singled out for attention in recent years. The number of women first becoming parents after age 30 or after age 35 has been steadily increasing and has caught the imagination of the media. Numerous newspaper and magazine stories have highlighted the issue. *Time* devoted a cover story to delayed parenthood, and Erma Bombeck has satirized it.

In addition to the media, the medical and business communities have expressed interest in the trend toward later parenthood. The medical concern centers on the increased risk of birth defects associated with advanced maternal age. Amniocentesis is routinely recommended for any pregnant woman past age 35, and sometimes for those past age 30. Since amniocentesis entails risk, is expensive, and requires sophisticated laboratory analysis, any increase in delayed childbearing is viewed with some concern.

Infertility (difficulty or inability to bear children) is a second medically related issue. Fecundity (reproductive potential) is widely acknowledged to decline with age, but the age at which the decline begins and its pace are not known. Studies based on historical populations suggest that fecundity begins falling sharply after age 35 (Bongaarts 1982; Menken 1985). A much publicized French study of women undergoing artificial insemination (Schwartz and Mayaux 1982) and data from the National Survey of Family Growth (Hendershot, Mosher, and Pratt 1982) suggest that fecundity begins declining in the late twenties and early thirties. These latter studies have been challenged on methodological grounds, but an editorial in the *New England Journal of Medicine* suggests that physicians should consider infertility when advising women on the best age to have children (DeCherney and Berkowitz 1982).

The concern in the business community has been very different and focuses on management. Consider women who are well established in their careers. They have often been trained at some expense to their employer, and typically are in a position of considerable responsibility within the corporation. The employers' concern arises because of the perceived incompatibility of the mother role and the career role. Such concerns have been reported repeatedly by *The Wall Street Journal* and other business-oriented publications. Often this concern is coupled with an implicit (and sometimes explicit) suggestion that women workers are unreliable and therefore ought not to be hired for positions of corporate authority. Note the following from a front page *Wall Street Journal* article:

They are the new dropouts. . . . The savvy that built careers sometimes proves inadequate when women return from maternity leave. Torn between loyalty to the company and responsibility for a child, they suffer fatigue and anxiety, making them less productive. Try as they might to slide back into the office groove, new priorities tug at their emotions. Some resolve the conflict by quitting (Towman 1983:1).

Our initial interest in research reported here stemmed from the question of delayed childbearing, and in particular from the sociological aspects of the question, How old is too old (Rindfuss and Bumpass 1978)? However, it soon became clear that an adequate explanation of delayed childbearing could not focus exclusively on delayed childbearers. Clearly one could not make the transition to parenthood at age 35 if one had already made the transition at any earlier age. This point is made formally in chapter 3; and in chapter 4 we show that there is much greater variability over time in childbearing rates at younger as opposed to older ages. The point to be made here is that an explanation of delayed childbearing must involve an explanation of why parenthood did not occur at younger ages.

The sociological work on the determinants of voluntary childlessness reinforces the argument that an understanding of either delayed childbearing or voluntary childlessness requires an understanding of the entire process of the transition to parenthood. This is perhaps ironic because most researchers initially interested in childlessness were interested in it as a number issue; that is, Why do some couples decide to have no children? Yet most researchers have moved to a timing explanation for this number question. The conclusions of those examining voluntary childlessness have been virtually unanimous: the voluntarily childless woman becomes childless by initially delaying the first birth, and then, after a number of years of delayed childbearing, deciding not to have any children. Thus our investigations of delayed childbearing and childlessness examine childbearing at all reproductive ages.

ON-TIME PARENTHOOD

Adolescent parenthood could be defined as births prior to age 18, 19, or 20—late parenthood as beginning at ages over 30 or 35. Adolescent and late parenthood are nonnormative events and have been singled out for much attention. We have recounted some of the reasons in the discussions above. Most Americans consider "on-time" parenthood as occurring sometime during a woman's twenties, give or take a few years. As demonstrated in subsequent chapters, this broad age span for normative parenthood is a distinctive feature of the modern American fertility pattern. Individuals are expected to delay parenthood until they are prepared to assume its obligations. This may imply saving money for expenses, acquiring a stable job, buying a home, or investing in education or training that will provide high and stable income in the future. Also, it may entail establishing a stable heterosexual relationship that is traditionally considered a prerequisite for parenthood.

On-time parenthood has received less attention than early and late parenthood, but has important implications nevertheless. First, family formation at these ages may be most sensitive to changing social and economic conditions (Namboodiri 1981). This greater responsiveness of on-time fertility coupled with most births occurring to women in their twenties, means that what happens at these ages drives the period trends. Social and economic conditions that remove barriers to family formation allow more to become parents sooner. For instance, Modell, Furstenberg, and Strong (1978) argue that favorable economic conditions and innovative social programs such as the GI Bill and Social Security removed many barriers to early family formation, leading to earlier and more universal parenthood in the immediate postwar period. In contrast, harsh social and economic conditions can create barriers to family formation by making it harder to find a secure job or buy a home. The Depression years of the 1930s typify a context unfavorable to family formation that produced a late age at marriage and parenthood. In short, women and men in these periods responded to broader social and economic forces by adjusting the timing of parenthood. The American normative context encourages and expects such adjustments.

Variability in on-time fertility can have important consequences too. The twenties are an important decade of change in most individuals' lives, and parenthood at the beginning of the twenties can have quite different implications than parenthood at the end of it. Consider two hypothetical couples: couple A consists of a mother aged 19 at the birth of her first child and a father aged 21 at the birth; couple B consists of a mother aged 24 and father aged 26 at the birth. Thus, the difference in age at parenthood between the couples is only five years, and neither couple represents an extreme case. For every cohort born in the twentieth century, between 10 and 20 percent first became mothers prior to age 19, and at least 25 percent were not yet mothers at age 25.

Irrespective of its content or quality, couple A will have less experience to draw on at the beginning of parenthood. This experience can be expected to provide knowledge and maturity that can be child-rearing resources. For instance, the wife in couple A will be less likely than the 24-year-old mother to have lived away from her parents for any length of time before having children. She would not have had much time to acquire and practice the skills of running her own household. Thus, she must acquire household management skills about the same time she acquires parental skills. Similar considerations apply to the fathers in our hypothetical couples.

Couples A and B also could have substantially different educational, work, and marital experience while in their early twenties. These differences could affect their subsequent life course, their performance as parents and, as a result, the behavior, skills, and aptitudes of their children.

Conversely, early age at parenthood can facilitate a more active interaction with an extended family because it shortens the length of the generation. Other things equal, the shorter the time interval between generations, the greater the probability that parents, grandparents, and even great-grandparents will be alive—and thus, the possibility exists for more contact with the extended family. A shorter generation may also make it easier for generations to empathize with one another, increasing the quality as well as the quantity of contacts.

If we consider a third couple where the woman and man become parents at ages 29 and 31 respectively, the potential differences could be greater. The added five years relative to couple B means the husband and wife are considerably farther along the age-income profile, are more likely to have savings, may have purchased a house, and, in general, will have considerably more stability and maturity.

OVERVIEW OF THE STUDY

The following chapter develops our conceptual model of the first-birth process in considerable detail. Briefly, we see the parenthood transition as intimately connected with the unfolding life course. Early experiences affect later behavior; both affect subsequent plans and aspirations. Individuals attempt to time parenthood to fit with this unfolding life course so that the most demanding roles, or aspects of them, do not compete with parenthood. Of course, waiting times to conception, miscarriages, and contraceptive failures make precise timing of parenthood difficult. Understanding the relationship between parenthood timing and the life course requires careful consideration of the broader social context within which these events occur. The social context defines the preferred timetable for key transitions including parenthood, the range of alternatives to parenthood, and the severity of the sanctions for nonconformity. Racial or ethnic groups, international comparisons, and different time periods provide contrasting fertility-relevant contexts.

Chapter 3 describes the secondary data sources and analytic strategy used in this monograph. The variety of questions we address calls for data on a range of periods or cohorts, with information on the timing of parenthood within an individual's life course and with substantial individual-level characteristics to represent the shape of the life course and the social context. No single data source contains all of these elements. Thus, we use a variety of data sources in combination to address given hypotheses. Our analytic strategy must also be able to incorporate each of the conceptual dimensions above. To do this we use life table methodology, extended to allow for the introduction of multivariate control.

Chapter 4 uses vital registration data to describe historical trends in the timing of parenthood and examines possible macrolevel determinants of these trends. Vital registration data for other countries is also included for a comparative perspective. We show a striking similarity between the timing of the first birth today and that observed during the Great Depression of the 1930s. Thus levels of delayed childbearing have a recorded historical precedent in the United States. Further, international comparisons show that these levels are not extreme. Determinants of U.S. trends are clearly period factors as evidenced by the pervasive changes one observes when the data are arrayed by calendar year. The precise period factors primarily responsible are more difficult to determine, especially for the more recent period. However, we stress the difficulty of family formation in a period characterized by high material aspirations, high inflation, high unemployment, and the consequent rapid increase in families dependent on both spouses as wage earners.

Using a series of eight fertility surveys conducted between 1955 and 1980, in chapter 5 we examine the determinants of parenthood by age, for a long series of birth cohorts, with a substantial number of important individual level characteristics such as religion and educational attainment. This chapter demonstrates most fully the utility of our conceptual approach. As in the case with overall fertility (see Rindfuss and Sweet 1977; Sweet and Rindfuss 1983) differential first-birth timing by education, religion, and other variables remains relatively constant while period factors exert strong pervasive effects. Moreover, there is strong variability by age in the influence of social structural variables. These variables tend to affect *when* women have first births not *if they* become parents. For instance, Catholics are less likely to have births at young ages but more likely to have them at older ages. Thus, on balance, Catholic women are only slightly more likely to be permanently childless.

Chapter 6 contrasts the levels, trends, and determinants of parenthood timing for whites and blacks. Historically, blacks have begun childbearing earlier than whites but a larger proportion of them remain permanently childless. A major debate has focused around the causes of this differential in permanent childlessness (N. J. Davis 1982; Farley 1970; McFalls 1973; Tolnay 1985). Our own analysis shows sharp divergence in the behavior of blacks and whites in the most recent period. In the late 1970s, blacks began childbearing earlier and were more likely than whites to experience parenthood at most subsequent ages. As a result the long observed higher childlessness of blacks almost certainly will be reversed for black women now in their late twenties or early thirties. Some hypotheses for these recently divergent patterns are suggested and preliminary examinations reported.

Chapter 7 focuses on the modern fertility patterns of the United States and Japan using aggregate and individual-level data. This chapter most clearly demonstrates the importance of social context. The Japanese begin childbearing later than Americans—teenage childbearing is nearly non-existent in Japan. But, very few Japanese women remain permanently childless. Moreover the factors affecting parenthood timing vary sharply across the Japanese and American contexts; the process is fundamentally different. The greater availability of socially approved, nonfamilial roles in the United States probably explains a large share of the observed differences. The availability of such nonfamilial roles has long been one feature distinguishing East from West. We also examine the timing of the first birth vis-à-vis marriage in the United States and Japan. This analysis points toward a lingering difference in the basis and meaning of marriage in these two modern societies.

In chapters 8 and 9, we focus on data from a representative sample of those in their senior year of high school in 1972. Longitudinal data for these respondents were collected between 1972 and 1979. These data allow us to study the paths through which background variables influence early adult activities and, in turn, the transition to parenthood. Current activity state—the respondent's current primary role—is an extremely powerful predictor of the transition to parenthood and mediates a sub-stantial portion of the influence of background variables. Yet the career paths of young adults are much more varied and complex than we ex-pected. Further work in this area is high on our future research agenda.

In chapter 9 we analyze respondents' timing intentions—When do childless men and women expect to have their first child? We argue that time-bound intentions accurately reflect actual fertility decisions and we show that such intentions have substantial predictive validity. Intentions to delay childbearing are associated with the respondent's reports of the importance of family, career, and leisure, with sex roles, and with reports of what the respondent expects to be doing at age 30. Clearly, respondents perceive the important implications of first-birth timing for other adult roles.

In chapter 9 we also incorporate these sex-role attitudes and life-style aspirations into the model of delayed childbearing presented in chapter 8. We expected that background factors, operating partly through current activity state, influence sex-role attitudes and aspirations. All variables, in turn, influence the transition to parenthood. We find that sex-role aspira-tions and attitudes operate largely independent of background variables (like parents' socioeconomic status) and current activity states (like being in school or currently working full-time). Thus this chapter raises an issue for further research: What experience not included in our current model is responsible for sex-role attitudes and life-style preferences which, in turn, influence the transition to parenthood?

Our final chapter reviews major findings and themes, and discusses their implications for future fertility change and, more broadly, for future social change.

2
Conceptual Overview

Becoming a parent is sometimes the result of a long and careful decision-making process, and sometimes the unintended consequence of the decision to have sexual intercourse coupled with an aversion to or disregard for contraception and abortion. Not becoming a parent can be the result of a similar decision-making process, or the unhappy consequence of biological factors out of the individual's control. The decision to have a first birth and the actual first birth may occur within the same 12-month period, or couples may debate or postpone the parenthood decision for 30 years, during which time they and society will have changed substantially. The characteristics and preferences of the individuals involved obviously are important, as is their being enmeshed in larger groups that have a stake in the reproductive outcomes of their members.

Any investigation of the sociological and demographic determinants of the transition to parenthood must take into account the complexity of the process in both conceptualization and data analysis. In this chapter we present the theoretical assumptions and conceptual framework that guide our subsequent analysis. Where our treatment differs from that of others, we present the rationale for our approach.

NORMATIVE PARENTAL IMPERATIVE

In the late 1960s when concern about population growth in the United States was peaking, many were recommending coercive antinatalist policies, while others argued that free choice ought not, and need not, be infringed. Similar debates were being held with respect to domestic family-planning policies and family-planning aid to developing nations (e.g., Donaldson forthcoming). In what became the conventional socio-logical position, Blake (1972) maintained that the question was not prop-erly framed for the United States. American society is "pervaded by time-honored pronatalist constraints," she argued (p. 105). It makes little sense to talk of free choice when normative pressure is strong, and to call for antinatalist policies without examining existing pronatalist ones. Widespread concern about their own overpopulation has abated in devel-oped countries, and in some European countries has been replaced with concern about fertility's being too low. All the while, strong pressures to have children have persisted. Higher parity births are increasingly discretionary, but parenthood continues to be expected.

The societal concern with the necessity of reproduction is so strong that women (or men, for that matter) are unlikely to pass through the reproductive stage of their lives without either becoming a parent or contemplating it. Even though a person may become a parent or remain a nonparent as the result of unintended behavior, it is extremely unlikely that an individual would remain a nonparent without receiving a substan-tial amount of normative pressure to rethink that position or sympathetic concern over the biological fate one was dealt.

The normative pressure to become a parent can be felt in a variety of ways, both subtle and otherwise. Many institutions assume and encourage the linkage of middle-age adults and children. American churches typi-cally plan numerous family activities that essentially demand the presence of children before they are complete. Some religious groups including Catholics, Mormons, and certain Protestant fundamentalist groups are even more explicit in their pronatalism, making it clear that childbearing is an obligation of marriage. The American tax structure represents another example of societal pressure to become parents by "subsidizing" parents of young children with extra deductions. Even though the cost far outweighs the "reward," the reminder of the state's support for children is there every spring. The mass media and the arts continually demonstrate how deeply the ideal of parenthood is rooted in our popular culture. While the particular portrayals of parent-child themes vary sub-stantially, their ubiquitous presence reinforces the notion that parenthood is an expected adult role.

Traditional sex roles also encourage parenthood. Male and female roles are largely defined vis-à-vis their divergent parental roles. In a sense, parenthood justifies sex-role differentiation (e.g., Blake 1972). Talcott Parsons (1955) and Kingsley Davis (1971) see societal sanctions against homosexuality as important for defining sex roles and encouraging parenthood. Discrimination against women in nonfamilial areas has often been done in the name of promoting parenthood, and that very discrimination alters the costs and benefits of the choices women make.

At the interpersonal level, normative pressure can be experienced from a variety of directions. Spouses or potential spouses may want to have a child; they may find a new partner if their current one will not agree to parenthood. Parents are often anxious to become grandparents, and will make their desires known—sometimes with annoying frequency. Likewise, at weddings, funerals, graduations, and other extended family gatherings there will be an aunt, an uncle, a grandparent, or a cousin making inquiries or remarks about the nonparents of childbearing age. Also, as one's peer group ages and larger proportions have become parents, nonparents are faced with the choice of either accommodating to "family style" social activities or moving toward a nonparent peer group.

Perhaps the most extreme expression of the normative pressure to become a parent is the tendency to operationalize the definition of the transition to adulthood as the transition to parenthood. While this equation holds most forcefully among poor black women (e.g., Rainwater 1965, 1966; Stack 1974), components of it can be found throughout American society. For men and women, parenthood or impending parenthood is taken as a legitimate excuse for dropping out of school. Even though high school dropouts receive the most attention, it is not unusual for university professors to see a 32-year-old graduate student use impending parenthood as a justification for not completing a dissertation. Indeed, as the educational demands continue to increase in our society, we may see an increasing number of individuals using parenthood to justify dropping out of school (see Gerson 1985).

There are a variety of other symptoms of this normative pressure to become a parent. For example, Blake's (1979) attitudinal data show that most respondents agree that childlessness is not a desired way of life. There is no glamorous aura attached to it. Further, confronted with the lack of social support, nonparents formed their own support group during the 1970s as an organized way to challenge pronatalist pressure in the United States: the National Organization for Non-Parents (Barnett and MacDonald 1976).

To this point, we have provided anecdotal evidence on the normative pressures favoring parenthood. It is important, however, to provide a more formal discussion of this concept because sociologists have overused and abused the terms *norm* and *normative* (Mason 1983). In particular, Marini (1984) presents a strong case of how the term *norm* has been abused in the general area of the life course.

Norms involve two characteristics: (1) they are properties of groups not individuals, and (2) their violation results in the imposition of sanctions. With respect to the second requirement, some might challenge the assertion that there is a norm in the United States to become a parent. But, such challenges must concede that the sanctions can be quite mild and extremely difficult to measure:

In most cases sanctions are informal—an approving or contemptuous glance, an encouraging or derisive laugh, a sympathetic or embarrassed silence. Such seemingly trivial but pervasive sanctions enable human beings to control informally . . . a share of their own actions and reactions and the actions and reactions of others. . . . Indeed, the relatively unruffled fashion in which informal sanctions operate constitutes one of their most important societal functions—they control behavior in a relatively painless manner before more formal measures are necessary (Blake and Davis 1964:465).

Thus in the case of the transition to parenthood, individuals are not formally sanctioned if they reach age 45 still childless. Rather the sanctions are far more subtle: nagging, pity, exclusion from some activities, slightly higher tax rates, and other irritating mechanisms. There is no formal imposition of these sanctions (with the exception of the tax rate differences); rather they are applied somewhat haphazardly by a wide variety of individuals. Nevertheless, they are applied. Further, as Blake and Davis (1964) note, conformity to the norm can occur simply because it has been thoroughly internalized. Indeed, this was one of the lessons of the early work on childbearing socialization by Gustavus and Nam (1970). Finally, a variety of exceptions are considered valid, such as physiological constraints or genetic concerns. But since there are exceptions to virtually every norm, we do not take their presence to be problematic.

Our empirical research makes no attempt to document this normative pressure. We measure neither expectations regarding the need to become a parent, nor the sanctions brought to bear when one does not become a parent as soon as expected. Rather, the normative pressure to become a parent is taken as a strong and central assumption. Indeed, our empirical analysis is concerned with the reasons why some individuals postpone parenthood longer than others. The normative imperative to become a parent is the reason that these delaying factors are visible and important.

Despite the strong pressure to become a parent, it is not unbridled.

The degree of pressure may fluctuate across periods. But regardless of time period, as Ryder (1973b:61) has noted, U.S. society puts qualifiers on the normative imperative to become a parent:

norms specify that all people are expected to marry and have two children as soon as, and providing that, their economic circumstances permit. The economic constraint is couched in terms of the scale of living to which they aspire.

In short, people should wait until they can "afford" to have children before they make the transition to parenthood. This is not a new ideology in the West. In premodern Western Europe young adults delayed marriage and childbearing until they acquired access to farmland. Often they waited until they inherited family land.

Such was also the case with some of the early cottage industries where the nuclear family was the unit of production. Parents benefited from the labor capacity of their unmarried children and delayed marriage was encouraged, either until the children could afford their own means of production or until the senior generation was willing to retire. The breakup of familial modes of production opened opportunities for young adults and led to decreases in age at union formation (Lesthaeghe 1980). In the modern context, the implication is that individuals should have finished their education and have procured a secure, well-paying job. Traditionally, the latter injunction only applied to men, but increasingly it applies to both sexes.

An important component of being able to afford parenthood is being able to afford housing. The United States has a conjugal family ideology that stresses independence of the nuclear family from broader kin networks (Goode 1963, 1982). The young couple must have sufficient resources to rent or, as has become an increasing expectation, to buy suitable and adequate housing. The centrality of the financial responsibility aspect to marriage and childbearing is found repeatedly in the literature. For example, Modell (1980) argues that after World War II, when age at marriage was declining substantially, the economic prospects of young adults were improving perceptibly. This argument is also very similar to Easterlin's (1962, 1966, 1973, 1978) relative income hypothesis that asserts that individuals marry and have children sooner when their income prospects brighten. While Easterlin emphasizes the role of relative cohort sizes in determining the ability to set up a nuclear residence, we would point to the wide variety of other factors that impinge on the ability of a young person to start a family.

The requirement that parents be able to "afford" children (their costs are primarily borne by parents rather than an extended family or society at large) and the absence of a fixed definition of *affordability*, allows for—indeed necessitates—inter- and intracohort differences in timing of the transition to parenthood in the United States. The hard times of the Depression produced late ages at the transition to parenthood, and the good times of the 1950s produced earlier ages. However, affluent children go on to become parents at a substantially later age than poorer children (see chapter 8) partly because of their high material aspirations, typically coupled with high educational and career aspirations.

Thus, within the United States, there are strong normative pressures to become a parent, but simultaneously there are conflicting pressures to do so at a young age (in order to define oneself as an adult) and to do so at an older age (to be able to afford the child). This situation results in a substantial amount of variance in age at first birth compared with other societies (see chapters 4 and 7). The United States has one of the highest rates of adolescent fertility in the developed world (E. F. Jones et al. 1985), yet there are predictions (Bloom 1982) that rates of childlessness for the cohort of women currently in their early thirties may surpass 30 percent—which would also rank among the world's highest.

This wide variance stands in sharp contrast to most other societies. But the contrast is perhaps sharpest with Asia where many societies have shifted from an early age at parenthood to a late age with little or no increase in the variance of the distribution. Furthermore, the possibility of remaining childless voluntarily in response to economic or other circumstances is not considered an option within the calculus of choice in most Asian societies. Even Asian demographers are mystified by the current behavior of Americans. We explicitly contrast the transition to parenthood for American and Japanese women in chapter 7. For now, perhaps the best illustration is that despite the very forceful actions initiated by the Chinese during the late 1970s and early 1980s to reduce their population growth rate (Aird 1985; Banister 1984; Coale 1984; Keyfitz 1984), they never considered encouraging some couples to remain permanently childless. It was simply not in their catalog of options.

To summarize, the United States has a strong normative imperative toward parenthood coupled with several injunctions that ensure a wide variance in age at which the transition to parenthood occurs. Thus an understanding of the process of becoming a parent necessitates an examination of a wide age range. Further, even when individuals decide not to become parents, the strong normative imperative cautions against treating that decision as a permanent one.

So far, we have treated the normative context as unchanging and have not discussed the origin of American fertility norms. The origins are sufficiently distant that discussing them is necessarily highly speculative. Even though there is considerable variation in the forms they take, the normative motivation to become a parent is in evidence in all countries. Thus, the successive waves of immigrants who populated the United States arrived with a norm to become parents—even if the various exceptions and qualifiers differed depending on country and region of origin.

Ultimately, the reasons for pronatalist norms follow from basic demographic facts. First, societal survival depends on survival of an adequate population. Societies lose members through death and out-migration. Complete reliance on in-migration to maintain a sufficient population is very risky because sufficient numbers of migrants may not be available and immigrants pose a threat to the existing order. Instead, all surviving societies maintain a relatively constant stream of individuals making the transition to parenthood. The population threat is thus met through cohort replacement where new cohorts have been socialized to respect the existing order. This solution to maintaining population provides stability while allowing for change (see Ryder 1965). This fundamental prerequisite for societal survival provides one universal basis for pronatalism.

But the norms surrounding parenthood are not set in granite; rather, they are shaped by the structural forces and cultural heritage of society (e.g., Lesthaeghe 1980). Although it is still too early to tell what the eventual impact will be, there is some evidence that in the United States the normative pressure to become a parent has weakened recently, making voluntary childlessness more acceptable. Using cross-sectional, nationally representative samples, Veroff, Douvan, and Kulka (1981) claim that between 1957 and 1976, the perceived advantages of childlessness have increased while perceived disadvantages have declined. Nevertheless, the normative pressure to become a parent is still quite strong. Thornton and Freedman (1983:16) take a similar position:

social norms and values prescribing parenthood have weakened, making it easier to remain childless . . . [but] there is no evidence of an embracement of childlessness. Substantial portions of Americans continue to value parenthood, believe that childbearing should accompany marriage, and feel social pressure to have children.

Evidence of weakening normative pressure can be found in the power and growth of the feminist movement. Following on the heels, and using a similar appeal for equality as the civil rights movement, feminism provided an ideology that supported and legitimated more egalitarian roles. Men's roles changed as well. For the decade of the 1950s, Ehrenreich (1983) documents the intense pressure for men to marry, have children, and adopt the breadwinner role. In later decades, she claims that substantial portions of men have rejected the breadwinner role, and that ideological support for new life-styles has arisen. Numerous other studies have documented more egalitarian attitudes across the past two decades. Mason, Gzajka, and Arber (1976) examined four nationally representative surveys conducted between 1964 and 1974. They find substantial and pervasive "movement toward more egalitarian role definitions" (p. 573). Using the Detroit 18-year panel study, Thornton, Alwin, and Camburn (1983:211) find a "definite trend toward more egalitarian conceptions of women's roles." Development of these less traditional roles may imply greater choice regarding parenthood.

A broader argument for ideological change can also be made. Freedom and individuality are long-standing features of Western culture. Bellah et al. (1985:275) argue that we have entered "the latest phase of that process of separation and individuation that modernity seems to entail." Freedom and individuality have become the paramount cultural values in modern American society and the pursuit of personal happiness the paramount goal, they claim. Further, economic success is seen as the means necessary to pursue individual happiness. Clearly, economic success, personal freedom, and individuality are antinatalist. To the extent that these values have become stronger and more pervasive, they might encourage later and less parenthood.

While it is possible that these factors may have weakened normative pressures toward parenthood, we caution against assigning them the major causal role in recent fertility trends. The changes Bellah et al. (1985) noted, if they have occurred, have been long-term secular ones, not cyclical ones capable of explaining recent shifts in first-birth timing. In chapter 4 we show that the trend toward later parenthood preceded the powerful women's movement that emerged in the late 1960s and early 1970s. As Kingsley Davis and Pietronella van den Oever (1982) argue, the change in women's roles can be seen as an adaptation to changed conditions of life and new ideological movements a reaction to justify these new roles. In short, the women's movement and the shifting norms may be best seen as a response to social-structural and demographic change. Yet once new ideologies have gained legitimacy, they make the new behavior far more attractive.

PROCESS AND BECOMING A PARENT

Biologically, there is a long time period in which women can make the transition to parenthood. At the extreme, this can take place anywhere between menarche and menopause—a span of 30 to 35 years. Men have an even longer period within which to make this transition (e.g., Anderson 1975). This long potential time period necessitates theoretical assumptions regarding the nature of the fertility decision-making process. These assumptions in turn have important implications for the methods of analysis one uses and the results obtained.

The main issue revolves around the time frame individuals use in making childbearing decisions. One extreme is represented by some of the early microeconomic modeling of the childbearing process (e.g., Willis 1973). This approach assumes that men and women make all their fertility decisions early in life, along with decisions about future labor force participation, educational attainment, and consumption. (See Turchi 1975, chap. 2 for a discussion of this set of assumptions.) At the other extreme is Ryder (1973a:503) who argues that "from the standpoint of the actions necessary to fulfill their reproductive intentions, all a couple needs to have in mind is whether to permit the next ovulation to come to fruition." With respect to analytical approaches, the microeconomic approach would thus tend to minimize period factors (because the decisions are made early in life), emphasize cohort factors, and move toward making as many of the substantive variables endogenous as is empirically tractable. Conversely, the short decision-making time frame assumption would allow for a greater effect of period factors, minimize the issue of endogeneity, and stress the importance of time-varying covariates. While our position falls between these two extremes, for reasons discussed below, we feel that Ryder's account is a more accurate reflection of how fertility decisions are actually made.

Perhaps the best evidence regarding the reappraisal of childbearing decisions comes from research on the determinants of childlessness. Despite a fairly consistent norm in the United States that individuals ought to become parents eventually, there has been substantial variability in the twentieth century in the proportion of cohorts remaining childless. For example, 22 percent of the women born 1906–1910 remained childless. By contrast, only 9 percent of the women born in the middle of the Depression (1933–1937) remained childless. This variation is primarily the result of variation in voluntary childlessness rather than changes in the incidence of involuntary childlessness.

How do individuals and couples make the decision to remain childless? Researchers looking at the topic of voluntary childlessness from a macro- and a microperspective have reached the same conclusion: the typical voluntarily childless woman becomes childless by initially delaying the first birth and, then, after a number of years of delayed childbearing, deciding not to have any children.[1] (See Veevers 1979 for a review of the literature.) Using cohort data, Hastings and Robinson (1974) show that delayed childbearing is related to increased levels of childlessness. Similar findings can be found in Poston and Gotard (1977), Pitcher (1980), and Masnick (1980b). At the microlevel, Veevers (1973) found that of wives who remained childless, more than two-thirds did so by a series of decisions to postpone having children until some future time (also see Gerson 1985; Houseknecht 1979). Baum and Cope (1980) reported similar findings from Britain.

The sociological reasons for this relationship involve the various roles women occupy or can occupy. Mason's (1974) "role hiatus hypothesis" states that time spent in nonfamilial roles during early adulthood can alter women's sex-role attitudes and tastes for paid employment. These tastes for work allow employment partly to fulfill the needs traditionally met by motherhood (see Spitze 1978). Or as Cutright and Polonko (1977:60) suggest, "given opportunities to engage in alternate roles, some women will find other activities more rewarding than childbearing, and successive postponements will eventually result in voluntary childlessness." As women grow older, the difficulty of combining childbearing and labor force participation becomes more apparent (Stolzenberg and Waite 1977). Further, a woman's perception of the wages she can command increases in importance throughout the family life cycle (Waite 1980). Thus, as women age, they will have had more experience and have been in a diversity of roles. They carry this history with them, and this history has

---

[1]This is not to deny that some couples or individuals may decide very early to remain childless and actively work toward that goal. Rather, the point is that the vast majority follow the alternative path of a series of initial delaying decisions.

its own effects on fertility decisions (Rindfuss, Swicegood, and Rosenfeld 1985). As women age, and remain childless, the demands of their other roles increase and the potential incompatibility with parenthood becomes more apparent.

Given that individuals have imperfect forecasting ability, it would be inconceivable that they do not adjust their plans as events in their life unfold. This is borne out in the research on fertility intentions and expectations, where the repeated finding is that these intentions change in response to changes in the individuals' lives as well as change in period factors (see chapter 9; Morgan 1981, 1982; Westoff and Ryder 1977*b*). One implication of our assumption regarding change in fertility goals is that the distinction between voluntary and involuntary childlessness is difficult, if not impossible, to make. Consider the woman who voluntarily postpones childbearing until some point at which she decides to have children. Also assume that during the early part of her postponement she had the biological ability to bear children, but sometime during this period of voluntary postponement, she became sterile. Is she voluntarily or involuntarily childless? An argument could be made either way, but both would miss the main point that a process had taken place such that a woman had spent some time voluntarily childless and some time involuntarily childless.

Another implication of our assumptions regarding change in fertility goals is that time needs to be explicitly brought into the analysis. While this notion is widely recognized in the broader life course literature (e.g., Elder 1978; Modell, Furstenberg, and Hershberg 1976; Riley 1985), it typically has not been made explicit in fertility analyses. Time here has two dimensions: aggregate and individual. The aggregate dimension involves period and cohort factors, such as cohort size, wars, economic hardship, or natural disasters. The normative structure may vary across periods or cohorts. The individual time dimension represents the individual's past history, and would include such aspects as the individual's physical maturation process, including fecundity, and educational, job, and familial experiences. Thus, even though individual and aggregate time are accumulating simultaneously for any individual, they are conceptually distinct. Later in this book, we present analyses showing that both are important.

One of the central issues in examining the aggregate dimensions of time is deciding between a cohort or period emphasis. Given that we will also be examining individual time, cohort and period cannot be examined simultaneously—unless one is willing to make simplifying assumptions (Glenn 1976; Mason et al. 1973; Pullum 1980; Rodgers 1982). We explicitly address this topic in chapter 4. Related to this issue is the question of whether period or cohort factors exert an additive effect on the timing of the transition to parenthood, or *whether* they interact with various structural factors. Even though period effects have been found to be remarkably pervasive (Rindfuss and Sweet 1977; Sweet and Rindfuss 1983), the logic of the interactive argument remains sufficiently compelling that one cannot dismiss it; we examine this topic at several points.

Another example of changing period factors has been the development of modern contraceptives. The pill was first marketed widely in the early 1960s. The modern IUD became available in the mid-1960s. Finally, advances in techniques made sterilization more attractive. These various new methods of contraception are more effective than traditional methods, separate contraception from the coital act, and their use requires less motivation. As such, their introduction probably facilitated the increase in age at first birth that occurred during the 1970s. However, as we show in this chapter, a similar pattern of age at entry into parenthood existed during the 1930s—cautioning against placing too much emphasis on the availability of modern contraceptives. Certainly they are not necessary to achieve impressive levels of delayed childbearing.

With respect to the individual components of time, we are referring primarily, in the first instance, to social characteristics, rather than biological ones. As suggested above, the social aspects of individual time derive from the fact that as individuals age they accumulate experience (Rindfuss and Bumpass 1978). These experiences are relevant when the decision to become a parent is being evaluated or reevaluated. For example, with the passage of time, the significance of one's career may increase in the individual's value structure. Further, over time, an individual's interests, as well as friends' interests, may change or become more rigid. This in turn may facilitate or hinder the transition to parenthood. Finally, Neugarten and her associates (1965, 1973, 1985) present broader arguments that individuals' lives are ordered by societal norms regarding age-appropriate behaviors, roles, and statuses. There are roughly agreed upon timetables regarding familial and occupational events. Individuals typically compare their own progress with that appropriate for their group.

One implication of repeated change in childbearing intentions is that predicting the ultimate level of childlessness for a cohort still in its childbearing years is hazardous at best, and quite often misleading. The most sophisticated example of such forecasting is found in the work of Bloom (1980, 1982, 1984) using an adaptation of Coale's age at first marriage schedule (1971; also see Coale and McNeil 1972). The basic assumption is that cohorts follow a standard schedule in the transition to parenthood that depends on the age at which significant proportions begin that transition and the pace at which it takes place. The early experience of the cohort is then extrapolated to fill out the cohort's experience. As Bloom points out, this analytical procedure is based on the assumption that strong period effects do not intervene. As we show in chapter 4, however, the intervention of strong period factors has been a dominant feature in twentieth-century United States. Thus, successful prediction of ultimate childlessness levels depends on successful prediction of future period factors.

BIOLOGICAL CONSTRAINTS

Although our principal concern is with the social determinants of the timing of parenthood, we cannot ignore the reality that fertility is a biological process as well as a social one. A number of physiological constraints placed on the social process affect who can and cannot have children and the time when they can have them. It is useful to review these biological factors with reference to the way in which they impinge on our ability to examine the social aspects of the timing of fertility. In particular, it is necessary to recognize the large stochastic factor built into the examination of the timing of fertility owing to these biologically based constraints. Of course, some of these physiological factors are in turn affected by social customs—coital frequency is but one example.

Starting with the most elementary fact, only women bear children, and then only between menarche and menopause. For men, there is no clear point when the ability to produce a child begins, except to say that it is during the pubertal period. Similarly, there is no clear end point in the male's ability to fertilize an ovum. For both the beginning and end points in the male's reproductive span, there is variability across men in the age at which these transitions are made. Further, there is evidence that male fecundability declines with age (Anderson 1975) but little is known about the pace or determinants of this decline.

For the female, the onset of the reproductive years is signaled by the beginning of menstruation. Menarche generally occurs between ages 10 and 15. As we shall see in chapter 5, age at menarche has an effect on the timing of entry into parenthood. Following menarche, there is a phase, commonly termed the period of adolescent sterility, during which menstrual cycles are often irregular and anovulatory cycles (in which there is no ovulation) are frequent. The length and characteristics of this period of adolescent sterility vary from woman to woman, but relatively little is known about the nature and causes of this period of adolescent sterility (see Leridon 1977).

After the period of adolescent sterility, there is still considerable variation in the ovulatory cycle. Leridon (1977) outlines four types of variation in the ovulatory cycle: (1) the average length of the cycle varies from woman to woman; (2) for any given woman, the length varies from cycle to cycle; (3) the day on which ovulation occurs varies; and (4) these factors vary as the woman ages. Within each cycle, the time available for fertilization is short, approximately three days.

Given a conception, there is also variation in the probability of its resulting in a live birth. Leridon (1977) estimates that 40 percent of all conceptions experience intrauterine mortality during the first two weeks of gestation. Note, however, that a recent series of studies examining early pregnancy losses has reached quite divergent estimates, ranging from 8 to 57 percent (Edmonds et al. 1982; Miller, Glue, and Williamson 1980; and Whittaker, Taylor, and Lind 1983). All three studies were based on small samples of women, thus providing further reinforcement for the argument that intrauterine mortality is a strong contributor to the stochastic nature of the fertility process. After the first two weeks, between one-fifth and one-quarter of the remaining pregnancies will not result in a live birth (Leridon 1977). Intrauterine mortality varies with the age of the woman and increases quite rapidly after age 30.

If a conception results in a live birth, a nonfertile period follows. The length of this period varies. In particular, lactation or breast-feeding practices have a strong impact on its length.

Finally, sterility, whether voluntary or involuntary, can occur at any time and can be the result of a physiological factor in the male, the female, or both. The existence of and timing of the onset of sterility varies considerably across individuals. Clearly, the female reproductive period ends at menopause, which on average occurs at age 50. However, well before menopause, a woman's fecundability will decrease. Exactly when it begins to decrease has been the subject of considerable debate recently. In a highly publicized article, using data from an infertility clinic, DeCherney and Berkowitz (1982) argue that fecundability begins declining markedly after age 30. Bongaarts (1982) and Menken (1985), using biometric and demographic data, argue that it is not until past age 35 that a substantial decline in fecundability occurs. While this debate is not fully resolved, two things are now clear. First, fecundability declines markedly well before menopause. Second, the issue of "how late can a woman wait" has been widely discussed in the popular press and has now become a *social fact* considered by couples thinking about postponing their fertility. Even if this "social fact" turns out to be scientifically wrong, it will still have an effect.

To see the impact of biometric factors on the ability of social scientists to explain fertility-timing differences using sociological explanations, consider first a natural fertility situation—one where there is no deliberate use of any method of birth control to restrict the number of children born. Leridon (1977) has shown that if a group of women remained fecund and exposed to the risk of pregnancy during their reproductive period and did not breast-feed their offspring, their average number of children ever born would be about 17 or 18, but for individual women this would range from 10 to 25. Sheps and Menken (1973) showed that, assuming no change in fecundability, the correlation between successive birth interval lengths is less than 0.5. As Ryder (1979) has pointed out, such stochastic factors in the biological aspects of fertility make the social demographer's job difficult. Furthermore, it means that a sociologist interested in the *timing* of fertility will necessarily have results with lower levels of explained variance than those interested in the total *quantity* of fertility.

If sociological factors affecting fertility did so through effective and complete use of birth control, then one would expect the explained variance to increase. However, the increase is not as large as one might expect, because (1) all couples do not translate their intentions into the use of birth control, and (2) contraceptive methods also have a stochastic element associated with them. To illustrate this latter point, consider the estimates of extended use effectiveness reported by Westoff and Ryder (1977a) for various methods of contraception. The percentage of respondents who fail during the first year of exposure to an unintended pregnancy is:

Method	Percent
Pill	6
IUD	12
Condom	18
Diaphragm	23
Foam	31
Rhythm	33
Douche	39

A portion of this failure, of course, is because of nonbiological phenomena. For example, it has been well established that contraceptive efficacy varies with the intention of the user (e.g., to stop childbearing or to delay the next birth). However, a portion of this level of failure is also due to chance. Thus, even in a "controlled fertility" setting, one would expect the proportion of explained variance to be relatively low because of stochastic variations of biological origin.

STRUCTURAL FACTORS

In addition to temporal and biological factors, individuals make decisions (or nondecisions) about the transition to parenthood within a social-structural setting. By birth, ascription, and achievement, individuals are members of social groups that affect the transition to parenthood. They also take part in social processes that bear on the timing of parenthood. Here we only provide a brief overview of this class of influences. We return to this topic in later chapters, particularly chapter 5.

Temporally, the earliest structural factors are those that define many of the social groups individuals belong to. Race, religion, region of origin, ethnicity, wealth of family of orientation, and rural or urban background are perhaps the most common. Some of these factors, such as race or ethnicity, tend to define an individual's group membership for most, if not all, of life.

In the context of the transition to parenthood, group membership is important to the extent that shared values or heritage regarding the timing of parenthood exist. For example, one might expect that upper-class families stress the importance of postponing the transition to parenthood until sufficient maturity is gained to allow the individual to take part in managing the family assets or until sufficient educational credentials are achieved to allow entry into an appropriate career. Thus, family background might have both direct effects and indirect effects through such variables as education. Alternatively, group membership could be important because it affects the various intermediate or proximate variables. For example, Catholics traditionally have had a strong proscription against premarital intercourse, and we expect that this should result in a later age at first birth for Catholics.

Such background characteristics are also important to the extent that they either expand or constrain opportunities available to individuals in their adolescent and early adult years. If nonfamilial activities are constrained, as might be the case in a small rural town, then early parenthood might become a more attractive alternative. Conversely, the alternative opportunities available to affluent young people may make them reluctant to make the transition to parenthood at a young age.

There are numerous suggestions within the literature (e.g., St. John 1982) that the structural conditions within some of these groups are sufficiently diverse that the processes operate differently. In particular, it is argued that quite different processes may be operating within the various race and ethnic groups. For example, blacks are often less able to turn their educational attainment into career advantages, and thus education may have a weaker effect. Similarly, young black mothers are more likely to have relatives volunteer to take care of the child if the woman wishes to further her education or pursue her career (e.g., Furstenberg, Brooks-Gunn, and Morgan 1987; Stack 1974). Even though this help may take a wide variety of forms, it is likely to reduce the conflict between being a student and a mother simultaneously.

Of course structural conditions also vary widely across countries. While our concern here is with the transition to parenthood in the United States, it is most likely that the structure of the process is quite different from that which exists in other countries. This phenomenon, of course, is only made visible through explicit comparisons. In chapter 4 we compare U.S. trends with those of a variety of developed countries, and in chapter 7 we contrast the structure of the process in the United States and Japan.

In addition to those structural variables, like race or religion, that tend to define the social groups within which one interacts during childhood, a variety of characteristics during adolescence would be expected to influence the timing of the transition to parenthood. These characteristics might involve the family of orientation, such as number of siblings or whether the teenager is living with both parents. These characteristics might also involve the structure of one's peer group. In either case, the effects might be direct through preferences about the timing of parenthood and its appropriate intermediate variables or indirect through the effect on educational or career aspirations.

Subsequent to these early adolescent characteristics, a variety of late adolescent and early adult factors are important. Most of these factors revolve around other transitions to adulthood that the young man or woman is going through—particularly school completion or entry into the labor force. The transition to adulthood in these arenas tends to have a major impact on the transition to parenthood because the time demands of parenthood may make it incompatible with other roles.

These social-structural determinants of the timing of the transition to parenthood are factors we will repeatedly return to in subsequent chapters—particularly chapters 5 and 8. In many ways they form the traditional sociological concern with explaining fertility behavior because these social-structural factors tend to define the social groups within which individuals live out their life.

THE ROLE OF MARRIAGE

Traditional social demography would place entry into parenthood as a life cycle stage that occurs after marriage. Thus, one would first examine the determinants of age at marriage, and then analyze the length of time between marriage and first birth. In fact, this treatment has been so ingrained in demographic research that the interval between marriage and first birth is still inappropriately referred to as the "first-birth interval" when strictly speaking, it is not a birth interval at all.

However, there is now increasing evidence that treating marriage as conditional to parenthood is unsatisfactory and misleading. The first live birth has a fixed biological definition that allows for straightforward comparisons over time and across groups. While there may sometimes be recall error associated with infant mortality or giving an infant up for adoption, the underlying behavioral definition is conceptually unambiguous. This is not the case with marriage, which is a socially defined institution. While most societies have some sort of ceremony marking the beginning of a stable marital union, there is no functional consistency over time or across groups in the meaning of what this ceremony marks.

The traditional demographic model assumes that marriage marks the beginning of sexual intercourse and cohabitation and thus the potential for parenthood. But this clearly need not be the case. Several examples should suffice. For some of our examples we have deliberately moved outside the contemporary United States. Furthermore, we have picked some extreme cases to make the central point more visible: marriage is a socially defined institution, and this definition varies across time and social group. Certainly in the United States, the variation in the definition of marriage is substantially more subtle but nevertheless variation does exist.

In many Muslim countries, two marriage ceremonies take place. The first is the one reported as the date of marriage. The second is the one that permits intercourse and cohabitation. While these usually take place within a few days of one another, in some situations they may be separated from each other by months or years. Hindu India provides a rather extreme case. Child brides often remained with their own family until menarche or beyond. In fact, Driver (1963) reports average intervals between marriage and the first birth which exceed five years. These long intervals suggest adolescent subfecundity and infrequent coitus. In contemporary Cairo, the period between marriage and the start of cohabitation is often stretched into months and even years because of scarce and expensive housing. In Thailand, Chamratrithirong, Morgan, and Rindfuss (1988) find that many spouses do not live together immediately after marriage, and Goldstein, Goldstein, and Piampiti (1973) find the same for all currently married Thais. Less formal observations suggest that marital nonresidence is common in many parts of Asia and Africa.

Even in the United States, marriage does not necessarily imply coresidence. For example, in 1980, among females aged 18–24, 3 percent of the white currently married women and 11 percent of the black currently married women were not living with their husbands for reasons other than marital discord (U.S. Bureau of the Census 1985). This percentage is in addition to the 5 percent of white currently married 18–24-year-old women and 16 percent of black currently married 18–24-year-old women who were not coresident with their husbands because of marital discord. Unfortunately, beyond marital discord, the census does not inquire about reasons for living apart. However, a wide variety of reasons related to occupation, education, military service, and institutionalization are likely to be involved. The point is that we cannot assume that marriage is synonymous with coresidence. Furthermore, other social-structural groups undoubtedly reflect differences of the sort mentioned for blacks and whites, thus reinforcing our argument that marriage is socially defined. In the other direction, premarital intercourse is increasingly common in Asia (see Rindfuss and Morgan 1983), and even more so in the West. The proportion ever having intercourse at young ages (15–19) is increasing in a wide variety of Western countries (see J. A. Jones et al. 1985) while age at marriage has also increased (see Muñoz-Perez 1979; Rodgers and Thornton 1985). Studies of adolescents in the United States clearly show that intercourse occurs earlier than in the past (see Zelnik and Kantner 1980, for instance).

Unmarried cohabitation has also attracted considerable attention from sociologists, with the Scandinavian countries being singled out as the most extreme cases. Trost (1975), for example, reports that nearly all Swedish couples cohabit prior to marriage. In interpreting the Swedish experience it is important to remember that cohabitation has long historical precedent there (Hoem and Rennermalm 1985). Further, studies of cohabitation in Europe do not support the contention that marriage is becoming unpopular. Instead, cohabitation is viewed as one step in a marriage *process* (Carlson 1986). Anthropologists have long argued that African marriages should not be perceived as a single event but as a process that unfolds over months and years (see Comaroff and Roberts 1977; Evans-Pritchard 1951; Kuper 1970). The transition to marriage in Europe may be becoming blurred so that such a model may be increasingly appropriate there as well. In the United States, premarital cohabitation has also increased sharply over the past 15 years (see Glick and Norton 1977; Glick and Spanier 1980; Spanier 1983). While it has not approached the levels of the Scandinavian countries, its increased presence argues against a simple or fixed definition of marriage.

In short, there is no necessary relationship between first marriage and birth of the first child (Hirschman and Rindfuss 1982). In some cases, the first birth may precede the first marriage. During the 1970s, parenthood preceded marriage for about 10 percent of white women and 60 percent of black women. When this occurs, the presence of a child may make a woman less attractive in the marriage market thereby delaying marriage. In this situation causality is running from the timing of fertility to the timing of marriage. A premarital conception, however, may hasten a marriage or lead to a marriage that might otherwise not take place in order to legitimate the ensuing birth. Approximately 40 percent of premarital pregnancies resulting in births were legitimated in the 1970s (J. A.

Jones et al. 1985). Here, causality is still working from the timing of fertility to the timing of marriage, but it is leading to a younger age at marriage rather than an older one.

These two situations (premarital births and premarital conceptions) can be contrasted with what would be considered the more traditional situation in which sexual intercourse and cohabitation do not take place until marriage (or at least, premarital sexual intercourse is contraceptively protected). After marriage, the couple either decides to have a child as soon as possible or to wait. Presumably, the marriage decision itself did not take into consideration when the couple wanted to have their first child. In this "classic" situation, causality is clearly running from the timing of marriage to the timing of fertility.

So far we have given precedence to either the fertility or the marriage decision and assumed that one then influences the other. An alternative possibility, and one that may operate in many cases, is that first birth and first marriage decisions are joint, that is, a simultaneous decision is made about both. Perhaps the most recent version of such joint decision making involves cohabiting couples who "finally" decide it's time to marry and have children. But such joint decision making is not new. As we have noted elsewhere (Rindfuss et al. 1980), it is clearly implied in the now somewhat quaint, colloquial phrase for announcing an impending marriage: "it's time to settle down and have a family." Clearly, if it is a simultaneous and joint decision, then the question of causal direction is not even relevant.

Thus, what is the role of marriage in the transition to parenthood? Our argument is that it is variable. There is no necessary relationship between marriage and becoming a parent. Note that we are not arguing that marriage is either irrelevant or unimportant for childbearing; rather its importance varies across socially defined groups, as does the causal direction of the relationship. Given this situation, most of our analysis focuses on the timing of the first birth without reference to marriage. We do so because conceptually the first birth is a far more precisely defined and measured variable, and because the transition to parenthood (particularly motherhood) is a far more permanent transition. Further, just looking at those who have a first conception after marriage means that a substantial number of people are being excluded.

Even though most of our work does not incorporate marriage, many couples in the United States marry while still childless and the woman is not pregnant. For these couples there are important sociological issues with respect to how long after marriage they wait before becoming'pregnant. To make these issues as visible as possible, in chapter 7 we contrast the determinants of the length of this delay in the United States with the determinants in Japan. The differences are quite striking and further reinforce our argument that marriage is a socially defined institution.

SUMMARY AND WORKING MODEL

Figure 1 shows a working model of factors affecting the transition to parenthood. Not explicitly shown is the general normative structure that individuals ought to become parents. Even though there may be qualifiers on this norm (waiting until marriage, proscription about Catholic clergy not becoming parents, or needing to achieve a certain standard of living first), and the pressure may wax and wane over time, at present it appears to be a universal expectation of individuals. The quantity of parenthood has changed, but not the general expectation of it. Thus, although it is invisible, essentially impossible to measure, and widely debated, it is basically the fuel that keeps the process shown in figure 1 going.

Also essential is explicit attention to the passage of time, which can directly affect preferences for the transition to parenthood because the decision-making framework is changing. The passage of time can indirectly affect the timing of parenthood through the biological aspects of the process. Further, it is important to remember the assumption that individuals can and do change their minds about the transition to parenthood and its timing (until, of course, it actually takes place). It is this assumption that makes the passage of time of sociological interest at the microlevel.

The entire process potentially interacts with a series of factors. First consider period or macrofactors, such as rapid changes in the cost of housing. The possibility of a period factor interacting with the biology of the process may at first glance seem implausible. But the effects of famine (Chowdhury and Chen 1977; Langsten 1980) provide one example of such an interaction in a developing country context. Perhaps the radiation effects from the recent nuclear accident in Chernobyl, USSR, will provide a developed country example. The next layer of possible interactions involves such factors as race, ethnicity, or even nationality. These factors can interact with period effects or the structural process. Then at the center of the model are the various microsocial-structural factors.

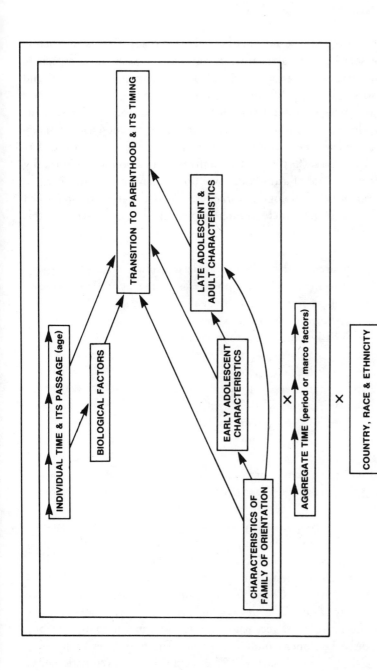

INDIVIDUAL TIME & ITS PASSAGE (age)

BIOLOGICAL FACTORS

TRANSITION TO PARENTHOOD & ITS TIMING

LATE ADOLESCENT & ADULT CHARACTERISTICS

EARLY ADOLESCENT CHARACTERISTICS

CHARACTERISTICS OF FAMILY OF ORIENTATION

AGGREGATE TIME (period or marco factors)

COUNTRY, RACE & ETHNICITY

X signifies a potential interaction

Fig. 1. Model of factors affecting the transition to parenthood.

Finally, note that we do not show the biological factors interacting with the social-structural factors. Some may question this, especially given the increased attention to fecundity impairments in general and those associated with pelvic inflammatory disease (e.g., Aral and Cates 1983; Cates 1984; Mosher 1986; Sherris and Fox 1983). At this point, however, there is not sufficient evidence to argue that these factors interact (in a statistical sense) with social-structural factors, nor are the differences between these factors and the effects of postponing childbearing clear (Menken 1985). Furthermore, we do not have direct measures on the vast majority of biological variables. Thus, the full exploration of such biological-social-structural interactions lies outside the scope of this work.

3

Data and Measurement

In this chapter we develop a measurement strategy for analyzing the transition to parenthood and describe the data sources used in the analytical chapters which follow. Our measurement framework relies on the logic of the life table but allows for multivariate control. We use a variety of data sources to examine a wide range of issues in the transition to parenthood. Because each data set has strengths and weaknesses, no single one would be sufficient to address fully the range of topics covered here. Several of our data sets allow comparison of numerous cohorts (the vital statistics data); some have fewer cohorts but with more detail or predictor variables (the 1980 June Current Population Survey); others have a still more modest range of birth cohorts but with more detail or individual-level characteristics (the series of United States fertility surveys); and finally one data set has extremely detailed microlevel data for a single cohort (The National Longitudinal Study of the High School Class of 1972). Thus, as we move toward more microlevel detail, we lose breadth of cohort experience. However, as we show in chapter 5, this is not a problem because the social-structural process appears to have been relatively stable over time. Additionally, this chapter treats a number of methodological issues that cut across several chapters.

DEFINING THE TRANSITION TO PARENTHOOD

A *birth* is an unambiguous event. Being biologically based, its meaning does not vary across time or space, or among various social groups. The *first birth* is not only unambiguous but a nonrepeatable, irreversible event. This unambiguous definition, coupled with the special experience of childbirth and the social meaning of this transition, results in an extremely high probability that the event will be remembered and accurately reported. It is the occurrence of the first live birth that we use to define the transition to parenthood.

But this definition is not without problems. First, there are two components to parenthood, a biological and a social one. Clearly, the biological component is the one measured in our definition. If we are interested in health consequences for mother and child, this definition is appropriate. But if we are interested in the effect of being a parent on other adult roles, then this biological measure may be problematic. Consider, for instance, a woman who adopts a three-month-old child at age 22 and has her first live birth at age 25. Our definition assigns age 25 as the age of transition to parenthood. For many reasons, it would be more appropriate to assign such a woman an age at parenthood that corresponded to the adoption date, the onset of social parenthood. Likewise, the biological mother of this adopted child, by allowing the child to be adopted, has abrogated the rights, duties, and obligations of *social* parenthood. Consequently, for those interested in the effects of social parenthood this mother might best be considered childless. Fortunately, for our purposes, the transition to social and biological parenthood is simultaneous for the overwhelming majority of women in the United States. This allows us to treat the date of the first birth as a reasonable, but not infallible, measure of parenthood—both its social and biological dimensions.

We should note, however, that the difference in timing between the transition to biological and social parenthood may be somewhat less clear-cut for men. First, since they do not go through a nine-month gestation followed by childbirth itself, at the outer limit men might not even be aware of when they make the biological transition to parenthood. Further, when a married or cohabiting couple splits up, the children typically stay with their mother. Thus, the correspondence between biological and social parenthood is likely to be far closer for women than for men. As with most fertility research, this monograph primarily focuses on the female transition to parenthood. In the later chapters, however, we do examine the process for men, and compare the two sexes.

First-birth timing is very important for a range of outcome variables. It signifies the proximity of the birth to various other important benchmarks. "Early or late childbearing" suggests a reference point. Early or late compared to what? We measure early or late relative to the woman's own birth. The age of the mother at her child's birth gives the timing vis-à-vis the mother's life cycle. The date of birth places the event in historical time, a period. Early and late childbearing can be defined in comparison with other cohorts or with other women in the same cohort. Here we examine comparative cohort careers—change in the pace (ages) at which various cohorts make the transition to parenthood. We also examine intracohort variability and determine which individual characteristics influence the likelihood of this transition at given ages.

While we highlight time elapsed since mother's birth, we do not analyze other potential benchmarks. Except for a short section in chapter 5, we do not examine age at menarche which signals the beginning of the fecundable period. Age at first intercourse which signals the beginning of pregnancy risk is absent from our empirical work. While both variables can be considered proximate determinants of first-birth timing, the first appears to have changed relatively little from the 1920s through the 1970s (Treloar et al. 1976). Prior to the 1920s, there appears to have been a decline in age at menarche, but the nature of the samples available means that there has been some controversy (e.g., Bullough 1981; Eveleth 1986; Tanner 1981). Nevertheless, the lack of change in recent years suggests that this variable has had little influence. The second variable, age at first intercourse, had not been asked about on the large nationally representative samples available during the course of this study. However, this omission may be of little consequence for much of our analysis, because the link between the timing of first intercourse and the timing of the transition to parenthood may be relatively weak in contemporary United States. During the 1970s, age at first intercourse was decreasing (Zelnik and Kantner 1980; Zelnik et al. 1981) at the same time that age at first birth was increasing (see chap. 4).

Our measurement of the timing of parenthood follows the well-known life-table framework. A conventional life table starts with a group of individuals (l_o) exposed to the event, d, being examined—here, a birth cohort that will be exposed to the risk of parenthood. With time, as the birth cohort ages, the group at risk of a first birth is depleted as members experience parenthood or are censored (withdrawn from risk because of interview, death, or curtailment of the study). Elapsed time for this group of individuals is treated in a discrete fashion of width n, and the beginning age indexed by x. The number of events occurring in a time interval is $_nd_x$. The basic building block of the life table is the $_nq_x$ function:

$$_nq_x = \frac{_nd_x}{l_x}$$

From the $_nq_x$ function, all the other functions of the life table can be derived. For our study, $_nq_x$ is the birth probability ($_nBP_x$): the probability of having a first birth between ages x and x + n for those still childless at exact age x. This probability of the transition to parenthood at age x will constitute the dependent variable for most of the analyses reported. Introduction of multivariate control is easily achieved (see chap. 5). The complement of $_nBP_x$ is the probability of remaining childless while age x, $_nP_x$:

$$1 - {_nq_x} = {_nP_x}$$

Given a series of birth probabilities from the youngest age at childbearing, say 15, one can use their complements to compute the proportion "surviving" the risk of parenthood at age x, for example, the proportion childless at age x (PC_x):

$$_1P_{15} \cdot {_1P_{16}} \cdot {_1P_{17}} \cdots {_1P_x} = PC_x$$

The proportion childless at age x gives an intuitively obvious measure of delayed childbearing to age x which can be compared across cohorts that have already reached age x.

Given $_nBP_x$ and PC_x, we can compute the proportion of those in a given cohort who have a first child at age x—the first birthrate (FBR_x):

$$_nBP_x \cdot PC_x = FBR_x$$

However, one measure from the conventional life table that cannot always be computed straightforwardly under our framework is e_x, the expectation of the "life" remaining at age x, or for our application, years remaining until parenthood. Computation of such a measure for women who have not yet aged beyond the childbearing years requires one to make assumptions about future behavior. One possibility is to take into account the past behavior of a wide variety of earlier cohorts (e.g., Bloom 1980, 1982, 1984; or Pitcher 1980). However, the problem with such approaches is that they implicitly or explicitly assume that future events will not influence the pattern of first births. We argue in the next chapter that this assumption is untenable in the American context.

For both methodological and substantive reasons, we do not focus on mean age at first birth, a commonly used measure of first-birth timing.

The most important methodological reason is truncation bias for the most recent cohorts. Failure to recognize truncation of variables can lead to severely biased results (see Morgan and Liao 1985; Rindfuss et al. 1983). For analyses of age at first birth, the question becomes, How much experience can be truncated before serious bias is introduced into estimates of trends and determinants? Clearly, so few births occur at ages 40 and above that truncation at these ages would have negligible effects. However, restricting the data to those who have already reached these older ages does not allow us to examine the behavior of women now in the midst of the childbearing years. At the same time, truncating at very young ages clearly produces misleading results. In figure 2, we show the mean age at first birth for cohorts 1910 to 1950, estimated from the 1975 and 1980 CPS surveys. All ever-married women as of the survey date are included.

Note that the 1950 cohort was aged 25 at the 1975 survey date and 30 at the 1980 survey. The 1975 estimate, therefore, excludes the 26–30 age behavior of this cohort while the 1980 estimate includes it. The effect of truncating this experience of age at first birth is severe—the estimates differ by nearly two years (see fig. 2). The discrepancy for the next most

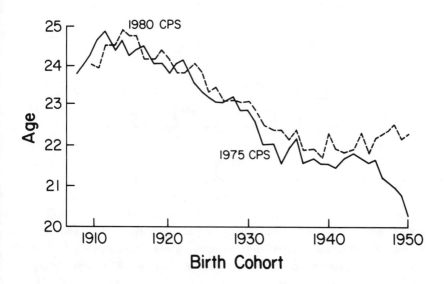

Fig. 2. Mean age at first birth by birth cohort:
Current Population Survey 1975, 1980.

recent cohort, the 1949 cohort, results from the exclusion of 27–31 experience; the 1948 discrepancy results from excluding 28–32 experience; and so forth. Note that the 1975 and 1980 estimates converge smoothly so that for the 1945 cohort there is little apparent bias. Put differently, excluding behavior at ages over 30 has negligible effects on overall trends in age at first birth. Our first-birth probability measures eliminate this age truncation problem.

There are also substantive reasons for not focusing on mean age at first birth. Our theoretical perspective (see chap. 2) emphasizes that the decision "to have a child now" is the appropriate analytical one, and that permanent childlessness generally results from a series of decisions to postpone childbearing. Some factors may affect fertility only at specific ages, a result that may not be as visible or as interpretable in a single summary measure across all ages. Also our interest often focuses on teenage childbearing or childbearing at older ages.

Thus, the transition to parenthood is represented as a series of conditional first-birth probabilities. These probabilities can then be manipulated to obtain the proportion childless at a given age, age-specific first-birth rates, or median age at first birth. We now turn to a discussion of the principal data sources used in the analysis.

VITAL REGISTRATION DATA

Trends in delayed childbearing are examined using vital statistics data. For a given cohort, the proportion childless at a given age (25, 30, or 35) measures the extent to which childbearing is delayed. Heuser (1976: tables 8a, 8b, and 8c) presents the distribution of women by parity at the beginning of each year 1917–1974 for individual cohorts by color. He also shows parity-specific birth probabilities and age-specific birth rates. This data set has recently been updated to 1980 and made available on computer tape.

The strength of this data source is the excellent measurement of first-birth timing over a very broad range of periods and cohorts. The birth registration system in the United States is widely acknowledged to be very complete and relatively error free (e.g., Shryock and Siegel 1971). The shortcoming of the vital registration data is the lack of individual-level characteristics—the data are disaggregated only by a white-nonwhite dichotomy, age, period, and cohort. To supplement this vital registration data, we obtained a number of potential aggregate-level determinants of these trends, the sources of which we discuss in chapter 4.

CURRENT POPULATION SURVEYS

A second data set that we use for several purposes is the 1980 June Current Population Survey (CPS). This data set has the advantage of being quite large (over fifty thousand households). It includes all women regardless of marital status and contains partial birth and marriage histories. The birth history contains information on the first four live births, and the last and next to last live births. We will only use data for the first live birth, and thus the incompleteness of the history is not a problem.

The most serious limitation of the 1980 June CPS (like earlier CPSs) is that information on many individual characteristics which may influence delayed childbearing has not been collected. The only relevant predictor variables included in the CPS are race, year of birth, ethnicity, education, and marriage history.

The primary advantage of the 1980 June CPS is its inclusion of all women aged 18 to 75, regardless of marital status. The older portion of the age range (those 60 and over) will not be included in our analysis so as not to contaminate results with the potential effects of differential mortality by parity, race, or cohort. But even after excluding the oldest respondents, the CPS still provides a very large sample.

The CPS sampling frame of all women contrasts sharply with most fertility surveys that are generally limited to ever-married women. The extent to which results from an ever-married sample are generalizable to the total population is unknown. In fact, the determinants of fertility might be quite different for ever- versus never-married women. Take the example of the effect of graduate training. Assume that graduate training led to delayed childbearing. Further suppose that disproportionate numbers of women with graduate training forgo marriage. Then an ever-married sample would underestimate the effect of graduate training.

The effects of excluding the never-married depend on (1) the degree to which the behavior of never- and ever-married women differs and (2) given some difference, the size of the never-married population. If the proportion never-married is small and/or their behavior is similar to ever-married, then the bias resulting from their exclusion will be minor.

Otherwise, excluding the never-married can produce misleading results. Since we will later be forced to use ever-married samples, the question becomes, Can we understand delayed childbearing by examining an ever-married sample? More specifically, will the observed levels and trends in delayed childbearing be affected by excluding the never-married? And will the socioeconomic determinants of delayed childbearing be the same for the ever-married and never-married samples? Some answers to these questions can be provided by the 1980 CPS, because it contains information on the timing of the first birth for all women regardless of marital status.

We have analyzed the 1980 CPS data twice: once on the full sample, and once on a sample of ever-married women. Comparison of results using these two samples indicates the extent to which the results for married women are representative of all women. Details are presented in appendix A and summarized here.

When comparing *levels and trends*, average age at first birth is not influenced by excluding the never-married because very few births occur to women who continue to remain never-married. The levels of four life-table measures *are* affected by exclusion of the never-married. Specifically, estimates of the proportion childless at age 25 and the birth probabilities at ages 25–29, 30–34, and 35–39 are sharply lowered by excluding the never-married. This result occurs because never-married women are more likely to be childless. However, cohort trends in the proportion childless or in the birth probabilities are very similar in both samples.

Within a multivariate framework, we also asked if potential determinants of delayed childbearing have similar effects in an all-women sample and an ever-married sample. The CPS data contain three likely determinants: birth cohort, education, and race (black or white). Estimated effects of these independent variables are quite similar across both samples, regardless of the fertility measure examined. Thus, for the birth cohorts we examine, the estimated determinants from an all-women sample also hold when it is restricted to an ever-married sample. This result is important in allowing us to use the fertility surveys.

THE U.S. FERTILITY SURVEYS

Beginning in 1955, a series of pioneering cross-sectional fertility surveys was conducted in the United States. Despite the many differences among them, each one used the earlier ones as a point of departure. Thus there is a considerable amount of continuity. We analyze the first six surveys in the series: the 1955 and 1960 Growth of American Families Studies (GAF); the 1965 and 1970 National Fertility Studies (NFS); and the 1973 and 1976 National Surveys of Family Growth (NSFG).[1] Table 1 is a summary of these three studies, the survey organizations that conducted them, and definitions of the universes. All six are acknowledged to be of high quality and, as we shall subsequently show, when restricted to the same universe they yield consistent results.

The primary advantage of these fertility surveys is that they contain information on a much wider range of social-demographic factors than the CPS data. In most cases the variables can be operationalized similarly across all six surveys[2] which allows us to extend the time period under analysis. To extend the series by pooling surveys, however, it was necessary to check for the presence of study effects. Such a check is necessary because these surveys have been conducted by various survey organizations and have had different principal investigators. Furthermore, the surveys targeted somewhat different populations of women. They also differ in their sampling frames, the manner in which certain information was obtained, and the timing of the survey itself. Nevertheless, these surveys have been put to similar purposes by different researchers and therefore have effectively been treated as if the differences that do exist among them are not critical with respect to the results obtained. If study effects are absent, we should obtain the same results when different surveys ask the same cohort the same retrospective questions about an earlier life cycle event.

We are able to check for study effects because each survey asked a series of retrospective questions, and there is overlap in the experience represented (see fig. 3). The horizontal axis is calendar year and the vertical axis is current age. The trapezoid created by the horizontal lines shows fertility experience that can be observed in the 1970 NFS; and the trapezoid created by the vertical lines shows experience which can be

---

[1]Detailed descriptions of these six surveys can be found respectively in the following: Freedman, Whelpton, and Campbell 1959; Whelpton, Campbell, and Patterson 1966; Ryder and Westoff 1971; Westoff and Ryder 1977*a*; French 1978; National Center for Health Statistics 1979.

[2]Some variables are measured differently. For example, in some cases we have education at interview and in others we have education at marriage; some surveys measure current religion, others religion of origin. We find no evidence that such variability affected our estimates of trends and differentials in first-birth timing.

TABLE 1.
NAME AND CHARACTERISTICS OF THE SIX FERTILITY SURVEYS—UNITED STATES

Study	Survey organization	Universe
1955 Growth of American Families (1955 GAF)	Survey Research Center, University of Michigan	White, currently married women, aged less than 40
1960 Growth of American Families (1960 GAF)	Survey Research Center, University of Michigan	Currently married women aged less than 45
1965 National Fertility Study (1965 NFS)	National Analysts	Currently married women aged less than 55
1970 National Fertility Study (1970 NFS)	Temple University	Ever-married women aged less than 45
1973 National Survey of Family Growth (1973 NSFG)	National Opinion Research Center	Ever-married women and never-married mothers aged less than 45
1976 National Survey of Family Growth (1976 NSFG)	Westat	Same as 1973 NSFG

observed using the 1976 NSFG. The intersection of these two spaces, the cross-hatched area in figure 3, illustrates experience sampled in both surveys. As this figure suggests, each survey contains data for different birth cohorts of women. However, the age range in each survey is sufficiently wide so that all cohorts of women born since 1916 are represented in several different surveys. The essence of our strategy is to examine the levels and determinants of the timing of first births and compare the results obtained in different surveys for the same cohorts of women (i.e., the study comparisons are made on women eligible to be in more than one survey). We constrain the samples in a way to ensure that (1) the women would have been eligible to be included in any of the surveys involved; (2) the fertility events under consideration would have occurred prior to the earliest survey. These constraints are outlined in detail in Swicegood, Morgan, and Rindfuss (1984). Their application results in a sample represented by the cross-hatched area of figure 3.

We test for two different types of study effects: mean shifts and predictor effect shifts. In the first type of study effect, the question is

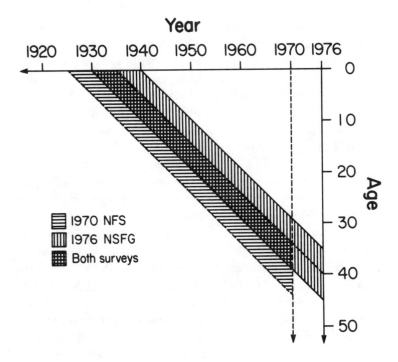

Fig. 3. Fertility experience sampled in 1970 National Fertility Study and 1976 National Survey of Family Growth.

whether or not the mean level of the dependent variable is the same across studies for comparably defined sets of women. When multiple data sources are compared in the social sciences, replication is frequently restricted to this type of question (see Santi 1980 and T. W. Smith 1982 for exceptions). The second type of study effect indicates whether the effect of some predictor variable on the dependent variable varies across studies for comparably defined sets of women. In other words, is there an interaction with study?

The comparisons we make involve grouping studies into two sets:

1. 1970 National Fertility Study (NFS), 1973 and 1976 National Survey of Family Growth (NSFG)
2. 1955 and 1960 Growth of American Family (GAF), 1965 National Fertility Study (NFS)

Comparisons are made within each set but not across sets. The 1955 and 1960 GAF, and 1965 NFS have to be analyzed separately because the cohorts involved are considerably earlier than the other studies, and more important, because all three are restricted to currently married women. Several different aspects of the timing of the first birth are examined. First, for those who had a first birth, at what age did they have it? Childless women are excluded, and the dependent variable is a straightforward continuous variable: age at first birth. Age at first birth is used here even though it is not used in the substantive portions of this monograph because our interest here is methodological and age at first birth has been widely used in prior studies. A second set of first-birth timing variables is how likely is a woman to remain childless until age 25 and until age 35? Finally, we examine a series of first-birth probabilities among those women who have remained childless until given ages. Here the two dependent variables are the probabilities of having a first birth by age 30 and 35 given childlessness at ages 25 and 30, respectively. We assess study effects across a variety of delayed childbearing variables[3] because the effect of the various predictor variables changes across these different formulations (see chap. 5), thus suggesting the possibility that any potential study effect could change similarly.

Before moving to the results, several comments on their interpretation are warranted. First, we have not specified particular hypotheses about where and why study effects should appear but instead test all possible ones. By chance alone such an approach will produce an occasional, statistically significant estimate. Such effects are far less troubling than a consistent pattern of study effects for a given variable. Second, our statistical tests are based on the assumption of simple random sampling. Since all modern national samples are clustered, the power of these tests is overestimated and significance levels are very liberal (see J. A. Davis 1982). We chose an overall approach and liberal tests because our goal is to assess the reliability of these demographic surveys broadly.

Since the details of this analysis and the implications have been presented elsewhere (see Swicegood et al. 1984), here we only focus on the general findings that have implications for this study.

We first examined differences in *levels* as measured by age at first birth and four life table measures. Of the ten possible differences (five measures

[3]Because some of the fertility variables are continuous and some are dichotomous, different statistical techniques had to be used. When the fertility variable was continuous, means were used as the descriptive statistic and the multivariate technique is ordinary least squares regression. When the fertility variable was a dichotomy, percentages were used as the descriptive statistic and the multivariate technique is logistic regression. See Swicegood et al. (1984) for details.

and two sets of surveys) only one is significant at the .05 level. The estimated level of childlessness at age 35 varies across the three earlier surveys (the 1955, 1960 GAF, and the 1965 NFS). But this difference is not significant if we choose a .01 instead of a .05 significance level. In short, the levels of fertility delay are quite comparably measured in these six surveys.

Next we asked whether the effects of various hypothesized determinants (of the timing of the first birth) are consistent across the studies. Inconsistent relationships might arise from sampling variability, but other sources of variation are perhaps more likely. In particular, a number of concepts presumed to be related to the family formation process are assessed somewhat differently in each of the surveys. Differences exist in question wording, ordering, and content. With respect to such factors as farm background, these differences can be considerable. In other instances, such as race or age, they are small.

Cells in table 2 show the set of possible study effects. The first panel shows which predictor variables have effects that vary across the first group of studies. Of 45 possible interactions tested, only six are significant. Furthermore, four of these six significant interactions involve just one variable, contraceptive use prior to the first birth. Given that the study variable only interacts with both region and fetal mortality once in five trials, we are reluctant to draw substantive conclusions about these interactions. Instead, such interactions appear to be the occasional type that arise because of sampling variability. Results from the other group of studies tell essentially the same story—lack of consistency for the effects of contraceptive use and quite consistent results for the other variables.

Several conclusions can be drawn from these results. First, the results obtained for the contraceptive use prior to the first birth variable are disappointing. Despite the aggregate stability of contraceptive use before the first birth using the first four fertility surveys (Rindfuss and Westoff 1974), it is clear that this variable is unreliably measured at the individual level. We find no consistent effect of this variable on timing of the first birth across studies. The sign even changes in some cases. These results suggest that new strategies need to be devised to obtain contraceptive information for the period prior to the first birth. Based on these results, we have excluded contraceptive use prior to the first birth in our subsequent analyses.

Second, with respect to timing of the first birth, the results are remark-

TABLE 2.
SIGNIFICANT STUDY EFFECTS BY PREDICTOR VARIABLE AND
FERTILITY INDICATOR—1970 NSF, 1973 AND 1976 NSFG;
1955 AND 1960 GAF, 1965 NFS

Predictor variable	Age at first birth	Childless at 25	Childless at 35	Birth probability at 25–35	Birth probability at 30–35
		1970 NFS, 1973 and 1976 NSFG			
Education					
Farm background					
Region			*		
Religion					
Race					
Intact family					
Cohort					
Fetal death		**			
Contraception	*	*		**	*
		1955 and 1960 GAF; 1965 NFS			
Education		**			
Farm background					
Region					
Religion					
Race					
Intact family					
Cohort					
Fetal death	**				
Contraception	**	**		*	

*Significant at .05.
**Significant at .01.

ably similar across surveys. Changing the study director, survey organization, question wording, the time over which events have to be recalled,
and other aspects of the survey do not affect the conclusions that the
researcher reaches. This general finding allows us to combine the fertility
surveys which provides larger sample sizes and longer time series. The
analysis in chapter 5 uses a pooled sample from these surveys.

Another potential methodological problem is the truncation on age at
marriage that arises in the fertility studies because they are either cur-
rently-married or ever-married samples. Figure 4 helps illustrate the problem. Again, the horizontal axis is calendar year and the vertical axis is

current age. We use the 1970 NFS, an ever-married sample, as an example. Those age 25 in 1970, the 1945 birth cohort, must have first married at ages less than or equal to 25 in order to be included in the sample. Twenty-year-olds must have married by age 20 in order to be included. Clearly those married by age 20 or 25 will not be representative of those who will ever marry. Our solution to this problem is to analyze only those over age 35 at the survey date. The implicit assumption is that those who marry by age 35 are representative of those who will ever marry. This decision was based on prior work (Rindfuss and St. John 1983; Rindfuss et al. 1980) and on our examination of truncation bias using all-women and ever-married samples selected from the 1980 CPS (appendix A). Thus, from the 1970 NFS we can observe, without bias, the 1925–1935 birth cohorts. The other five surveys provide unbiased observations of earlier and later cohorts.

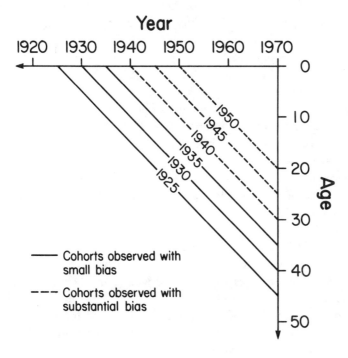

Fig. 4. Age at marriage bias inherent in ever-married survey conducted in 1970.

THE NATIONAL LONGITUDINAL STUDY OF
THE HIGH SCHOOL CLASS OF 1972

The National Longitudinal Study of the High School Class of 1972 (NLS) is a large and detailed study funded by the National Center for Educational Statistics (NCES) and widely used by scholars in the sociology of education field. However, it is only recently being used by other sociologists (e.g., Haggstrom et al. 1984). Because this data set may be less familiar to our readers than the other data sets we use, we describe it in somewhat greater detail.

The first data collection took place in the spring of 1972 when panel members were seniors in high school. Follow-ups were conducted in the fall of 1973, 1974, 1976, and 1979. An additional follow-up was conducted in 1986.[4] The data set is large (over twenty thousand cases), rich in detail, and contains information for both sexes.

Approximately three-quarters of the members of this study were born in 1954 and 20 percent in 1953. Thus there is relatively little age variance, but they are very strategic cohorts. First, they represent a recent set of cohorts. Members have been delaying entry into parenthood more than any set of cohorts since those born in 1910–1915, who were in their early twenties during the Great Depression. These cohorts (1953 and 1954) have experienced a substantial amount of political, social, and economic change. During their years in grade school, the civil rights controversy was at its peak. During their high school years, activism over the Vietnam War and feminist issues were major social movements. During their early adult years housing prices rose substantially, and toward the end of their twenties they faced extremely high interest rates that accompanied economic stagflation.

Although the primary purpose of the NLS was to examine the relationship between educational experiences and career outcomes, we use this rich source of information on schooling and early career experiences to identify which career lines are associated with delayed childbearing, and to determine factors affecting the likelihood of being in a given career line. This research is possible because the third and fourth follow-ups

---

[4]Again the 1986 data collection is being supported primarily by NCES. But the National Institute of Child Health and Development (NICHD) has awarded a grant to Robert Michael and Robert Willis to allow inclusion of questions on marital and fertility histories, resource flows outside the household, and intergenerational transfers.

contain information on family status and fertility intentions and, most important, the fourth follow-up contains a birth history.

The base year (1972) data were collected by the Educational Testing Service of Princeton, N.J., and all follow-up data have been collected by the Research Triangle Institute of Research Triangle Park, N.C.

The sample design was a highly stratified two-stage probability sample with schools, and then students, as first- and second-stage sampling units. The sampling universe contains all 1972 twelfth graders enrolled in public, private, and church-affiliated high schools in the United States (the 50 states and Washington, D.C.). In the 1,009 schools participating in the base year, 16,683 (of 19,144) seniors completed questionnaires.

The first follow-up added 4,450 high school seniors of the class of 1972 representing types of schools unable to participate earlier. These respondents were asked additional background questions to fill in information collected for others in the base year questionnaire.[5] Of the 23,451 potential respondents, 21,350 completed the first follow-up questionnaire. Additional members who did not complete the first follow-up did participate in subsequent follow-up. (See Riccobono et al. 1981 for more details.)

Throughout, response rates were remarkably high given (1) the length of each questionnaire and (2) that the follow-ups were initially mail-out, mail-back procedures, followed by telephone reminders. The fourth follow-up received information from 89 percent of those who were sent the questionnaire. The corresponding number for each of the earlier follow-ups was well over 90 percent.

The NLS contains a wide variety of information. In the base year, each student provided information on personal family background, educational and work experience, plans, aspirations, attitudes, and opinions. In addition, respondents took a 69-minute test, composed of six subtests, measuring verbal and nonverbal ability. Base year data were also obtained from a student's school records, including high school curriculum, grade-point average, credit hours in major courses and, if applicable, position in ability groupings, remedial-instruction record, involvement in certain federally supported programs, and scores on standardized tests.

With two major exceptions, the follow-up questionnaires were of

---

[5]While not everything that was originally included in the original baseline questionnaire was included for these additional panel members, the critical pieces of information that we need were. Thus we are able to include these additional panel members in our analyses.

similar design. Most of the questions involved the respondent's activity state as of October 1 of each year since the last follow-up. These activity states include school, work, military, and so forth. Even though a complete continuous time, event history was not obtained, the choice of October 1 is an excellent one for our purposes. At the ages being considered here (roughly 18–25), individuals are prone to engage in some of these activities for a very short duration. The summer months are the ones most likely to find individuals in very temporary activities: summer jobs, a refresher course at school, or touring Europe by bicycle. By October 1, those who are students are likely to be back in school full time. The job market would have solidified such that those who are unemployed at that point will probably spend more than just a few days in that state. And those who finished school the previous spring with the intention of joining the military would likely be in the military by October 1.

The amount of information obtained for these activity states varied. Consistent with the study's being sponsored by the National Center for Education Statistics, information is richest for those who were in school, ranging from the name of the school itself to how individuals are financing their education. However, the information available on all the activity states is more than sufficient for our purposes.

The baseline questionnaire, and each of the first three follow-ups also included information about marriage and fertility. However, the information obtained was not very detailed, and even a mildly complex history would be incomplete based on data from these first four questionnaires. Fortunately, the 1979 follow-up contained a complete fertility history.[6] Since there is widespread evidence that such information can be accurately collected retrospectively (e.g., see the previous section of this chapter), these fertility data can be merged with all the information contained in the previous four rounds. Unlike the activity states, all respondents can be classified on a monthly basis as to whether or not they have become parents. This provides us with considerably more flexibility in the specification of our parenthood variable than with the activity states.

While this is a rich data set that allows detailed examination of the determinants of the timing of parenthood, there are several limitations. It is only a sample of those who reached their senior year in high school.

[6]The 1979 follow-up did not include a comparable marriage history. Thus even if there were theoretical grounds for having marriage as a preparenthood stage (see chap. 2) such data would not be available for NLS 72.

Thus high school dropouts are excluded. As such, it is a sample more appropriate to examining delayed childbearing than early childbearing. Indeed, this is how we use it in chapters 8 and 9.

Finally, we reiterate that NLS 72 is restricted to a small set of birth cohorts, and we will not know with certainty how generalizable our results are to other cohorts. But, this is an extremely interesting cohort with respect to the timing of fertility. It appears that their age pattern of first birth will be quite similar to those who bore children during the depression (see chap. 4). Further, our principal interest in the NLS 72 is to examine structural effects on the transition to parenthood. Our findings from chapter 5 suggest that structural relationships are reasonably stable over time. A similar study of the high school class of 1980 is currently under way. Thus, future researchers will be able to check our results against more recent cohorts.

CONCLUSION

To summarize, we measure the transition to parenthood as a series of conditional first-birth probabilities. These probabilities can then be manipulated mathematically to obtain the proportion childless at a given age, age-specific first-birth rates, or median age at first birth. This operational procedure flows from our theoretical conceptualization of the entire first-birth process.

Given the fairly broad scope of our interest in the transition to parenthood, no single data set is sufficient. Instead we employ a variety of data sets—exploiting the strength of each and using the strengths of others to minimize the weaknesses of each. Thus, in what follows, the results from any one data set are more compelling because of the corroborating evidence from the others. We now turn to our substantive results.

4

Trends of Transition Timing

Lay persons and scholars devote substantial attention to parenthood not only because it has important consequences but also because of its considerable variability. In the United States, changes in parental timing have been particularly evident since World War II. Here we begin with a brief overview of U.S. trends in the transition to parenthood, and then place them in a broader historical context. Finally, given the recent prominence of delayed childbearing, we focus on its trends and determinants.

Because recent trends are substantially different for whites and blacks, we examine the timing of the transition to parenthood only for whites here. We investigate black-white differences in chapter 6. Throughout, recent changes are viewed from a broad historical perspective to determine if they are indeed unprecedented. The main data source used in this chapter is the series provided by the vital registration system and described in chapter 3.

OVERVIEW OF U.S. TRENDS

Trends in overall fertility patterns in the United States are by now well known. At the beginning of the twentieth century, total fertility rates were continuing their general long-term decline, which had its origins in the late eighteenth or early nineteenth century (e.g., Coale and Zelnik 1963). Fertility levels reached a low point during the Great Depression. Following World War II there was a sustained increase in fertility which continued during the 1950s. The 1960s brought a decrease in fertility, again, which continued until the early 1970s—reaching levels lower than any ever experienced in the United States.

Since changes in timing of the first birth are such a large component of the overall changes in fertility (Ryder 1980*a*), it is not surprising that trends in the timing of fertility tend to mirror the overall trends. In table 3 we show the percent childless by age for the 60-year period 1920–1980. Looking first at age 25, which represents the most volatile age, one can see that the proportion childless increased during the 1930s, reached a low point during the 1950s and has been increasing since 1960. In 1980 more than twice as many women were childless at age 25 than was the case in 1960. Similar trends can be found at older ages, but, because of the cumulative nature of the childlessness measure, the time lag is somewhat greater. For example, the low point in childlessness at age 35 was not reached until 1970.

Several additional points need to be made regarding these general trends. The first involves adolescent childbearing. This topic has galvanized the attention of American policymakers for the last decade. In particular, fertility among very young teenagers has received the most attention. Such concern is justified in that there are consequences for both mother and child as a result of childbearing at such a young age (see chap. 1). What is somewhat surprising from table 3 is why the concern now for adolescent childbearing? For all teenagers, there has been a decline since the 1950s in the proportion making the transition to parenthood. And at the very youngest ages, during this 60-year period (1920–1980) there has been relatively little change in the proportion becoming parents. Put differently, teenage childbearing has a very long history in the United States. Recent attention has more to do with young childbearing being increasingly out of wedlock and not because of its increased incidence.

High levels of childlessness were common at the beginning of this time period (table 3). From 1920 through 1950, approximately one in five white women was still childless at age 40. While part of this may be the result of the Great Depression, it is also clear that it is a pattern well established before the 1930s. The women who were 40 in 1920 were in their prime childbearing years at the turn of the century. Modell, Furstenberg, and Strong (1978) point out that the single adult was a significant part of the American population in the nineteenth and early twentieth century.

Finally, table 3 illustrates how important ages 20–29 are in the transition to parenthood. Despite all the attention given to both extremes of the childbearing distribution, ages 20–29 are the prime years for making

TABLE 3.
PERCENTAGE OF WHITE WOMEN CHILDLESS BY AGE AND CALENDAR YEAR—1920–1980

Age	Year												
	1920	1925	1930	1935	1940	1945	1950	1955	1960	1965	1970	1975	1980
17	97	97	97	97	97	97	96	95	95	96	96	96	96
20	81	78	80	83	82	81	75	71	69	73	77	80	81
25	45	44	46	51	51	45	36	31	26	27	35	45	55
30	29	27	28	30	34	29	21	16	15	12	14	20	28
35	24	23	21	23	24	25	19	14	11	11	9	10	15
40	23	22	21	19	21	21	21	16	11	9	9	8	10

SOURCE: Heuser (1976) and recent vital statistics volumes.

the transition to parenthood. For the cohorts represented, the proportion becoming parents in their twenties ranges from 46 through 65 percent—with much of this occurring between ages 20 and 25. Our analysis in subsequent chapters will often focus on these "on time" ages because of their central importance.

THE UNITED STATES IN INTERNATIONAL PERSPECTIVE[1]

A variety of period factors have affected the timing of the transition to parenthood in the United States. However, the United States is not isolated from the rest of the developed world. Clearly, many social, economic, and political events that affect the United States also affect other developed countries. The high interest rates of the late 1970s and early 1980s were experienced by many other nations, as were high rates of inflation. The women's movement is found in various guises in most developed countries. Furthermore, communication improvements have intensified this linkage among developed nations.

A variety of social, political, cultural, historic, and economic differences also exist among developed nations. Thus, even if all developed nations experienced the same events, those events would be filtered through the varying social, economic, and historical perspectives that make each nation unique. These different filters may produce different effects. Furthermore, some events clearly impinge more on certain countries than others. For example, even though many countries contributed support to the United States' involvement in Vietnam, presumably its impact was far more severe on the United States than any other developed country.

In short, reasons exist for similarities and differences in parenthood timing across developed nations. By examining United States trends in a comparative context, we should gain a better understanding of the forces affecting parenthood timing within the United States. In this section, we compare trends in the proportion childless and first-birth probabilities for 11 developed nations. In addition to the United States, they include Austria, Ireland, Sweden, Belgium, Italy, England, Japan, West Germany, Hungary, and Portugal. These countries have time-series data sufficiently long to warrant inclusion.

[1]This section was prepared with assistance from David Bloom, who supplied the data for all countries except the United States, Sweden, and Japan. His help is appreciated.

Data for each country come from its vital registration system. Since differences exist across countries in coverage and definition, we exercised caution in making these cross-country comparisons. For example, the English vital registration system does not publish information on the birth order of illegitimate offspring. Thus, the English rates presented here include only legitimate first births. However, given the broad, general points with respect to the U.S. pattern that we will be making, such differences can be safely ignored.

Trends in the proportion childless at ages 20, 25, 30, and 35 are shown in the four panels of figure 5. To highlight the United States relative to the other ten countries, the trend for the U.S. has been drawn considerably bolder than that for any of the other countries. Looking at the first panel, proportion childless at age 20, one can see that throughout the entire 30-year period, the United States stands out as having a high proportion of women who are parents by age 20. Westoff, Calot, and Foster (1983) noted that during the 1970s the rate of white teenage childbearing in the United States was among the highest in the developed world. The first panel of figure 5 makes it clear that this has been a long-standing difference. Only in the last few years has Hungary had a higher proportion of teenage parents, undoubtedly reflecting the strong pronatalist policies recently promulgated there. If we had data for other eastern European countries, like Rumania, Czechoslovakia, Yugoslavia, or East Germany, we expect that they too would show increased proportions of teens becoming parents during the latter part of the 1970s.

A second feature found in all four panels of figure 5, although it is most prominent at age 25, is the amount of variation from decade to decade in the proportion childless in the United States relative to other countries. The other countries, by way of contrast, tend to exhibit less change from year to year or decade to decade. And, for most of those experiencing change, there is a tendency for it to be unidirectional rather than apparently cyclic as in the United States. Of all the countries shown, England comes closest to the U.S. pattern. These international differences in parenthood-timing trends are not the same as those for overall fertility. While the baby boom was strongest in the United States, Australia, and Canada, it is quite evident in most European countries (see Campbell 1974).

A final noteworthy feature of figure 5 is that the difference in the proportion childless between the United States and the other developed countries is approximately maintained across the progressively older age groups shown in the four panels. This finding suggests that countries do not "catch up" to one another. Countries that start out with high levels of delayed childbearing tend to have higher levels of childlessness at the end of the childbearing years. There is one exception to this generalization. Japan starts out with extremely high proportions childless at age 20 and has extremely low proportions childless at age 35. In chapter 7 we explicitly examine the contrast between Japan and the United States.

DELAYED CHILDBEARING IN THE UNITED STATES

While the United States has one of the highest rates of teenage childbearing in the developed world, as the previous section showed, the most striking feature of recent U.S. trends is the increase in the proportion of women who are delaying parenthood. Focusing more closely on the U.S. data, we examine the demographic components of this change. Recent changes imply that an increasing number of women will remain permanently childless, but increasing numbers will also have births at older ages. Subsequent analysis shows that these and other predictions should be offered cautiously since period effects have in the past, and could again, cause rapid, dramatic, and pervasive change in parenthood timing.

We presented the rationale for focusing on delayed childbearing in some detail in chapter 1. Briefly, the 1970s witnessed sharp increases in the number of older women giving birth for the first time. Between 1966 and 1976 the number of first births to women over age 30 increased by almost one-third. Such increases have led to a number of medical, demographic, and economic issues. The medical issues involve the risks of childbearing at older ages, for mother and infant. Demand for infertility treatment is also an issue. The demographic issues focus on the implications of fertility delay for subsequent childbearing and for marital disruption, to provide just two examples. Economic and social issues include the consequences of childbearing for older, more career-oriented women.

Central to any discussion of these issues is an understanding of the demographic causes of the increase in first births among older women. The number of first births occurring to women aged 30–44 (FB_{30+}) is determined as follows:[2]

---

[2]We focus here on women aged 30–44 because this age group has generated the most concern. Subsequently, we expand the age range.

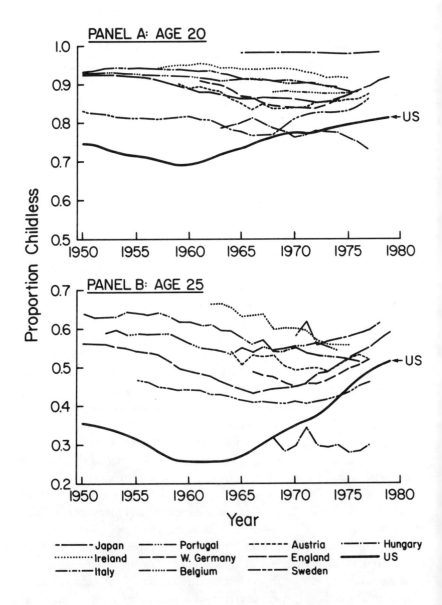

Fig. 5. Proportion childless at ages 20, 25, 30, and 35 for various developed nations—1950–1979.

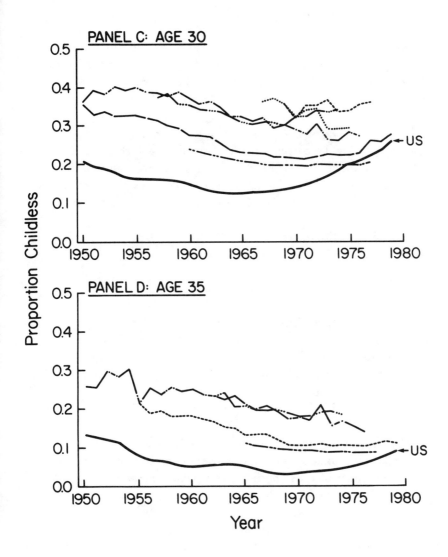

Note: Countries and dates shown vary depending on data availability.

$$FB_{30+} \quad = \quad W_{30+} \; * \; FBR_{30+}$$

where W_{30+} is the number of women aged 30–44 and FBR_{30+} is the rate at which women aged 30–44 are having first births. The first-birth rate (FBR_{30+}) can itself be further decomposed as follows:

$$FBR_{30+} \quad = \quad PC_{30+} \; * \; BP_{30+}$$

where PC_{30+} is the percent childless at ages 30–44 (the percentage still at risk of having a first birth) and BP_{30+} is the probability of first birth among those women still childless at ages 30–44. Thus, the overall number of first births to women aged 30–44 is the product of three terms:

$$FB_{30+} \quad = \quad W_{30+} \; * \; PC_{30+} \; * \; BP_{30+}.$$

CHANGES IN THE NUMBER OF WOMEN AGED 30–44

The number of first births to women over age 30 increased by almost one-third between 1966 and 1976, while the number of women aged 30–44 increased by only 6 percent, indicating that increasing population size has been a relatively small factor in the overall increase in the number of first births to older women. However, between 1976 and 1990, this situation has and will change dramatically as a result of earlier fertility trends.

The shift in the number of white women aged 30–44 between 1966 and 1976 was caused by the exit of those cohorts born between 1922 and 1931, and entry of those born between 1937 and 1946. From 1922 to 1931, fertility levels fell gradually; the total fertility rate fell from 2.97 to 2.31. From 1937 to 1946, there was a similar gradual increase in fertility, with the exception of the sharp, postwar increase in 1945 and 1946. Thus, the overall change in the number of women aged 30–44 was relatively small between 1966 and 1976.

Between 1976 and 1990, however, the story is quite different. The cohorts exiting the 30–44 age group will be those born between 1932 and 1945. These cohorts, particularly those born in the period 1932–1940, are among the smallest born in the twentieth century. The entering cohorts, those born between 1947 and 1960—the Baby Boom—are among the largest in American history. Between 1976 and 1990, the average cohort entering the 30–44 age group will be 53 percent larger than the average cohort leaving this age group. Thus, even though the W_{30+} component had only a small positive impact on the total number of first births to women aged 30–44 during 1966–1976, this impact is now being felt and will continue to be felt throughout the 1980s. In the absence of other changes, we can expect increases in the number of first births to older women.

THE PROPORTION OF WOMEN REMAINING CHILDLESS

The proportion of women remaining childless at older ages has increased sharply for recent cohorts of white women. Figure 6 shows the proportion of women childless at ages 25, 30, and 35. These proportions reflect the degree to which cohorts have delayed fertility, but do not distinguish between intentional and unintentional delays. Note that current levels of fertility delay have a precedent in that they approximate (at age 25) or approach (at ages 30 and 35) the level of delay experienced by women of prime childbearing age during the Depression (1910–1920 birth cohorts). This close approximation of the percentage of childless women currently in their childbearing years to that of women of childbearing age during the Great Depression is striking. Further, as table 3 suggests, if we could extend the series in figure 6 farther back in time, there would be still earlier cohorts that resemble the cohorts currently bearing children.

Figure 7 presents the proportion of women who were childless at ages 20 to 39 for a cohort experiencing the Depression (1910 cohort), a cohort contributing to the Baby Boom (the 1932 cohort), and the latest available data (through 1979) for two recent cohorts (those of 1950 and 1954). The Depression and Baby Boom experience set the referents for more recent experience. Increasingly, more recent cohorts seem to be following the "Depression pattern" of fertility delay (also see Masnick 1981*b*). In fact, the 1954 cohort pattern is virtually indistinguishable from the Depression one. If the 1954 cohort continues to follow this pattern, then approximately 20 percent of women born in 1954 will remain permanently childless.[3] In contrast, fewer than 10 percent of the Baby Boom cohort fall into this category. Of course, any projection of the proportion child-

---

[3]Bloom (1982), however, projects significantly higher levels of permanent childlessness for these cohorts—a topic we turn to later.

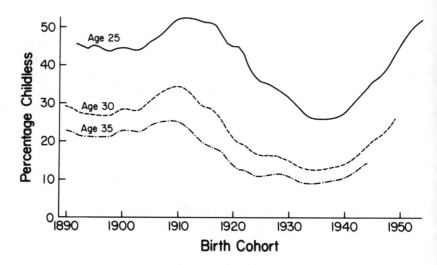

Fig. 6. Percentage childless for white birth cohorts at ages 25, 30, and 35.

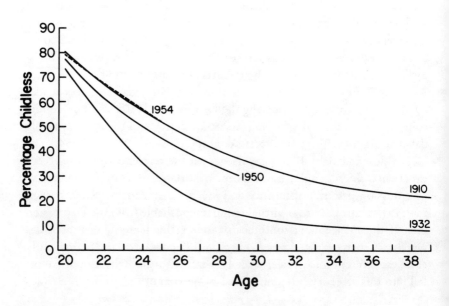

Fig. 7. Percentage childless by age for selected white birth cohorts.

less for cohorts still in their childbearing years is subject to error. The more years of childbearing remaining to a cohort, the greater the possible error. Historical precedent warns that sharp increases and decreases in the proportion childless have occurred in the recent past and could occur again.

BIRTH PROBABILITIES

If a woman reaches a given age childless, what is the probability that she will have her first child at that age? This is the birth probability (BP). Clearly, birth probabilities at younger ages have been falling, thereby producing larger proportions of women who are childless at ages 25, 30, and 35, as already shown in figure 6. Further, reports in the popular press suggest that birth probabilities at higher ages have risen sharply. The *Wall Street Journal* (Towman 1983:23), for instance, raises late motherhood to "epidemic proportions" and quotes a vice president of an executive recruiting firm as saying that "almost every married woman executive in her thirties is either pregnant or planning to be." Actually, results presented below will show that for white women as a group, birth probabilities at older ages are declining—given that women over 25 are childless, they are less likely to have a first birth than was true a decade ago.

Figure 8 shows first-birth probabilities at ages 25, 30, and 35 by birth cohort. At each age, these birth probabilities are approximating historically low values and show clear declines over the past two decades. Once again, the recent trends are similar to those found during the Depression years.

To highlight the effect of contemporaneous social and economic conditions on family formation, we have replotted the birth probabilities in figure 8 by year of observation instead of birth cohort (top panel of fig. 9). The trend lines show similar fluctuations, apparently in response to the childbearing environment at the time of observation—period phenomena. This point can be made more explicit by raising the birth probabilities at age 30 and 35 by a multiplicative constant, as shown in the second panel of figure 9. Clearly, women at each age are responding similarly to the prevailing environment. Put differently, period factors affect all women, regardless of age group. Thus, determining the proportion remaining

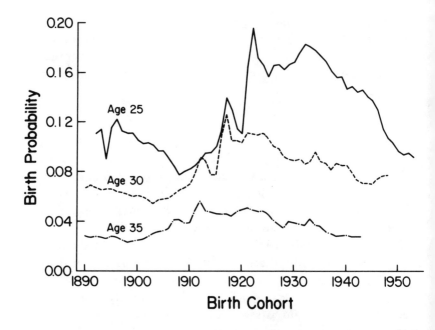

Fig. 8. First birth probabilities at ages 25, 30, and 35 for white birth cohorts.

childless for a cohort still in the childbearing years is likely to be an extremely error-prone exercise—unless, of course, the prevailing environment remains the same. As suggested in chapter 2, period factors have an overwhelming effect on trends.

The results shown in figures 8 and 9 have important implications for two quite different lines of research, both of which emphasize cohort rather than period change. The first is Easterlin's relative income or relative cohort size hypothesis (Easterlin 1962, 1966, 1973, 1978, and 1980). Easterlin argues that the marriage and fertility plans of young men are influenced by their relative economic prospects, as indicated by their current income in comparison to their parents' income while they were growing up. Parents' income references the consumption standard of the family of origin and represents young men's material aspirations. When young men judge their relative income to be favorable, marriages will occur earlier and fertility will rise. The macroversion of this hypothesis places considerable emphasis on cohort size. Men from large cohorts will have poor economic prospects and men from small cohorts will have

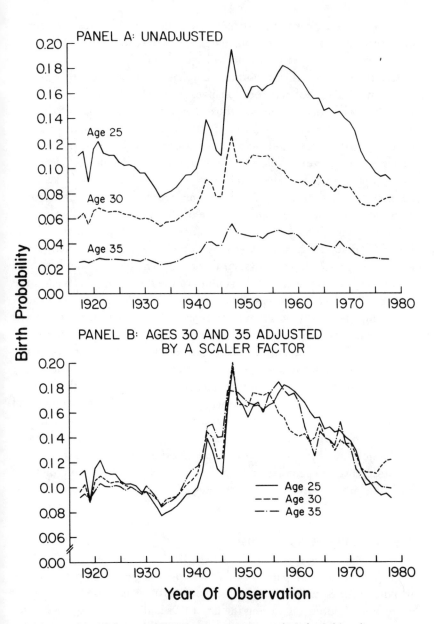

Fig. 9. First birth probabilities at ages 25, 30, and 35 for whites by year of observation.

bright economic prospects. Further, the system tends to have a built-in perpetuating mechanism because large cohorts tend to have small off-spring cohorts, who in turn tend to have large offspring cohorts.

Clearly the Easterlin hypothesis emphasizes a cohort rather than a period mechanism of temporal change. The size of one's cohort stays with that cohort as it ages, and thus its effects ought to be visible at all ages. As figures 8 and 9 make clear, this simply has not been the case. Rather, a variety of period factors have affected all age groups. Thus, for example, in the years following World War II, all cohorts (large and small) were affected by the postwar prosperity. Although not examined here, we would expect that similar findings would hold for first-marriage rates—the other key outcome measure of the Easterlin hypothesis.

The second line of research for which these results are relevant is Bloom's (1980, 1982, and 1984) adaptation of the Coale-McNeil (1972) first-marriage schedules to first-birth timing. The basic model has three parameters that represent the beginning of the distribution as well as the horizontal and vertical scales. Since the model is parametric, projections of incomplete cohorts is a natural exercise. Indeed, Bloom has projected that recent cohorts might experience an ultimate childlessness rate of 30 percent—a level higher than ever experienced by any cohort of white women in the United States. Fundamental to Bloom's predictions is a model of cohort change, and that once a cohort is far enough along on the trajectory of the first-birth process no period factors would alter the trajectory. Again the results in figures 8 and 9 argue against such an assumption. Period factors have substantially altered the trajectories of past cohorts, and it is not unreasonable to expect the same in the future. Put differently, depending on future period factors, Bloom's predictions could be either over- or underestimates.

DO COHORTS CATCH UP?

Do cohorts that delay parenthood catch up via higher birth probabilities at older ages? Some predict an upsurge in fertility as those women who postponed childbearing during the late 1960s and the 1970s begin having children.[4] In 1980 over half of the white women aged 25 were childless

---

[4]The most reasoned and sophisticated version of this argument is found in Sklar and Berkov (1975). However, the same argument is found repeatedly in the popular press today.

(see table 3). Fifteen years earlier the comparable figure was 26 percent. Childbearing among these women, should it occur, would result in a substantial increase in the number of births, and in turn would have a significant effect on institutions ranging from day care provision to the Social Security system. A second view emphasizes that fertility delay leads to greater levels of childlessness and lower overall fertility (Rindfuss and Bumpass 1978; Veevers 1979). This argument asserts that fertility delay allows women to develop interests that compete with childbearing, thus fostering further delay and, eventually, producing increased childlessness and small families.

From figure 6, it is clear that those cohorts that have delayed fertility to age 25 or 30 also have higher proportions of women childless at age 35. This pattern persists to ages 40 and 45 (not shown in fig. 6). Substantial fertility delay is not completely made up—cohorts that initially delayed their fertility never surpass those cohorts that did not.

But given that cohorts do not surpass those which delay less, do they catch up at all? Or, given two cohorts, one with substantial delay to age 25 and one with a relatively low proportion childless at this age, which will experience higher birth probabilities at later ages? For example, for the 1905 cohort, the proportion childless was reduced from .442 to .209 (or 47 percent) between the ages of 25 and 44. However, the 1925 cohort had only .355 childless at age 25 and this was reduced by 70 percent to .103 by age 44. For this comparison, then, the 1905 cohort fell farther behind rather than catching up.

If cohorts make up delayed childbearing, then the proportion childless at older ages should be positively related to birth probabilities at these ages; and if postponement breeds further postponement, then negative relationships would obtain. The first model in table 4 shows the estimated effects of the (logged) proportion childless at exact age X on the (logged) birth probability while age X. Regardless of age, higher proportions childless are associated with lower birth probabilities. The last column shows that a 1.0 percent increase in childlessness at age 25 reduces the likelihood of a birth between ages 25 and 39 by .199 percent. Cohorts delaying childbearing not only fail to catch up but generally fall farther behind.

The estimated negative effects, however, do diminish in size with age. At age 25 a 1.0 percent increase in the proportion childless is associated with a .907 percent decrease in the birth probability. A similar increase in childlessness at age 39 only reduces the birth probability by an estimated .048 percent.

To further explore this issue, the powerful influence of period factors shown in figure 9 must be taken into account. The antinatalist forces producing the high proportion arriving at age 25 childless are also likely to be little diminished during the cohort's twenty-fifth year. However, period factors change over longer time periods so that the proportion childless at older ages is less strongly related to current period factors. For example, the proportion childless at age 39 will bear little relation to current period factors, but instead represents the cohort's full history of period experience—especially that experience during the prime childbearing years of the early and mid-twenties. In sum, then, cohorts do not catch up, at least partly because antinatalist (or pronatalist) pressures are often similar in adjacent periods. By the time period conditions change substantially, many women are "too old"—in a social sense—to have children (Rindfuss and Bumpass 1978), and others are too old in a biological sense.

This interpretation leads to a more refined question. Do cohorts catch up or further postpone net of dominant period-specific factors? To answer this question, one must select a "measure" of period or devise a procedure to control for its effects. There is no one accepted way to do this. Below, we use three distinct strategies that provide similar answers to the question posed. Each approach has its drawbacks, but all three yielding similar findings gives confidence in the results. In model 2 we have chosen measures of economic performance (per capita gross national product [GNP] in 1958 dollars), unemployment (percentage of the civilian labor force unemployed), and inflation (consumer price index) as measures of relevant period factors.[5] A dummy variable was also included to allow for an additive shift in birth probabilities during World War II (1940–1944). Model 2 in table 4 shows the effects of these factors (measured in year T-1), and the proportion childless at age X on the birth probability at age X. The effects of three of these period controls are consistently strong and in the predicted direction. Low unemployment and inflation, and rapid economic growth are associated with higher birth probabilities *at all ages* between 25 and 39. The war variable has no significant effect. Net of these factors, the proportion childless leads to further delay in the twenties and some catching up in the thirties. The

[5]Measures of per capita GNP and unemployment and inflation rates are from *Historical Statistics of the United States, Colonial Times to 1970* (U.S. Bureau of the Census 1979) with additional data from the yearly *Statistical Abstract of the United States.*

positive coefficients at ages 32 to 39 are not statistically significant but there is a clear pattern.

Results of model 2 must be tempered by its inherent shortcomings. First, the four control variables are unlikely to represent period effects fully. Second, our model constrains the effects of these control variables to be constant over nearly half a century of fertility experience. Strategies to which we now turn do not suffer these shortcomings, but they have others. Model 3 controls for the cyclic trend pattern in birth probabilities by introducing successive powers of the trend variable. Such a procedure is commonly used for eliminating secular trend or cyclic variation in time series (for a demographic application see Preston and McDonald 1979; for discussion of the method see Johnston 1972:186–189). The shortcoming of this approach is that it is clearly ad hoc. Without identifying the period factors precisely, we do not know how to assess the likelihood of future change in them. Also, the rule for determining how many successive powers are sufficient to control for period is quite arbitrary.

The only substantively interpretable parameters in model 3 are the effects of the proportion childless. The effects mirror those in model 2, but there appears to be considerably more catching up at older ages (e.g., the positive effects at ages 35, 37, and 39 are stronger). We are unsure why stronger results are found, except to note that it is likely that we are capturing more of the effects of period variability than was the case in model 2. Unfortunately, the ad hoc nature of this approach is not substantively informative as to the nature of these period effects. Nevertheless, we want to emphasize the similar pattern and direction of effects in models 2 and 3.

Models 4 and 5 adopt the strategy often used in age-period-cohort problems, that is, we place an identifying restriction on one variable. In this case, we control on age (by our definition of the dependent variable), place a constraint on period, and estimate the cohort effect (catching up). The period constraint forces the change in the fertility of a younger (model 4) or older (model 5) cohort in year t to represent the period influence. Residual variation can then be explained by cohort factors. Like the previous ones, this approach has shortcomings. First, Namboodiri's (1981) work shows that not all age groups respond as strongly to period factors. Specifically, the 20–24 age group was found extrasensitive to environmental shifts. Birth probabilities for those aged 20 and 22 provide the period controls at ages 25 and 27, respectively, in model 4. Consequently, these estimates are suspect. Second, note that the effect

TABLE 4.
GROSS AND NET EFFECTS OF THE PROPORTION CHILDLESS AT AGE X ON THE BIRTH PROBABILITY WHILE AGE X

Dependent Variable: X =	(log) Birth Probability for Cohorts C at Age X							
Independent Variables:	25	27	30	32	35	37	39	25–39
Model 1								
(log) % childless	−.907*	−.582*	−.339*	−.289*	−.171*	−.121	−.048	−.199*
Model 2								
(log) % childless	−.685*	−.375*	−.073	.011	.034	.085	.109	
(log) CPI	−.382*	−.301*	−.499*	−.750*	−.864*	−.831*	−.877*	
(log) GNP	.439*	.411*	.718*	1.032*	1.115*	1.131*	1.147*	
(log) UNEMP	−.190*	−.177*	−.168*	−.173*	−.201*	−.204*	−.221*	
War dummy variable	.145	.182	.060	−.033	−.020	−.007	−.033	
Model 3								
(log) % childless	−.530*	−.402*	−.382*	−.371	.180	.509*	.496*	
trend[a]	−.097*	−.110*	−.120*	−.119*	−.080*	−.054*	−.055*	
$(trend)^2$	.0061*	.0076*	.0091*	.0093*	.0055*	.0034*	.0031*	
$(trend)^3$	−.00012*	−.00017*	−.00022*	−.00023*	−.00011*	−.00005	−.00004	
$(trend)^4$	.0000008*	.0000012*	.0000017*	.0000017*	−.0000006	.0000001	−.0000000	
Model 4								
(log) % childless	−.075	−.092	.045	.049	.036	.019	.028	

	25	27	30	32	35	37	39	25–39
(log) birth probability for *younger* cohort observed in same year	.882*	.661*	.805*	1.007*	1.103*	.999*	.940*	
Model 5								
(log) % childless	–.434*	–.212*	–.068*	–.043	–[b]	–[b]	–[b]	
(log) birth probability for *older* cohort observed in same year	.806*	.748*	.784*	.890*	–[b]	–[b]	–[b]	

Dependent Variable: X =

(log) Birth Probability for Cohorts C at Age X

Independent Variables:	25	27	30	32	35	37	39	25–39
R^2 Model 1	.63	.50	.27	.19	.07	.04	.01	.14
R^2 Model 2	.80	.69	.57	.58	.58	.60	.62	
R^2 Model 3	.82	.78	.80	.82	.85	.88	.83	
R^2 Model 4	.90	.81	.83	.86	.90	.91	.86	
R^2 Model 5	.92	.91	.90	.91	—	—	—	
Cohorts Included	(1893–1953)	(1891–1951)	(1888–1948)	(1886–1946)	(1883–1943)	(1881–1941)	(1879–1939)	(1891–1939)

*Significant at .05 level.

[a] The trend variable has the 1891 cohort variable equal to '1' with adjacent cohorts scored 0 and 2, etc. Stated differently, the trend variable equals year of birth minus 1890. Such a constant shift in the trend variable, of course, does not affect the coefficients of interest (the effects of the proportion childless).

[b] The period controls at these ages are birth probabilities at ages 40 and over. We doubt if the proportionate change assumption holds at these ages and chose not to estimate these effects.

of the proportion childless is weakest in models 4 and 5 compared with models 2 and 3. This may occur because cohorts born only five years apart share similar experiences. As a result, some of the joint change attributed to the period component may actually be because of similar proportions childless in cohorts separated by only five years. Period influence would thus be overestimated at the expense of cohort phenomenon—such as the proportion childless. Despite these problems, the percent childless again has a negative effect at the younger ages, which diminishes and becomes positive at the older ages.

In sum, the similarity of results across procedures suggests the results are robust. Regardless of procedure, period factors exert the dominant influence on birth probabilities. Similar results have been reported at other parities (see Namboodiri 1981; Pullum 1980; D. P. Smith 1981). The same conclusion emerges from figure 9. Cohorts catch up or fall further behind depending primarily on period factors in their later years of childbearing. As a result, *cohorts display no catching up* at any of the ages analyzed here.

We also ask a more refined question: Do cohorts catch up net of the dominant period factors? We find, net of these period factors, that cohorts with high proportions childless have lower first-birth probabilities during their late twenties and catch up slightly during their thirties as shown in models 2 through 5. Thus, there is no simple answer to this more refined question of whether postponement leads to further postponement or to catching up. Indeed, one process tends to cancel the other. But the dominant process varies by age in an intuitively appealing way. During a woman's twenties, when career or self-fulfillment goals are being pursued, postponement of childbearing allows further investment in these nonfamilial areas which, in turn, may promote additional delays of childbearing. By the early to mid-thirties, concern about the biological clock running out, together with the normative influence to have children, prompts some catching up. Overall, given that childbearing occurs much more frequently in the twenties than in the thirties, a cohort's ultimate level of childlessness is clearly increased by postponement of childbearing during the twenties.

The catching up that does occur in the thirties is of interest, however, given the hazards associated with late childbearing. Based on the behavior of past cohorts, birth probabilities at ages over 35 will most likely increase slightly over the next decade, if period factors remain unchanged. This slight increase, coupled with the larger cohorts approaching their mid-thirties and larger proportions of these cohorts delaying childbearing, implies substantial increases in the number of first births to women over age 35 throughout the rest of this decade.

Of course, this projection could err in either direction. Period factors are a primary determinant of birth probabilities at any age, and we have no reliable way of predicting what the future holds in this regard. Period factors may shift substantially in the coming decade. It is also possible that the underlying relationships could change. One possibility is a reaction to the widespread discussion of delayed childbearing that has been taking place, a discussion that has often focused on the problems attendant to combining motherhood and career. As more "successes" are highlighted and solutions outlined, the current generation could adopt a fertility schedule at older ages that would substantially catch them up to the parenthood levels of earlier cohorts. Conversely, a change in fecundity patterns because of pelvic inflammatory disease or other factors (Aral and Cates 1983; Menken 1985; Mosher 1986; Sherris and Fox 1983) could undercut the ability to catch up.

AGGREGATE DETERMINANTS

Given the substantial fluctuations in the timing of entry into parenthood during the twentieth century, and the absence of an equilibrating mechanism by which the delaying cohorts catch up, what then are the macro-factors that are determinants of these trends?

The shape of the trends themselves and the models in table 4 suggest the importance of changing economic conditions. The work of such economists as Butz and Ward (1977, 1979) and Devaney (1983) examining the determinants of overall fertility levels, as opposed to the timing of the first birth, also stresses the importance of changing economic conditions. Consequently, our preliminary work began by regressing annual measures of economic growth, unemployment, and inflation on measures of delayed childbearing. Earlier analyses also clearly showed the disruptive effects of World War II. While models containing such variables explained considerable variance (not shown here), the estimated parameters were often counterintuitive and quite volatile. They varied depending on which of these variables were in the model, as well as when additional factors were introduced. Such results clearly indicate a mis-specified model. Either important variables have been omitted or other constraints imposed by the model are unacceptable.

In this preliminary work, we had constrained variables in the models to have constant and additive effects across all cohorts. There are substantive reasons for expecting that both of these constraints are inappropriate. Moreover, given the multicollinearity among the determinants and considerable autocorrelation for all variables, we have concluded that the separate effects of economic growth, inflation, unemployment, military mobilization, and so forth cannot be estimated with any confidence from these data. Instead we explain variation in the observed time series with a set of period-specific causes. However, it should be made clear that this analysis only demonstrates that a particular set of period causes could have produced the observed data. It does not rule out alternative hypotheses. Although post hoc, this approach holds that the specific factors affecting childbearing can vary substantially from one period to the next. Carlson (1979:526) reaches a similar conclusion in an analysis of a time series of divorce rates.

Period variables used to describe variation in first-birth probabilities are defined below:[6]

WWI-ENL (World War I enlistment) = 1 if year is 1918; 0 otherwise

DEP (the Great Depression) = unemployment rate if year is 1928 through 1945; 0 otherwise

WWII-MOB (World War II mobilization) = 1 if year is 1942 through 1945; 0 otherwise

WWII-ENL (World War II enlistment) = number in the military (in thousands) if year is 1942 through 1945; 0 otherwise

PW (postwar period) = 1 if year is greater than 1945; 0 otherwise

PW-UN (postwar unemployment) = the unemployment rate if year is greater than 1945; 0 otherwise

PW-IN (postwar inflation) = inflation rate if year is greater than 1945; 0 otherwise.

CHANGE = 1 if cohort reached age 19 prior to 1945 and age 25 to 35 prior to 1963. C1 equals 1 if CHANGE equals 1 and year equals 1946 through 1953; 0 otherwise. C2 equals 1 if CHANGE equals 1 and year equals 1954–1963; 0 otherwise.

---

[6]Sources for GNP per capita, inflation, and unemployment are in note 5. Enlistment figures for the World War II period are from U.S. Bureau of the Census (1979).

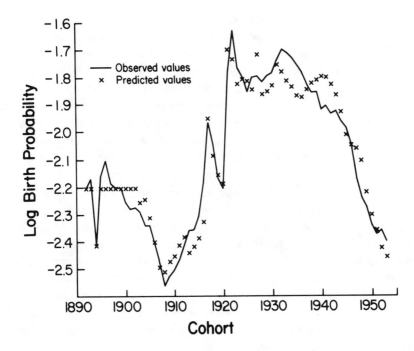

Fig. 10. Observed birth probabilities and values predicted from
period factors—age 25.

Table 5 shows the estimated coefficients obtained from regressing
(using OLS) the birth probabilities at age 25, 30, and 35 on the variables
defined above.[7] This set of factors explains most variation (over 90 percent) in birth probabilities at each age. Figure 10 shows the close fit of
observed to expected values at age 25. Results at other ages are very
similar and are not shown here.

The coefficients in table 5 show the expected effects. The effects of
war enlistment (WWI-ENL and WWII-ENL) are strongly negative at
younger ages and become insignificant at age 35. (The size of the WWI
and WWII effects should not be compared because the metrics are not
the same.) The unemployment rate from 1928–1945, DEP, nicely captures

[7]Autocorrelation is not severe in these models—in all cases the Durbin-Watson statistic
does not allow one to reject the hypothesis of no autocorrelation. As a result, parameters
are estimated using ordinary least squares (OLS).

the negative effect of the Depression on birth probabilities. The mobilization for World War II, WWII-MOB, leads to much improved economic conditions and outlook, even net of sharp declines in the unemployment rate. The mobilization also may have led some to consummate relationships earlier than they otherwise would have.

In the postwar period, higher unemployment and inflation are associated with lower birth probabilities (except at age 30 where unemployment has no effect). The most complex variable, and perhaps the most substantively interesting variable, is CHANGE. This variable reflects sharp changes in the socioeconomic environment. At age 25, for instance, cohorts that reached age 18 prior to 1945 had higher than expected fertility (given postwar trends in unemployment and inflation) in the postwar period. Almost certainly these cohorts assessed current socioeconomic conditions in comparison with recent experience—the Depression and war years. Older women, those aged 30 to 35, in the immediate postwar period also displayed much higher fertility than one would predict given conditions and subsequent postwar fertility behavior. Another way to describe this behavior is to say that socioeconomic conditions improved markedly and those in the childbearing years responded to the improved economic context. This change effect is not the same as the Easterlin relative income effect, although it shares similarities. Easterlin maintains that young couples gauge their current circumstances against those prevailing during their formative years. Our data suggest that *all* women gauge the current socioeconomic environment with respect to the recent past.

The sharp impact of the CHANGE variable can be seen clearly in the two panels of figure 11. Here we have plotted expected birth probabilities for ages 25 and 35 from models which include and exclude the estimated effect of CHANGE. The area between the dashed and solid line shows the fertility increase that cannot be explained by objective levels of inflation and unemployment in the postwar period. Instead, this increase in fertility may be attributable to the strong contrast between pre- and postwar economic conditions.

Just as the original Easterlin argument had tremendous intuitive appeal, so does this broader relative economic times argument. Individuals do not necessarily examine the present objectively but rather use the past to filter it. For example, an unemployment rate of 7 percent might be viewed with alarm if it had averaged 2 percent in the preceding decade. In contrast, the same unemployment rate might be viewed with optimism

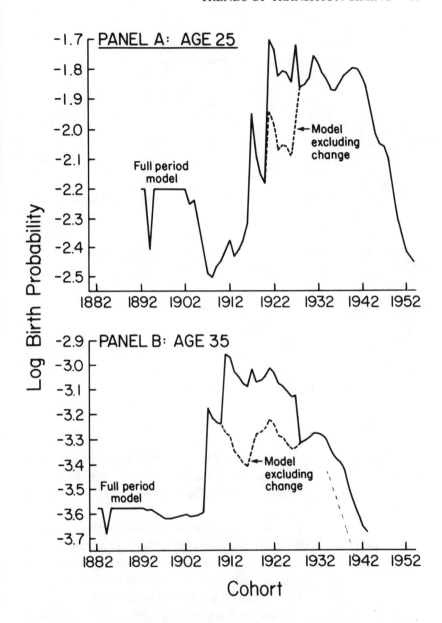

Fig. 11. Predicted birth probabilities from full period model and a model excluding the "change" variable: panel A—age 25.

TABLE 5.
ESTIMATED PERIOD EFFECTS ON FIRST-BIRTH PROBABILITIES

| | Dependent Variable: | | First-Birth Probabilities at Age: | | | |
| | 25 | | 30 | | 35 | |
Period effects	Beta	SE	Beta	SE	Beta	SE
WWI-ENL	−0.208*	(.074)	−0.167*	(.069)	−0.104	(.081)
DEP	−0.012*	(.002)	−0.004*	(.001)	−0.002	(.002)
WWII-MOB	.432*	(.108)	.454*	(.099)	.446*	(.117)
WWII-ENL	−0.032*	(.011)	−0.022*	(.010)	−0.008	(.012)
PW	.717*	(.074)	.325*	(.080)	.624*	(.086)
PW-UN	−0.036*	(.015)	.004	(.015)	−0.051*	(.016)
PW-IN	−0.089*	(.007)	−0.033*	(.007)	−0.046*	(.009)
Change: C1	.248*	(.040)	.325*	(.040)	.323*	(.044)
C2			.197*	(.038)	.211*	(.036)
Intercept	−2.203		−2.723		−3.582	
N	62		62		62	
Cohorts						
R^2	.934		.922		.918	

*Significant at .05 level.
NOTE: SE is standard error.

if the average in the preceding decade had been 15 percent. Nevertheless, some caution needs to be exercised in interpreting these change variables. They may simply represent other variables not adequately measured in the model.

Finally, net of these three postwar variables, fertility is significantly higher in the postwar period. This might reflect higher fecundity related to improved health and nutrition. Or it could simply be that, net of the measured period factors, the socioeconomic environment is much better in the postwar period than prior to the prewar years examined.

As in the previous section, we again test for an effect of the proportion childless on the birth probability. If we add the proportion childless at age x to the models predicting the birth probability at age x (table 5), we find little evidence of a positive effect at older ages (results not shown here). This result is consistent with that reached in the previous section.

This latest model (shown in table 5) contains explicit terms which capture the fertility response to changed socioeconomic conditions. If socio-economic conditions change sharply then the fertility response can be substantial. In other words, there was substantial catching up after World War II in response to a more pronatalist socioeconomic context. We should exercise caution before concluding that there will be catching up under other circumstances—if economic conditions worsen or remain the same. Additional inflection points are required for more certain answers on this issue, but we find little evidence of catching up net of the strong period factors. The most important finding is clear enough: period con-ditions are of overwhelming importance and there will be little catching up among cohorts who delayed their first birth if socioeconomic condi-tions do not change.

In sum, the time series of first-birth probabilities can be explained by the disruptive effects of war (the negative effect of enlistment and the positive effect of mobilization) and the prevailing economic environment as judged by subsequent experience. These findings suggest that substan-tial future improvements in economic conditions would increase birth probabilities at all ages. Young couples would not feel obligated to delay as preceding cohorts did and older couples would "catch up" on fertility delayed. These results are entirely consistent with those described in the preceding section. Period effects are dominant. Whether cohorts make up delayed fertility depends on changes in period factors.

DISCUSSION AND SUMMARY

Our analysis demonstrates the critical role played by period effects. Explanation of changes in childbearing patterns must focus on the relation between the prevailing socioeconomic context and fertility. A second major finding is that current levels of delayed childbearing have a recorded historical precedent in the United States, and do not seem extremely high by European standards. In sum, fertility delay in the West is a time-hon-ored, normatively approved response to harsh economic conditions.

While current levels of delayed childbearing appear to approximate those of the 1930s, obviously the two periods are not identical. Indeed, economic conditions were quite different. The Depression witnessed widespread unemployment, bank failures, and business bankruptcies. Prices, including housing, declined. The deprivation was widespread and severe because no safety net of social services was in place. In the 1970s, more moderate levels of unemployment were coupled with sharp increases in inflation and, subsequently, in interest rates. The deprivation was less visible because of the safety net of social services constructed at least partly in response to the Depression.

Parallels between the two periods, however, do suggest some similarities between the family formation environment present during the Depression and that confronted by more recent cohorts. Buying a home, finding a secure job, and achieving an adequate income were difficulties common to both periods. An unemployed auto worker receiving benefits in the 1970s was probably no more likely to consider starting a family then than a similar worker without benefits would have been in the earlier period.

Further, couples in the more recent period do not compare the current childbearing environment to that of the 1930s; rather, the postwar period of the 1950s and 1960s is the referent. Economic conditions were markedly better in the immediate postwar period and social programs such as Social Security and the G.I. Bill removed obstacles to early family formation (see Modell, Furstenberg, and Strong 1978). In view of this comparison, and continually rising expectations with regard to the standard of living one ought to achieve, the social and economic climate of the 1970s can reasonably be characterized as harsh for young people. The cost of home ownership in 1981, for example, was over two and a half times that in 1970, approximately 30 percent greater than the growth in real family income, itself supplemented by the increasing prevalence of two earners. Thus, a pivotal element of the American Dream, owning one's own home, has now slipped out of the reach of many Americans. To keep pace with inflation, many young couples were forced to adopt a two-income strategy that conflicts with parenthood.

It is unfortunate that more detail is not available for the period prior to the Depression, but we do know that high levels of childlessness existed prior to it. Until more of this historical detail is filled in we are reluctant to overplay the comparison between the 1930s and 1970s. However, in both time periods it was difficult for young individuals to start a family.

Economic conditions, while the most readily quantifiable, represent only one aspect of fertility-relevant contexts. Social change in other guises also is likely to be important. We reserve most comments on the importance of such broad social change for later in this book, but noneconomic factors may also have played a role in producing recent trends in delayed childbearing. Development of modern contraceptive methods, changing views of the woman's role in society, and increasing rates of marital disruption are factors often mentioned.

In summary, pervasive period effects and historical trends in the initiation of childbearing suggest comparison of the family formation environment of the Depression with the 1970s. Significant change in the economic circumstances of the more recent period has produced a noticeable increase in the proportion of women remaining childless at all ages. Our analysis warns against calling delayed parenthood a recent phenomenon, or identifying the pill, women's liberation, or increasing marital disruption as the sole explanation for this trend. Yet, each of these recent developments may help to perpetuate the pattern of childbearing that emerged in the 1970s.

Concomitant with this trend toward delayed childbearing, indeed flying in the face of it, has been the persistence of young teenagers becoming mothers. Not only does the United States have one of the highest rates of teenage pregnancy in the world but it has continued despite all the social and economic forces moving American women toward later and later childbearing. While one often hears complaints about American welfare programs, welfare cannot be a sufficient explanation because European programs tend to be substantially more generous. Perhaps the explanation is more complex involving social programs and an American Horatio Alger ideology that anyone (and everyone) can achieve high educational and occupational attainment. In such a setting, becoming an adolescent parent is one of the few "legitimate" ways of dropping out. We return to this theme in chapter 6.

With respect to the future, one has to take into account that past trends in delayed childbearing and childlessness are the cumulative result of period factors. Birth probabilities at most ages are responsive to these factors, making prediction of a cohort's future fertility behavior, based on its behavior to date, extremely suspect. Only if period factors remain constant would such predictions be accurate. History suggests this prospect is an unlikely one.

Nevertheless, given the pace of change in the relevant socioeconomic factors, we can make some reasonable short-term projections. We know that high proportions of the cohorts now entering their thirties are childless and that these are very large cohorts, comprised of women born during the Baby Boom of the 1950s. These two demographic factors combined imply increased numbers of children being born to older women, *and* increases in the proportion of women remaining permanently childless. Without a substantial change in the relative economic climate, we also expect continued delayed childbearing among those entering their twenties. In short, the trend toward older ages at parenthood should continue in the near future.

The long-term prospects with respect to delayed childbearing and childlessness are much less clear. They depend on long-term trends in socioeconomic and political conditions and these are difficult to predict. To the extent that the general economy is depressed, specifically the job and housing markets, and/or if there is a massive military mobilization, we can expect a continuation of high levels of delayed childbearing and childlessness.

If, however, general socioeconomic conditions improve substantially, then we face the same demographic situation that produced the Baby Boom: relatively small cohorts entering the early childbearing years and relatively large cohorts postponing childbearing. First-birth probabilities among older childless women increased in response to the post– World War II prosperity. If older childless women increased their first-birth probabilities and the younger cohorts simultaneously moved away from the delayed childbearing pattern, a substantial increase in period fertility rates would result. This increase could occur despite the possibility that the actual number of births experienced by successive cohorts of women would change relatively little. This, in fact, is what happened during the Baby Boom.

5

The Intersection of Temporal and Structural Dimensions

Researchers have adopted different approaches that address a variety of questions in examining the first-birth process and other young adult transitions. The three most common approaches are time-series, cross-sectional, and life course studies. For example, the preceding chapter was based on a time-series approach. These three approaches do not necessarily represent distinct theoretical or methodological perspectives; rather they tend to coalesce around available data which in turn dictates the factors and processes that are given particular emphasis. All three have yielded considerable insight. Unfortunately, insights gained from one approach have not always informed the work of the others, thus limiting our understanding of the entire process.

This chapter moves beyond the time-series approach of the preceding chapter and incorporates elements and insights from all three approaches mentioned above. Our conceptual framework acknowledges the importance of timing and micro- and macrolevel determinants. Our methodological strategy allows all three types of variables to influence the first-birth process. Finally, our data, consisting of pooled fertility surveys spanning 1955 to 1980, provide a lengthy time series merged with micro-level fertility data and individual background characteristics. Thus, our work is a hybrid of time-series, cross-sectional, and life course analyses allowing simultaneous examination of *structure, process,* and *trend.*

CONCEPTUAL FRAMEWORK

The first-birth process itself has two distinct aspects: biological and social factors (as noted in chap. 2). Women[1] make decisions (or nondecisions) about whether and when to have the first child. Fecundity also varies across individuals, and over time for any given individual. For several reasons, we necessarily focus on the behavioral outcome of the process, the first birth itself. First, accurate measurement of a woman's fecundity is impossible, short of asking her to stop using contraception and then recording how much time elapses before conception occurs (Rindfuss and Bumpass 1978)—clearly an unacceptable strategy. More important, as discussed in chapter 2, the process of deciding to remain childless blurs the distinction between voluntary and involuntary childlessness.

The sociological variables influencing the timing of the first-birth process have been studied from three different perspectives. The first, the time-series tradition employed in the last chapter, has generally emphasized aggregate phenomena and, for this reason, we will refer to it as "aggregate time."[2] One of the earliest concerns, and perhaps the most basic, involves the demographic correlates of fertility trends (e.g., Ryder 1969). Within this tradition, the description and interpretation of trends in childlessness is the aspect of the first-birth process that has received the most empirical attention (Hastings and Robinson 1974; Masnick 1980b; Poston and Gotard 1977). There has also been considerable emphasis placed on social and economic factors influencing changing period fertility rates. The Easterlin (1978) hypothesis is perhaps the best known, but other suggested explanations include: (1) changing contraceptive availability (see chap. 2) including introduction of the pill and IUD and increased popularity of sterilization, (2) changing social values as embodied, for example, in the women's movement and changes in female labor force participation, and (3) changing circumstances facing young

---

[1]Men and women are involved in the childbearing process, but for ease of exposition it is convenient to refer to just one sex. Since women are the actual childbearers and since the empirical work in this chapter only includes women, this discussion refers to women. In later chapters (8 and 9), we extend the analysis to include men.

[2]We adopt the term *aggregate time* rather than the more conventional *period* or *cohort* because the two latter terms have come to assume a much more specialized meaning. Time-series analysis can be done within either approach, often with the same data. (See chap. 4.) Here it is the aggregate dimension of both that we wish to emphasize.

adults including variation in the cost of housing (Bumpass 1973; Butz and Ward 1977; Ryder 1979; Westoff 1978).

The cross-sectional approach has been primarily concerned with differentials, arising out of the general sociological concern with the effect of group membership on individualized behavior. The bulk of the explanatory variables examined fall into the social-structural category, and we refer to this general class of theoretical questions and empirical variables as "social structural." Empirical work on the first-birth process in this tradition generally isolates extremes of the process, childlessness or adolescent fertility. Two recent exceptions are Rindfuss and St. John (1983) and Trussell and Bloom (1983). The childlessness research has typically found that the same variables that correlate with low fertility also correlate with high levels of childlessness (Freshnock and Cutright 1978; Gustavus and Henley 1971; Thoen 1977; and Veevers 1979).

Finally, the life cycle perspective is one of the earliest approaches used to examine timing of the first birth. This approach originated with rural sociologists (Loomis and Hamilton 1936) and came to be identified with the work of Glick (1947, 1955, 1977; Glick and Parke 1965). Initially, this life cycle approach focused on the description of the conjugal family and its stages, one of them the initiation of childbearing. Recently, a number of investigators (Chudacoff 1980; Masnick 1980*a*; Masnick and McFalls 1976; Modell, Furstenberg, and Strong 1978) have begun to examine the interconnections among various life course events. Related to this work is the expanding number of studies concerned with the timing and order of events in an individual's life (Elder 1975, 1978; Hogan 1980; Marini 1978; Rindfuss and Bumpass 1978; Winsborough 1978).

This life course perspective tends to emphasize individual aspects of time rather than its aggregate aspects. The concern is with how long individuals or groups spend in a given life state. Both age and duration are important gauges of "individual time."

Prior research clearly shows that all three dimensions are important. Moreover there are strong theoretical reasons to expect that the effects of variables in one dimension might depend on those in another. Such an examination of interactive effects can best take place in an analysis that includes elements from each dimension. The conceptual model outlined in chapter 2 can easily subsume these three dimensions suggested by prior research traditions. Social-structural variables include ascribed and achieved characteristics. These characteristics can help set individual life course trajectories and can affect them at subsequent ages. In some cases, social-structural variables can represent entirely different social contexts, especially when the variables identify groups with relatively little social interaction. The aggregate time dimension also can represent changing social contexts. The nonfamilial opportunities available to women are an example of one aspect of the changing social context represented by more recent periods. Others include economic conditions, military mobilization, and various social and political movements. Finally, our life course model takes into explicit account individual time, which includes physical maturation, social expectations, and legal definitions.

To demonstrate the advantages of looking at disparate factors simultaneously, consider, for instance, the effects of religion in the social-structural dimension and the long-run secularization trend in the aggregate-time dimension. Although there have been dissenting voices (N. E. Johnson 1982), most observers have either predicted or documented a decline in Catholic versus non-Catholic fertility differences (Freedman 1962; Westoff and Jones 1977, 1979). This set of results suggests that the effect of religion would vary with period such that the effect is diminished in more recent time periods.

The effects of social-structural variables might also interact with individual time. For instance, high levels of education should reduce the probability of a first birth in a woman's early twenties because she is more likely to be establishing a career. By her early thirties, however, the same woman may be anxious to "make up" for lost childbearing time. Similarly, the effects of aggregate time might vary with individual time—the effect of period factors might be stronger at some ages than at others. The effect of a historical event such as the Korean War on the first-birth process, for example, presumably would be stronger among women in their late teens or early twenties than among those aged 30 or more. While we found little evidence of such an age-period interaction in the previous chapter, it may appear when other factors are taken into account.

DATA AND METHODS

The data used to examine the importance of aggregate time, individual time, and social-structural dimensions of the first-birth process are the six national studies of fertility conducted in the United States since 1955 (see chap. 3). To extend the time series as far as possible, we have pooled

TABLE 6.
NUMBERS OF RESPONDENTS IN POOLED DATA FILE BY BIRTH COHORT AND STUDY

Birth cohort	Study						
	1955 GAF	1960 GAF	1965 NFS	1970 NFS	1973 NSFG	1976 NSFG	Total
1915–1919	588	449	346				1383
1920–1924	88	622	702				1412
1925–1929		144	714	712	129		1699
1930–1934			208	908	944	475	2535
1935–1939				256	784	862	1902
Total	675	1215	1970	1876	1857	1337	8931

all six surveys. Our examination of the quality and comparability of these surveys indicates that they can be pooled. These results were summarized in chapter 3.

Because none of the six surveys include never-married nonmothers, it is important that we do not bias our results with respect to age at marriage (see chap. 3; Ryder and Westoff 1971). In the United States, the vast majority of women who marry prior to the end of the reproductive period do so before age 35. Thus, we restrict our sample to women aged 35 or older at the time of the interview.

Initially we also restrict the sample to white, native-born women, based on evidence that the structure of factors affecting the first-birth probabilities differs for whites and blacks (see chap. 6; St. John 1982; St. John and Grasmick 1985). We return to the issue of the structure of black first-birth timing later in this chapter. Further, because foreign-born women may have experienced their first birth elsewhere, it is quite possible that the factors affecting the process (including immigration itself) differ.

Table 6 shows the distribution of our pooled sample by study and five-year birth cohorts. By pooling the data, we are able to examine cohorts from 1915–1939. Respondents in each birth cohort are obtained from at least three surveys, and sometimes four.

Information on the social-structural dimension is obtained from a set of questions on background and adolescent characteristics included in each of the surveys. To pool across all six surveys, we restricted the

TABLE 7.
MEASUREMENT OF SOCIAL-STRUCTURAL VARIABLES IN THE MODELS

Variable	Description	Proportion in full sample
Education		
0–8	Dummy variable coding.	0.124
9–11	0–8 will be omitted category	0.205
12		0.462
13–15		0.116
16+		0.093
Farm	Farm background coded 1; others 0	0.311
Catholic	Catholics coded 1; others 0	0.267
South	Southerners coded 1; others 0	0.321
Household composition	If not in intact family at age 14 coded 1; others 0	0.170

analysis to those variables comparably measured in each study.[3] Fortunately, many of the background variables expected to affect the first-birth
process are included in all six surveys. Table 7 shows their measurement
and the distribution of the pooled sample on these variables.

The justification for these social-structural variables on the timing of
family formation is well established in the literature (e.g., Marini 1978;
Rindfuss and St. John 1983; Rindfuss, Bumpass, and St. John 1980;
Ryder 1973b). We discussed the importance of education above. Religion
is also likely to affect the time when women become mothers. Unfortunately because of data constraints, the only religious distinction that we
can examine is that between Catholics and non-Catholics. To the extent
that Catholic effects are present, we expect that these women will be less
likely to have a first birth at younger ages and also less likely to remain
permanently childless. In short, they will delay entry into parenthood
but they will make the transition. Lower birth probabilities at young ages
are consistent with a long tradition of late age at marriage for some

[3]One variable, household composition at age 14, was not measured in one of the surveys,
the 1955 GAF. We created a dummy variable for the household composition for 1955 GAF
respondents. However, it is of no substantive interest, thus we do not include it in the
tabled results.

Catholic groups, such as the Irish. Late ages at marriage would tend to delay the first birth. Further, Catholic doctrine prohibits sex outside of marriage. To the extent that Catholics adhere to this doctrine, premarital pregnancies and early age at first birth would be reduced.

This situation provides a good example of where the effect of marriage would be expected to be different across groups. We would expect Catholics to be far less likely than non-Catholics to have a child outside of marriage. Thus, while we are not explicitly examining marital effects here, the differential impact of marriage is part of the explanation. At older ages and following marriage, Catholic doctrine stresses the importance of procreation and prohibits the use of any contraceptive method other than rhythm. The recent convergence of Catholic and non-Catholic contraceptive behavior (see Westoff and Jones 1977) suggests that the timing differential between religious groups may narrow across the most recent cohorts. However, the most recent cohort we examine, those born 1930–1934, is likely too old to be influenced by this recent convergence.

Delayed childbearing is expected to be less extensive among women residing in the South, having farm backgrounds, and growing up without both parents. Early motherhood may seem more attractive than pursuing a career when educational opportunities are limited, as they are (or at least have been) in many rural areas (Duncan and Reiss 1956) and in the South. Likewise, attractive, nonfarm, female career opportunities may be scarcer in rural areas and in the South. These characterizations may be changing, but they are likely to hold for the cohorts we examine. Prior research shows that rural women have first births earlier (Duncan 1943) and that fertility was higher in the South than in other regions during the period when cohorts in our sample spent most of their childbearing years. Since the late 1950s, fertility levels of Southern women appear to be lower than those of their counterparts in the rest of the nation (Rindfuss 1978). Of course, these lower levels do not necessarily derive from a faster pacing of first births. Finally, girls not living with both parents when they were aged 14 may have had a somewhat less desirable home life. Further, a girl with one parent will have fewer resources than one living with both parents. Resources provide educational and career opportunities which can compete with the motherhood role.

Individual time enters into the analysis through explicit recognition that the first-birth process can unfold over a period spanning two decades or more. Prior to the end of the reproductive period, at any age, any woman who has not already done so can have a first birth. We divide the first-birth process into a series of conditional probabilities (see chap. 3), using the age boundaries[4] shown below:

Age group	Percent childless at beginning of interval	Of those childless at beginning, percent having first birth in interval
0–19	100.0	24.4
20–21	75.6	26.4
22–23	55.6	31.2
24–25	38.2	31.4
26–27	26.2	29.3
28–29	18.5	24.4
30–34	14.0	40.6

Within each of these segments, typically one-quarter or more of those still eligible to have a first birth have one in that segment.

We treat this series of conditional first-birth probabilities as a set of dependent variables to be analyzed. Since these dependent variables are dichotomies, we use a logistic regression procedure (Harrell 1980). The predictor variables are birth cohort and the social-structural variables shown in table 7. Within each analysis of the conditional first-birth probabilities, we allow birth cohort to interact with the social-structural variables to see if the effect of the latter is dependent on aggregate time. By comparing effects of birth cohort and the social-structural variables across the various conditional first-birth probability models, we can see if the effects of these sets of variables depend on individual time. This approach is essentially a multivariate life table (see Guilkey and Rindfuss 1984) or a discrete time survival analysis (Allison 1982). This procedure is flexible and relatively assumption free.

In our results, we present beta coefficients from the logistic regressions. These coefficients represent reductions or increases (depending on the sign) in the log odds of the conditional probability of having a first birth in the segment. All the predictor variables are categorical, and thus the coefficients should be interpreted relative to the reference category. It may be helpful to remember that coefficients of 1.0 and 0.5 represent

[4]These boundaries were chosen to highlight the main part of the first-birth process, the 20s, while still allowing examination of either end.

respective increases of approximately 2.7 and 1.6 times the odds of having a first birth in the interval.

Three final methodological issues should be mentioned. The first is the question of whether there is a causal effect from the first-birth process back to education. Among the variables we examine, this is the only one for which such a causality issue arises. Although there is some disagreement about this in the literature (e.g., Marini 1978), most recent research suggests there is no direct effect of the first-birth process on the amount of education a young woman receives (Haggstrom et al. 1981; Rindfuss, Bumpass, and St. John 1980; Zelnik and Kantner 1978). Further, most of the theoretical arguments and empirical evidence for a reverse causal effect center on young teenagers (e.g., Hofferth and Moore 1979). We approach our analysis as a series of conditional first-birth probability models, and only in the first age group (15–19) might a reverse causal path be present. Thus, for the majority of our analysis, the causal direction is unambiguous; and even in the youngest group, most evidence suggests there is no feedback from age at first birth to education. For these reasons, we assume that education has causal priority to the first-birth process, but caution needs to be exercised when interpreting the results for the youngest age group.

Our measure of aggregate time is labeled birth cohort. We do this for ease of presentation because as a woman ages her cohort remains fixed, but the relevant period changes. However, cohort as an index of aggregate time also represents period. Note that both period and cohort cannot be in a model predicting an event at a given age.[5] Thus, at every age, the cohort variable could be relabeled for the relevant period; as such one would understand them to represent the influence of unique historical factors associated with a particular period of time. Since period factors tend to be more important than cohort factors in explaining U.S. fertility trends (see chap. 4; Namboodiri 1981; Pullum 1980; D. P. Smith 1981), our interpretations will often be in terms of period factors. Consequently, the translation from cohorts to periods should be kept in mind. We return to this issue later.

Finally, we reiterate that age at marriage is omitted from the analysis. The reason is that there exists substantial theoretical (e.g., Hirschman and Rindfuss 1982) and empirical evidence that age at marriage and age

---

[5]This is the variant of the age, period, cohort problem (see Glenn 1976; Mason et al. 1973; Pullum 1980; Rodgers 1982).

at first birth are reciprocally interrelated, and, with the data available, we cannot defensibly untangle this relationship. This issue was discussed more completely in chapter 2.

POOLED RESULTS

To set the stage for the more detailed analysis of the first-birth process, we examined the effect of social-structural and aggregate-time characteristics on the probability of having a child by age 35. Over 92 percent of the women in our sample had a birth by age 35. Since birth probabilities past age 35 are extremely low (Heuser 1976), examining the probability of having a child by age 35 is essentially the same as examining the determinants of permanent childlessness.

We first examined a series of models where each of the structural variables was allowed to interact with cohort. However, adding various sets of interaction terms did not significantly improve the fit of the model. In other words, the effects of the structural variables on the probability of having a child by age 35 have not changed over the time period analyzed.

We show the additive effects of the social-structural variables and cohort on having a child by age 35 in table 8. Looking first at the structural variables, it is clear that as a group, they tend not to affect whether or not a woman becomes a mother by age 35. This may be surprising, given the effects these variables have on other fertility-related variables. Large differences do exist among cohorts, however. Those cohorts with relatively few childless women by age 35 were those that were in their teens and twenties during the relatively prosperous 1950s and 1960s; those with a relatively large proportion childless experienced the Great Depression while they were in their peak childbearing years. This is the same pattern documented with vital registration data in chapter 4.

The only structural variable that has any effect on the probability of having a child by age 35 is education. Women who have attained at least a college degree are substantially less likely to become mothers than other women. These are precisely the women who enter careers that effectively compete with the prospect of childbearing for the woman's time. However, even among college graduates, childlessness is rare.

TABLE 8.
EFFECTS OF SOCIAL-STRUCTURAL AND AGGREGATE-TIME CHARACTERISTICS ON
LIKELIHOOD OF HAVING HAD A CHILD BY AGE 35

Variable[a]	Beta
Education	
9–11	0.351*
12	−0.042
13–15	0.027
16+	−0.510**
Farm	−0.082
Catholic	−0.015
South	−0.082
Household composition	−0.070
Birth cohort[b]	
1915–1919	−0.664**
1920–1924	−0.576**
1925–1929	−0.365**
1930–1934	−0.104
Model χ^2	91.5
N	8876

*Significant at .05.
**Significant at .01.
[a]See table 7 for description of these variables.
[b]Cohort 1935–1939 is omitted category.

FACTORS AFFECTING FIRST-BIRTH TIMING.

With these results in mind, we now turn to the detailed analysis where both structure and aggregate time can interact with individual time as well as with each other. First, for the seven age segments examined (20, 20–21, 22–23, 24–25, 26–27, 28–29, and 30–34), we ran a series of models which allowed cohort to interact with each of the five structural variables in turn.

In general, the social-structural variables' influence has not changed over time. In only three cases did addition of a cohort by structural variable interaction term significantly increase the fit of the model at the

0.01 level: (1) education by cohort at age 22–23, (2) South by cohort at age 28–29, and (3) Catholic by cohort at age 30–34. The latter two effects tended to be of a relatively small magnitude and substantively uninterpretable. Furthermore, in no case does the same structural variable interact with cohort at two adjacent ages. Given this situation, we conclude that the effects of these structural variables on the first-birth process have been relatively stable over time. This is the same conclusion reached when period fertility rates are examined (Rindfuss and Sweet 1977; Sweet and Rindfuss 1984).

The only exception to this lack of interactions involving aggregate time is the one between education and aggregate time. The pattern of the education interaction is substantively appealing. Further, the same pattern is found at age 20–21, and would be significant if we used a more liberal significance criteria. To examine this interaction more closely, we used the 1980 June CPS—a larger data set that unfortunately lacks the range of predictor variables found in the fertility surveys. With this larger data set which covers more cohorts, the education by cohort interaction is visible at several adjacent ages. We present these CPS results later. Since the interactions are confined primarily to the CPS findings, we present our results from the pooled fertility surveys without interaction terms.

In table 9, we show effects of the social-structural variables and aggregate time on the entire first-birth process. In interpreting table 9, remember that each column represents a separate logistic regression analysis. Effects of the social-structural variables change with age. Both magnitude and direction of their effects change substantially across individual time. The pattern of change is theoretically and intuitively appealing.

Before discussing individual effects, it should also be noted that the overall fit of the model, relative to a model of no effects, tends to decline with age. Because χ^2 is directly proportional to sample size, this decline is partly a function of sample size declining with age. Modifying James Davis's (1982) procedure, we adjust for sample size as follows:

$$\text{adjusted } \chi^2 = \frac{\chi^2 * 3500}{N}$$

The constant, 3500, is arbitrary and approximately represents our median sample size. The degrees of freedom do not change across ages, and thus no adjustment on this dimension is necessary. The final row of table 9 shows this adjusted model χ^2.

With these adjustments, there is still a tendency for the fit of the model to decline with age. There is, however, a strong upturn at age 30–34. To see if this upturn was the result of moving from a two-year to a five-year width, we ran a model for ages 30–31 and 32–33. The explanatory power diminished but was still higher than adjacent categories in the late twenties. We suspect that the early thirties are a significant assessment point in a young woman's life, and that childbearing decisions are reviewed then.

Given the nature of the variables examined, it is not surprising that the fit of the model declines with age. With the exception of education, Catholicism, and aggregate time, these variables are fixed well before a woman begins childbearing. As the woman cumulates experience, the effect of such background characteristics should be diluted. We do not have any indicators of what these women were doing in their twenties. Thus, this finding may simply be the result of unmeasured heterogeneity. We doubt, however, that unmeasured heterogeneity is the total explanation. As age increases, the proportion of a woman's contemporaries who are still childless decreases. For example, at age 28 fewer than one-fifth are still childless. At such a point, the normative pressures to have children may diminish. Those who might have exerted the pressure may have given up the still childless as being "hopeless."

Looking at the effects of the coefficients themselves, it is clear that education has a powerful effect on the first-birth process. Up until the mid-twenties, education has a strong inverse effect. The strength of this effect diminishes as one approaches the mid-twenties. Afterward, education has a positive effect. Thus, education has a substantial effect on *when* women become mothers. Table 9 indicates that the "proper" time to become a mother is several years after finishing school—certainly not before or not too much after.

These education effects are more apparent when examining the predicted cumulative proportion having had a child by various ages. (See Guilkey and Rindfuss 1987 for details of this procedure.) We show these predicted probabilities in table 10, where all other variables in the equation were set to their mean levels. At age 22, there are substantial differences among the five education groups. Those with the lowest level of education are four times more likely to have made the transition to parenthood than the college graduates. That such a small proportion of college graduates become mothers prior to the typical age of graduation reinforces our emphasis on the incompatibility of student and parent

TABLE 9.
EFFECTS OF SOCIAL-STRUCTURAL AND AGGREGATE-TIME CHARACTERISTICS ON CONDITIONAL PROBABILITY OF HAVING A FIRST BIRTH AT VARIOUS AGES (BETAS)

Variable[a]	Having First Birth at Age						
	<20	20–21	22–23	24–25	26–27	28–29	30–34
Education:							
9–11	0.056	-0.034	0.166	0.195	0.370	0.213	0.240
12	-1.409**	-0.250**	0.084	0.356*	0.472**	0.279	0.310
13–15	-2.402**	-0.598**	-0.036	0.502**	0.571**	0.440	0.745**
16+	-3.548**	-1.684**	-0.490**	0.276	0.703**	0.534*	0.466
Farm	0.144*	0.087	0.005	-0.015	0.111	-0.079	-0.405**
Catholic	-0.618**	-0.233**	-0.156*	0.062	0.177	0.176	0.231
South	0.276**	0.017	-0.045	0.090	-0.162	-0.397**	-0.124
Household composition	0.225**	0.045	0.060	-0.038	-0.181	0.019	-0.233
Birth cohort:[b]							
1915–1919	-1.152**	-1.053**	-0.855**	-0.348**	-0.537**	0.306	0.695**
1920–1924	-1.074**	-0.893**	-0.718**	-0.153	-0.143	0.149	0.451*
1925–1929	-0.698**	-0.395**	-0.266**	-0.263*	-0.058	0.120	0.230
1930–1934	-0.293**	-0.259**	-0.130	0.032	-0.054	0.213	0.160

Model χ^2	1679.8	375.6	141.0	36.8	38.9	22.8	45.2
N	8,876	6,718	4,966	3,426	2,344	1,654	1,256
Adjusted Model χ^2	662.3	195.7	99.4	36.6	58.9	48.2	126.0

*Significant at .05.
**Significant at .01.
[a]See table 7 for description of these variables.
[b]Cohort 1935–1939 is omitted category.

TABLE 10.
PREDICTED CUMULATIVE PROPORTION HAVING HAD A CHILD BY
AGE AND EDUCATION[a]

| | Age | | |
Education	22	26	30
0–8	33	66	78
9–11	32	69	82
12	28	68	82
13–15	21	65	82
16+	8	51	77

[a]All other variables in equation have been set to their means.

roles. By age 26 these differentials had diminished substantially, and by age 30 only the two extreme groups are different.[6]

Farm residence, living in the South, and not living in an intact family at age 14, all increase birth probabilities at ages less than 20 and tend not to affect the first-birth process thereafter. In all three cases, the sign of the effect at the later ages tends to be the opposite of the sign at ages less than 20. The Catholic effect, in contrast, remains strong in the expected direction until the mid-twenties, consistent with the pattern of later age at union formation among Catholics. By age 30, however, the predicted probability for having become a parent is exactly the same for Catholics and non-Catholics: 81 percent.

Coefficients for the aggregate time effects on birth probabilities at the early ages clearly reflect the extensive delayed childbearing during the Depression, but it appears that the effects of aggregate time interact with age. However, this is not the case once one realizes that cohort also measures period influence, that period factors dominate with respect to first-birth probabilities (see chap. 4), and that period has to change as the cohort ages. To make the effect of period more visible, we reestimated the models shown in table 9 for all birth probabilities of two-year widths, using two-year time periods as predictors. The results (betas) we show in table 11, for the period variables only—although all the structural variables were also in the model. Coefficients for birth probabilities 20–21 and

[6]Some caution should be exercised in interpreting the lowest education group because they have less education than the legal minimum. Suffice it to say that this is a small and heterogeneous group.

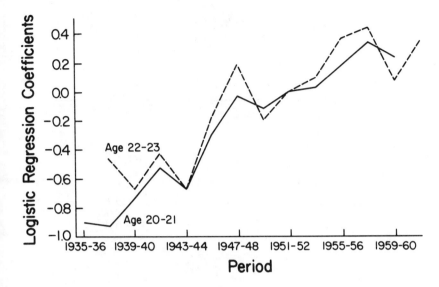

Fig. 12. Effects of period on birth probabilities at ages 20–21
and 22–23—1935–1962.

22–23 are graphed in figure 12. These results strongly suggest that the
effects of aggregate time do not interact with individual time, evidenced
most clearly at the younger ages. However, even at the older ages, one
sees a similar pattern of coefficients from column to column. Thus, period
effects during the time covered in this analysis result in important shifts
in the entire first-birth distribution, without affecting other relationships
in the process.

TRENDS IN EDUCATION EFFECTS

We now return to the question: Have some educational groups shown
disproportionately strong trends toward delayed childbearing? Examination for such differential change is important because it allows us to assess
hypotheses about the macrolevel causes of these trends. For instance,
some researchers credit the women's movement and expanding occupational opportunities in recent years with providing a major thrust toward
delayed childbearing. If this is the case, then we should expect that the
most highly educated women—those most affected by these changes—

TABLE 11.
PATTERNS OF FIRST-BIRTH PROBABILITIES BY PERIOD—1915–1939 BIRTH COHORTS
OF NATIVE-BORN WHITE WOMEN[a]

Period	Having First Birth at Age				
	20–21	22–23	24–25	26–27	28–29
1935–1936	-.899**				
1937–1938	-.926**	-.464**			
1939–1940	-.733**	-.670**	-.439		
1941–1942	-.527**	-.430**	-.172	-.291	
1943–1944	-.671**	-.675**	-.243	-.439	.305
1945–1946	-.294*	-.183	-.153	-.028	.160
1947–1948	-.030	-.191	.179	.398	.425
1949–1950	-.117	-.197	-.471*	-.298	.156
1951–1952	b	b	b	b	b
1953–1954	.025	.096	117	.325	-.171
1955–1956	.185	.365**	-.067	.432*	.144
1957–1958	.336	.434**	.341	.038	.361
1959–1960	.232	.072	.231	.114	.184
1961–1962		.352	-.106	.281	.151
1963–1964			.304	.313	.021
1965–1966				-.307	-.123
1967–1968					.144
Model χ^2	385.8	170.6	59.3	58.5	28.1
N	6,718	4,966	3,426	2,344	1,654

*Significant at .05.
**Significant at .01.
[a]Models also include all variables shown in table 9.
[b]Reference category.
NOTE: Blank cells indicate data point not available or deleted from model.

would show the stronger trends. Indeed, Wilkie (1981:583) claims that "delaying parenthood is a recent strategy adopted by women interested in careers, especially those with higher education."

To examine this interaction further, we use the 1980 Current Population Survey (CPS). The CPS sample includes all women, and thus, we can examine more recent cohorts without biasing our results with respect to marriage timing. Also, the sample includes women of a wide age range, allowing observation of a broad spectrum of birth cohorts. This range is important because the fertility survey analysis above examines first-birth timing only up until the late 1960s when changes in the social and economic climate were just becoming apparent. The 1980 CPS sample allows us to investigate more recent fertility behavior. Finally, this sample is very large, thus making more refined statements about trend possible. As noted in chapter 3, the major limitation of the CPS data is the scarcity of background variables. Here, we examine differential change in birth probabilities by educational level without controlling for other social-structural factors.

Although our analytic strategy is the same as that used earlier in this chapter, the statistical technique is different. We have used minimum logit chi square regression (see Theil 1970) because it greatly reduces the cost of computing with such a large data file. However, the choice of technique does not affect the results since both logit estimators are asymptotically equivalent (Fienberg and Mason 1978).

The question of interest is: Have there been different education effects by cohort? At the younger ages, where the education effects are stronger, the answer is yes. At older ages, there is only a weak education effect that does not vary substantively or significantly by cohort. We arrived at this conclusion by fitting several different models to the cross-classification of birth probability by cohort by education. While much of the observed variance can be explained by an additive model, we find an interpretable and clearly significant pattern of differential change at ages 20, 20–21, 22–23, and 24–25. At these ages, interaction terms between cohort and education are necessary to describe the data adequately, but we find that a constrained interaction model fits the data nearly as well as a saturated one.[7] The differential change in this constrained model, takes the form $b_1\text{COHORT} + b_2\text{COHORT}^2$, where COHORT is a linear scoring of cohort, e.g., those born 1915–1919, 1920–1924, . . . 1950–1954 are scored 0,1, . . . 7 or 0,1, . . . 6, depending on the number of cohorts included in the analysis. The resulting patterns appear in figure 13 (panels A–D), where we have plotted the change in birth probability by cohort, net of the additive education effect (the birth-probability derivative with respect to cohort; see Stolzenberg 1979).

The pattern in figure 13 shows that the intercohort differences are greatest for those with the most education. Stated differently, well-educated women respond more strongly to the prevailing socioeconomic climate. They delayed fertility most in response to the more recent period conditions, as well as in response to the Depression, and least in the post–World War II period. The extent to which college-educated women have delayed childbearing in the 1970s is consistent with the hypothesis

[7]Details of this model fitting are available in Rindfuss, Morgan, and Swicegood (1984), table 6.

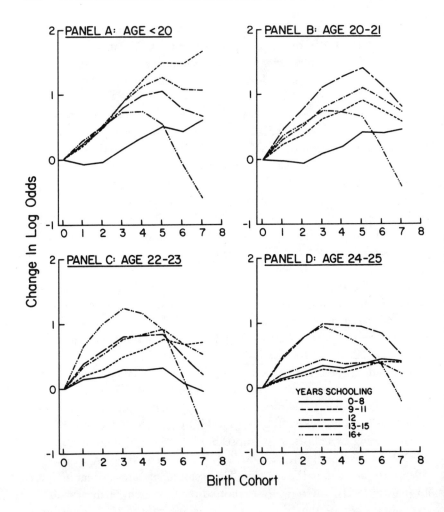

Fig. 13. Change in likelihood of a first birth by education and birth cohort—
ages 20, 20–21, 22–23, and 24–25.

of expanding opportunities for women. This evidence, however, must be weighed against the relative similarity of delay for college-educated women now as compared to the 1930s, when a different opportunity structure for women existed. We again see that delayed childbearing is not a new strategy, but the direction of change is such that expanded opportunities are likely to be an important part of the explanation for recent trends.

OTHER ADOLESCENT FACTORS

Analyses reported so far examine variables measured in all six fertility surveys. We now focus on the effects of age at menarche which can only be estimated using the 1965 and 1976 fertility surveys, and youthful cigarette smoking which was measured only in the 1970 NFS. Both variables are associated with an early transition to parenthood and both variables raise intriguing issues about peer group effects during adolescence. Thus, even though these results are primarily suggestive, they help fill in a potentially important component of the conceptual model presented in chapter 2—the role of adolescent behavior and experience.

AGE AT MENARCHE.

Menarche marks the beginning of a woman's fertile years and of her physical transformation from girl to woman. The timing of menarche also is related to the timing of subsequent adult behavioral transitions, such as age at first intercourse, age at first marriage, and age at first birth (Buck and Stavraky 1967; Kiernan 1977; Presser 1978; Ryder and Westoff 1971; Udry 1979; Udry and Cliquet 1982; Zelnik et al. 1981). Age at menarche and at first birth are linked although in a country like the United States they may be separated by a decade or more.

Since age at menarche is essentially a biological event and age at first birth is a biological and social event, their linkage may involve biological pathways or social pathways. In fact, both have been suggested in the literature. Biologically, it is possible that women who experience early menarche may also be more fecund, and other things being equal, will be more likely to become mothers at an early age. This difference in fecundity may be the result of temporary effects on fecundity related to differences in the length of adolescent sterility, or may be the result of permanent differences in fecundity levels.

Sociologically, menarche may signal to the woman, her parents, and her friends that she is becoming an adult and is ready to engage in a series of adult behaviors which culminate in becoming a mother. The variation in age at menarche will tend to cut across other age-graded transitions within society. For example, if the postmenarcheal seventh-grader is more likely to be dating than the premenarcheal seventh-grader, these differences in early dating behavior may lead to permanent behavioral differences between the two groups, or such differences may diminish once all have passed menarche.

Unfortunately, age at menarche was not asked in all the fertility studies that we have been examining—only the 1965 NFS and the 1976 NSFG. As before, these two surveys were pooled, and a series of conditional logit regression equations were examined. Age at menarche was categorized into five groups, with the following distribution:

Age at menarche	Percentage distribution
9–11	19
12	23
13	30
14	15
15+	13
	100

Table 12 shows the results. The χ^2 difference row shows the improvement in fit gained from adding the menarche variables (which consume four degrees of freedom) to the models estimated earlier (see table 9). Only at age 20 is there a substantially significant effect. Also only at age 20 is the pattern of coefficients interpretable. The observed effects show that increasing age at menarche decreases the log odds of a teenage birth. Specifically, compared with those experiencing menarche at age 13, those with earlier age at menarche are more likely to have a teenage birth; those later than 13 are less likely. The only individually significant coefficient is the 15+ category. Tests (not shown) indicate that one cannot legitimately constrain the other coefficients to equal 0.0, nor can the age at menarche categories be scored as a linear scale. Instead, adequate description of these effects requires a nonlinear effect (e.g., movement to an older menarche category reduces the log odds on a teenage birth by –.10), and a heightened effect of moving from category 14 to 15+ (movement across the categories lowers the log odds by –.43).

In sum, increasing age at menarche reduces the likelihood of a teenage birth, especially for those with age at menarche 15+. Beyond the teenage years, however, there is no significant effect of age at menarche. Hence, the effect of age at menarche on timing of entry into motherhood is temporary, occurring either through the biological pathway affecting the length of adolescent sterility, or through the social pathways affecting adolescent dating behaviors.

TABLE 12.
LOGIT REGRESSION COEFFICIENTS FOR EFFECT OF AGE AT MENARCHE
ON FIRST BIRTH[a]

Age at menarche	Having First Birth at Age						
	<20	20–21	22–23	24–25	26–27	28–29	30–34
9–11	0.19	–0.11	0.15	–0.18	–0.28	–0.18	–0.21
12	0.06	0.10	–0.18	–0.13	–0.20	0.26	–0.26
13							
14	–0.14	0.14	0.09	–0.01	–0.12	–0.31	0.05
15+	–0.66*	0.11	0.25	0.03	–0.02	0.25	–0.04
χ^2 difference[b]	35.66*	3.85	8.48	1.89	2.23	5.37	1.89
N	3808	2837	2074	1453	998	719	550

*Significant at .05.
[a]In addition to age at menarche, we included the following variables in the analysis: education, rural-urban background, religion, region, whether respondent was in an intact family while growing up, and cohort.
[b]Measures improved fit of model to data resulting from inclusion of age at menarche variables. Including these variables sacrifices 4 degrees of freedom.

YOUTHFUL SMOKING.

In earlier research (Rindfuss and St. John 1983), cigarette smoking at a relatively young age (less than 15) was found to be associated with a comparatively early entry into the mother role. As argued there, clearly cigarette smoking is not the causal factor. Rather, smoking at a young age is probably indicative of the peer group to which the young woman belonged during her early adolescent years. One would expect that early cigarette smokers would be more likely to associate with other early smokers. Further, Reynolds and Nichols (1976) suggest that a direct relationship exists between cigarette smoking and various personality traits. Smokers tend to be less well adjusted and more likely to engage in antisocial behavior than nonsmokers. Fracchia, Sheppard, and Merlis (1974) suggest that early smokers are more likely to engage in other "adult" behaviors at a relatively early age. Consequently, one might expect early smokers to initiate sexual intercourse, marriage, and entry into the labor force at relatively young ages. These, in turn, are likely to lead to a young age at parenthood.

The reasoning above suggests that youthful smokers are more likely

TABLE 13.
LOGIT REGRESSION COEFFICIENTS FOR EFFECT OF SMOKING AT AN EARLY AGE
(≤15) ON FIRST BIRTH[a]

	Having First Birth at Age					
	<20	20–21	22–23	24–25	26–27	28–29
Early smoking	0.43*	0.35	−0.43	−0.20	−1.62*	−1.94*
χ^2 difference[b]	3.92*	1.68	1.52	0.21	6.61*	5.57*
N	1851	1381	971	620	425	283

*Significant at .05.
[a]In addition to smoking at an early age, we included the following variables in the analysis: education, rural-urban background, religion, region, whether respondent was in an intact family while growing up, and cohort.
[b]Measures improved fit of model to data resulting from inclusion of "early smoking" variable. Including this variable sacrifices 1 degree of freedom.

to become adolescent mothers, but leaves open the question of the effect of youthful smoking on those who delayed childbearing past their teenage years. The question on age at initiation of smoking was only asked in the 1970 NFS, and thus the number of cases available for analysis is quite limited. Nevertheless, it is still possible to examine the effects of youthful smoking. Results are in table 13; again these effects are net of social-structural and aggregate variables analyzed earlier (see table 9).

As expected, women who begin smoking at or before age 15 are more likely to become adolescent parents than other women. However, among those who survive to their mid-twenties still childless, the adolescent smokers are substantially less likely to become mothers, an unexpected finding. Early smokers may be less likely to respond to the normative pressures to have a child which occur in the late twenties, but we would need additional information to argue this interpretation forcefully.

These effects of menarche and youthful smoking hint that adolescent behavior and experience can have important consequences for the parenthood process. Some of these effects may only operate on teenage fertility, as is apparently true for age at menarche; other factors may influence on time or late childbearing. Note also that these variables are not simply mediating effects of background variables, but provide additional explanatory power. Clearly, the complexity of the unfolding adolescent life course provides a promising area for subsequent research. Research on teenage childbearing frequently examines adolescent experience, but we have little evidence of how this crucial life course phase influences childbearing at subsequent ages.

RACIAL SIMILARITIES AND DIFFERENCES

To this point, we have considered various dimensions of the first-birth process for white women only, under the assumption that the structure of the process may differ across racial groups. Our analysis of a pooled sample of black respondents from the major U.S. fertility surveys indicates that the assumption is to some extent correct. In this section, we discuss the principal similarities and differences between blacks and whites.

Insofar as possible, we conducted parallel analysis to those presented above based on data from the pooled fertility surveys. Because there were very few black women interviewed in the 1955 and 1960 GAF studies, our sample of black women is limited to the 1920–1939 birth cohorts. A total of 2,736 black women were aged 35 or more at the time of interview and thus eligible for inclusion. The pace of first-birth timing for these women is shown below along with comparable numbers for whites:

Age group	Percent childless at beginning of interval		Of those childless at beginning, percent having first birth in interval	
	Blacks	Whites	Blacks	Whites
0–19	100.0	100.0	49.9	24.4
20–21	51.1	75.6	29.2	26.4
22–23	36.2	55.6	27.4	31.2
24–25	26.3	38.2	23.9	31.4
26–27	20.0	26.2	23.7	29.5
28–29	15.2	18.5	15.8	24.4
30–34	12.8	14.0	19.9	40.6

The considerably faster pace of the black first-birth schedule is readily apparent. The proportion of black women who became mothers by age

20 is about twice that for whites in the 1915–1939 birth cohorts.[8] Conditional first-birth probabilities are roughly similar for blacks and whites in their early twenties, but at older ages the likelihood of blacks having a first birth becomes increasingly lower than that for whites. As a result of this slower pace at older ages slightly over 10 percent of the black sample reached age 35 childless. The corresponding figure for whites is about 8 percent. As shown in chapter 6, the historical pattern of greater permanent childlessness among blacks is likely to be reversed for more recent cohorts of American women.

While there are substantial differences in the first-birth schedules for blacks and whites, the structure of the process is fairly similar across these racial groups. We estimated a set of logistic regression models for blacks that parallel those presented in tables 8 and 9 for whites. The effects of aggregate time as indexed by birth cohort were found to be quite similar for blacks and whites. At ages 24 and older, the first-birth probabilities for blacks tend to show somewhat greater intercohort variability (or period response) such that by age 35 differences in the proportion childless between the youngest and oldest cohorts in the analysis are substantially greater for blacks than for whites.

Results for the social-structural variables also suggest similarities in the structure of first-birth timing for blacks and whites. The black pattern of effects across individual time corresponds well with the white pattern for the background household composition and Catholic measures, although the effects for Catholics were not statistically significant. Remember that there are relatively few black Catholics. Black women from farm backgrounds tended to have slightly higher first-birth probabilities across all ages culminating in about 30 percent greater odds of having a first birth by age 35 than black women from nonfarm backgrounds. Surprisingly, all else equal, Southern black women were more likely to be childless at age 35 than non-Southern blacks. These patterns contrast with white women for whom farm and Southern background were both associated with a faster first-birth pace at younger ages and slower pace at older ages.

[8]Because we are using an ever-married sample, the percentage childless at each age will be an underestimate for all women (see appendix A). At age 35, black women in these cohorts in contrast to white women were more likely to be never-married by three to four percentage points. This would tend to make the underestimate relatively greater for blacks. However, the tendency would be counterbalanced by the greater likelihood that black women will bear an out-of-wedlock child.

Reasons behind these racial differences are not clear, but it may be that the extensive migration of these cohorts of blacks both to urban areas and out of the South are related to these differences. Certainly the fertility of urban blacks fell much earlier than did that of rural blacks because of differences in the rate of socioeconomic change. It is also possible that physiological factors or sterility played some role especially in higher childlessness observed in the South (see Tolnay 1985 for a review of the black fertility transition). The fecundity explanation would seem to fit with the lower birth probabilities observed for white and black Southern women during the later years of reproductive age.

Earlier we presented evidence showing the powerful influence of education on the timing of first births for whites. Education effects are also quite pronounced for black women, but they tend to be of smaller magnitude than those observed for whites. One exception to this general pattern concerns the probability of having had a child by age 35. Here, we find that black women with four years of college were particularly likely to remain childless by that age as compared to whites. This finding is consistent with the racial fertility pattern first noted by Lee and Lee (1959) for highly educated black women to have lower fertility than their white counterparts. However, the results presented in the next chapter suggest that this pattern has reversed itself among more recent cohorts.

In an overall assessment of the black-white comparisons, one is struck by the similarity of structure of the first-birth process given the substantial differences in the timing of those births. Unfortunately, beyond racial differences in educational attainment, our analyses do not point to factors that result in the much higher levels of adolescent fertility that characterize the black population. Moreover, because of the faster pace of first-birth timing for blacks, we are in a poor position empirically to analyze the correlates of first-birth probabilities at later ages for the group. After pooling data from six fertility surveys, we ended with only 351 black women who had not had a first birth by age 30. The logit model of the four-year first-birth probability for these women had no statistically significant predictors.

SUMMARY AND DISCUSSION

Our findings clearly indicate the importance of all three dimensions of the first-birth process. First-birth probabilities change as social-structural aspects, as aggregate time and individual time change. All three are essential ingredients in a complete understanding of the process. The effect of the social-structural variables varies substantially with changes in individual time but only minimally with changes in aggregate time. This latter finding allows separating aggregate-time or structural factors in the examination of the initiation of motherhood—a result we rely on when using data from the National Longitudinal Survey of the High School Class of 1972 in later chapters.

In general, period factors increase or decrease childbearing at all ages and for all subgroups within society. Although period factors operate pervasively throughout society and are among the most important variables explaining temporal changes, few clues to the nature of these period effects are obtained. The reason is that in any given period many changes are taking place which could explain period trends. During the 1970s, for example, the women's movement, increases in housing prices, rising interest rates, the Vietnam War (in the early part of the decade), and increasing economic uncertainty all could have produced declines in first-birth probabilities. To distinguish among these causes, we need to increase the length of the available time series or obtain comparable time-series data from multiple countries. Given the clear importance of period factors, such work should be high on the future research agenda.

The one interaction involving structural variables and aggregate time that we found was the education and aggregate time interaction, which is instructive with respect to the need for a long time series. Had we just examined the 1950s through the 1970s, we would have concluded that college education was having an increasing impact on the delay of fertility because of expanding opportunities for women in the 1970s. However, by extending the time series back to the 1930s, one sees that the effect of education in the 1930s is rather similar to that of education in the 1970s.

Women in both periods pursued a strategy of delayed childbearing, and in both periods this pattern was most pronounced among well-educated women. Explanations offered for the most recent trends have focused on factors unique to that period, such as the modern contraceptive regime or the women's liberation movement. That similar patterns emerged in the 1930s suggests these causal factors clearly are not necessary conditions for delayed childbearing, and in fact, they may have had only a minimal effect.

Structural factors that we examined tend to affect *when* women become mothers more than *whether* they become mothers. Further, the effect of these structural factors varies substantially by age. For example, highly educated women have the highest conditional first-birth probabilities at the later ages and the lowest probabilities at the earliest ages. In short, the effects are not proportional. Thus, these social-structural factors are primarily important from a life course perspective. They determine the amount of time spent without children—time that is critical with respect to establishing a career, establishing a relationship with a man, accumulating resources, establishing avocational interests, and to the maturation process in general. This delay, in turn, further affects fertility because the later couples start having children, the fewer they have.

Finally, the general predictability of the process declines with age. This situation may be the function of the lack of contemporaneous variables, such as the extent and quality of women's labor force participation (Gerson 1985), as well as fecundability. In short, it may be the result of unmeasured heterogeneity. But it also may be a function of the structure of the process itself. By the time a woman reaches her late twenties still childless, she has relatively few contemporaries still childless, and she has demonstrated her ability to resist the pronatalist pressures of society at large and of the various subgroups to which she belongs. The elapsed time—for example, having lived ten years in the adult role without becoming a mother—may have an important effect in its own right, an effect that would be a constant for all members of that group. Thus, it would not be surprising that our ability to predict her behavior diminishes. Given the relatively large pool of women currently at risk of childbearing (see chap. 4), and given the increased costs associated with later childbearing because of genetic counseling, amniocentesis, and other attendant medical factors, the reduced predictability increases the difficulty of policy decisions in this area.

6

Racial Similarities
and Differences

In this chapter, we examine racial trends in the initiation of childbearing. Although recent cohorts of white women have sharply delayed their first birth (chap. 4), we find that black women have done so much less. This differential fertility behavior has been noted by other researchers (Bloom 1982; Evans 1986; Michael and Tuma 1985), but systematic explanations have not been offered. Michael and Tuma (1985:26), for example, conclude their analysis with the following assessment:

We are struck by our lack of success in identifying reasons for black-white differences in teenage entry into marriage or in teenage males' entry into parenthood, despite the large number of family background variables included in our study.

In addition to providing further documentation of the diverging racial trends in the timing of first births, we consider various factors that might account for this divergence. We place particular emphasis on one explanation not explicitly raised in the previous literature. Empirical evidence presented below indicates that the differential racial trends in delayed childbearing are most pronounced for women of higher levels of educational attainment. This finding suggests that the divergent racial patterns of the 1970s may follow in part from the substantial socioeconomic improvement of better educated blacks during a time when better educated whites saw a reduction in their relative standard of living (Farley 1984). Thus, if blacks who benefited most from the reduced discrimination of the decade actually perceived their recent social and economic experience less harshly than whites, they may have been less inclined to delay their childbearing. In short, the socioeconomic convergences Michael and Tuma mentioned may be partially responsible for the demographic divergence.[1]

Of course, other plausible explanations for the black-white divergence exist, some of which complement our basic hypothesis. We discuss several of these explanations below. We also discuss potential consequences of these differential patterns. For example, future race differentials in family size and socioeconomic status may be affected. Finally we consider how these results challenge the view that majority/minority group fertility differentials will disappear as minority groups become more assimilated with respect to social and economic factors (e.g., Johnson 1979; Lee and Lee 1959; Sly 1970).

MEASUREMENT AND DATA

Our analysis focuses on two measures of timing used throughout this monograph: C_x, the proportion childless at age x; and BP_x, the first-birth probability, which is the proportion having a child while age x among those still childless at exact age x. C_x then can be taken as a measure of fertility delay to age x and BP_x a measure of continued delay while age x (see chap. 3 for further discussion).

The vital registration and Current Population Survey data we use are described in chapter 3. The vital registration data provide a long fertility time series for whites and nonwhites. The 1980 June Current Population Survey (CPS) allows us to compute measures of first-birth timing by race and wife's current level of schooling from a representative national sample. The 1980 CPS is appropriate because it includes a wide age range allowing examination of a long series of birth cohorts. It also includes both ever- and never-married women so that the more recent cohorts can be observed without an age-at-marriage bias. This aspect of the sample is especially important in examining first births for blacks, about half of which now occur outside of marriage (J. A. Jones et al., 1985; O'Connell and Rogers 1984). Finally, it provides a large sample that allows for more

---

[1]See Espenshade (1985:221–229) for a related argument with respect to differential racial trends in marital behavior.

reliable trend estimates. Where possible, we have made extensive comparisons of results from these two different data sources (CPS and vital registration), and they are similar.[2]

AGGREGATE TRENDS IN THE PROPORTION CHILDLESS

Using vital registration data, figure 14 shows the percentage childless at various ages by cohort and race. Panel A shows the proportion childless at age 20. Nonwhites consistently have more teenage first births than whites, with little apparent convergence across the entire time series.

At age 25 (see panel B) there is much greater variability in the white-nonwhite differential. For the pre-1920 cohorts, those reaching age 25 by 1945, the white-nonwhite gap had narrowed compared to that observed at age 20 (see panel A). Those passing through their early twenties during the postwar period of prosperity (c. 1925–1940) show virtually no differential—white first-birth probabilities at ages 20–24 rose substantially more than nonwhite ones so that whites had *caught up* with the earlier childbearing start of nonwhites by age 25. The more recent cohorts (c. 1940–1954), those passing through their early twenties in the late 1960s and the 1970s, show a dramatic divergence. Whites are increasingly likely to remain childless until age 25 while the pattern for nonwhites is one of oscillation over the same time period.

Panel C shows trends in the proportion childless at age 30. The earliest observed cohorts show no race differential. The wide race differential characterizing these cohorts at age 20 (see panel A) narrowed by age 25 and disappeared by age 30. Later white cohorts (c. 1915–1935) had *caught up* earlier (see panel B) and by age 30 showed lower childlessness levels than nonwhites. Again in the 1970s (c. 1940–1949) whites show sharp increases in delayed childbearing while nonwhites actually appear less likely to be childless by age 30 than at any point in the entire series.

Given the very low birth probabilities observed at ages over 35, childlessness at age 35 can be viewed as a rough indicator of permanent childlessness. Panel D shows these data for available cohorts. One can

---

[2]The CPS provides reliable overall estimates of C_x and BP_x. But the sample size is not sufficiently large to provide reliable estimates of BP_x when disaggregated by education. Consequently the analysis of race differentials by cohort and education is restricted to the proportion childless measure.

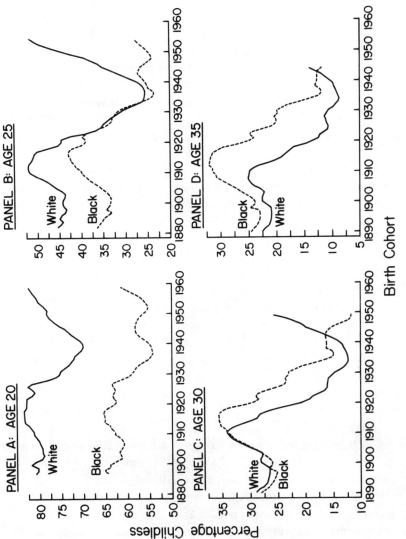

Fig. 14. Percentage childless at various ages by cohort and race.

see the greater childlessness of nonwhites over the entire period of study, except for the most recent birth cohorts.[3]

In sum, these trends show that nonwhites have consistently higher fertility while in their teen years. For most of the time series, whites experienced higher first-birth probabilities while in their twenties and thirties, reversing this childlessness gap by age 35. The pace at which whites closed this gap seems to depend on prevailing socioeconomic conditions—the gap closed by age 25 for those reaching this age during the peak Baby Boom years and by age 30 for those reaching this age in the pre–World War II years. In other words, whites showed stronger responses to these changing conditions than did nonwhites. Finally, at ages 25 and over, whites and nonwhites show quite different trends in the 1970s. Whites display sizable and increasing levels of delayed childbearing while only very recent cohorts of nonwhites exhibit even a slight tendency toward fertility delay.

AGGREGATE TRENDS IN BIRTH PROBABILITIES

Childlessness at ages 20, 25, 30, and 35 can be interpreted as intentional or unintentional fertility delay. We now examine continued delay: If a woman reaches these ages childless, what is the probability that she will remain childless while at this age? In figure 15 we show the trend in these birth probabilities from vital statistics data. Because such measures are very responsive to period changes they will add some clarification to the different white-nonwhite patterns observed in figure 14.

Panel A shows that, except for the Baby Boom period, nonwhites have higher birth probabilities at age 20. Panels B, C, and D show the opposite pattern at older ages (e.g., whites have higher first-birth probabilities)—except in the most recent period. In the 1970s nonwhites are *less likely*, compared to whites, to reach each age childless (see fig. 14) and given that they do reach these ages childless they are *more likely* to have a first birth (see fig. 15). This scissors pattern at older ages shown in figures 14 and 15 has important implications. It implies, for instance, that women born in the 1950s will show a reversal of the historically observed greater

[3]Bloom (1982) suggests that rates of childlessness for nonwhite women may be overestimated for nonwhite birth cohorts because of underregistration of first births. However, he does not argue that these rates do not exceed those of white women.

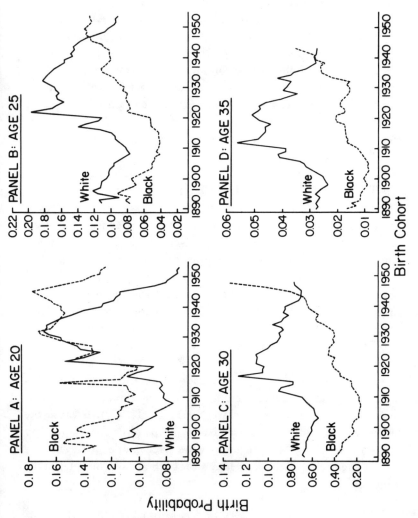

Fig. 15. First birth probabilities at various ages by cohort and race.

childlessness of nonwhites (also see Evans 1986:fig. 4). Net of changes at other parities, this change will widen the existing racial fertility differential in completed family size. We discuss further implications of these trends below.

Note that the diverging white-nonwhite trends in first-birth probabilities appear to be only temporary at age 20 (panel A). Nonwhite cohorts born after 1952 show declining first-birth probabilities, as do whites, instead of the diverging pattern seen at older ages. Perhaps these most recent nonwhite cohorts will continue to approximate the patterns of whites so that the diverging patterns at older ages will be short-lived. Of course, only future data will allow a firm conclusion on this point, but the large racial differential in birth probabilities at age 20 that remains for recent cohorts is not suggestive of a rapid convergence at older ages.

EDUCATIONAL DIFFERENTIALS BY RACE

We next examine trends in the timing of first births by educational levels to obtain clues as to the source of racial divergence in the 1970s. Education differences are likely to be interpreted differently depending on what one thinks education measures. In previous work (Rindfuss, Bumpass, and St. John 1980), we have argued that the student and mother roles tend to be incompatible because both are time and energy demanding. Thus these roles tend to be held sequentially. Given this interpretation, years of schooling has constant meaning across cohorts. Years in school represents time not available for other roles.

To examine differential trends by education we turned to the CPS data described above. These trends were modeled using minimum logit chi-square regression techniques (Berkson 1953; Theil 1970). Because the data in figures 14 and 15 established that the patterns for whites and blacks are different, we searched for a preferred model for each race separately. The preferred model selected for both racial groups takes the following form:

$$y = b_1 \text{ Cohort} + b_2 \text{ Educ} + b_3 \text{ Educ(Coh)} + b_4 \text{ Educ (Coh}^2)$$

where:

y = the log odds of childlessness at age 25

Cohort = a set of 7 dummy variables for 5-year birth cohorts, 1915–1954, where cohort 1915–1919 is the reference category

Educ = a set of 4 dummy variables for years of schooling: 9–11, 12, 13–15, and 16 + ; education 0–8 is the reference category

Educ(Coh) = a set of 4 variables for the interaction between education categories and cohort where cohort is a linear coding 0–7

Educ(Coh²) = a set of 4 dummy variables for the interaction between education and cohort squared where cohort is a linear coding 0–7.

This model is the same one used for whites in chapter 5, and is discussed in somewhat greater detail there.

Because the model contains interaction terms, individual coefficients are not easily interpretable and one should examine the derivative of the log odds with respect to a chosen factor (see Stolzenberg 1979). In figure 16, we plot the expected log odds which, because of the interaction of all factors, take the same pattern as the derivative (with respect to cohort).

For those of low educational attainment, 9–11 years, trends are very similar for whites and blacks, but there is some modest divergence for the latest cohort. Equally interesting is the absence of a trend toward delayed childbearing for either racial group in the most recent period. In fact, for white and black women of low educational attainment, childlessness at age 25 has been declining. Social programs constructed in the postwar period, the social "safety net," may have eased the economic crisis or economic uncertainty of lower-status persons causing less intentional fertility delay. Also, improved fecundity associated with improved health and health care could explain this common pattern. Nancy J. Davis (1982:440) argues convincingly that fecundity changes could not explain the aggregate pattern—increased childlessness for early birth cohorts of this century followed by declining childlessness—since there was "a gradual improvement in health levels of both white and black women of childbearing age during [this] period." This gradual improvement in health, however, does match the trend for those of the lowest education level.

The other panels of figure 16 show that, at the higher education levels, black and white patterns diverge in recent years. For women who com-

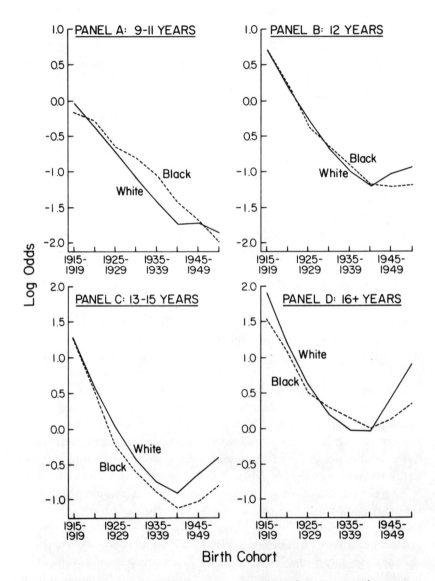

Fig. 16. Log odds on childlessness at age 25 by cohort, race, and years of schooling completed.

pleted 12 years of schooling, likelihood of childlessness at age 25 declines up through the 1940–1944 birth cohorts. While younger cohorts of white women then begin to reverse the trend, the corresponding cohorts of blacks show no evidence of fertility delay. Panels C and D reveal a more pronounced racial divergence for women with education beyond high school. Beginning with the 1945–1949 cohorts, both blacks and whites in these educational categories show trends toward increased delay. However, white women exhibit this tendency more clearly than do blacks.

To this point we have treated education in terms of number of years of schooling. This method is consistent with a conceptualization of its effects on fertility as a matter of occupying time that otherwise might be filled by nonstudent roles including that of mother. But education is also a measure of general socioeconomic status. In this sense, years of schooling has changed its meaning across the time span examined because of the increasing educational attainment of successive cohorts. For example, the 1980 CPS educational distributions indicate that for a woman in the 1915–1919 cohort 11 years of schooling would place her in the 43d percentile of her cohort. For the 1950–1954 cohort this same level of schooling would place a woman in the 14th percentile of her cohort.

To represent how the socioeconomic dimension of education has changed over time, we constructed a relative education measure: the woman's years of schooling completed relative to others in her birth cohort. Again, we used logistic regression analysis. The preferred models *for both races* allow for an unconstrained aggregate trend (represented by dummy variables for each cohort). The effect of relative education is represented by a linear and squared term allowing for nonmonotonic education effects. Interaction terms allow the effect of education to vary by cohort. In the interaction terms, cohort is scored 0–7; relative education is scored as above.

Figure 17 shows the log odds on childlessness at age 25 by cohort, race, and relative education. The panels of this figure contain the estimated cohort trends for those women at the 15th, 30th, 60th, and 90th educational percentiles. If anything, the results shown in figure 17 are even stronger than those in figure 16. At the lower levels, the trends are quite similar for the two racial groups. For those of higher status, there is an increasingly pronounced white-black divergence and an increasingly strong recent trend toward delayed parenthood. As in chapters 4 and 5, we caution against calling delayed parenthood a recent strategy. Levels

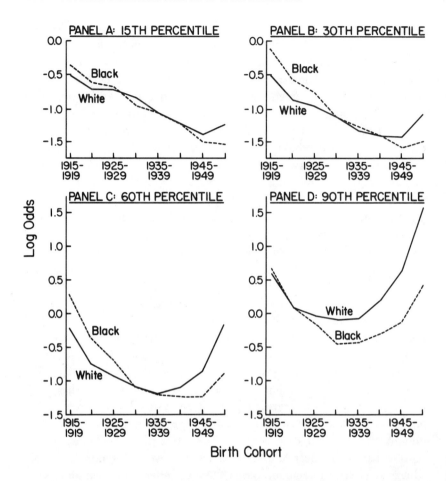

Fig. 17. Log odds on childlessness at age 25 by cohort, race, and relative
education percentile.

of fertility delay experienced by the most recent cohorts are similar to
those observed for the 1915–1919 cohorts, those reaching their twenties
during the Great Depression. Moreover, those of higher status increased
the tempo of their fertility most during the Baby Boom and have contributed disproportionately to the trend toward delayed childbearing in the
1970s.

This greater responsiveness of the more educated at first narrowed and
then widened educational differentials. This greater responsiveness pre-

TABLE 14.
COHORT TRENDS IN RELATIVE EDUCATION[a]

Cohort	Whites (1)	Blacks (2)	Difference (1)–(2)
1915–1919	62.1	36.8	25.3
1920–1924	63.4	38.7	24.7
1925–1929	63.6	43.3	20.3
1930–1934	64.5	50.0	14.4
1935–1939	63.6	52.5	11.1
1940–1944	63.3	50.0	13.3
1945–1949	62.7	52.7	10.0
1950–1954	62.6	53.6	9.0

[a]Relative education is the mean percentile rank on years of schooling completed within each cohort. The mean percentile for the full cohort need not be 50.0 because all those with a given level of schooling are assigned the cumulative percentage value at that schooling level.

sumably reflects their greater ability or desire to alter their family-building schedule. In chapter 4 we argued that changes in the economic circumstances of young adults help explain the aggregate trends (also see N. J. Davis 1982). These educational differentials, like those in chapter 5, suggest that the more educated are most responsive to such changes.

Can the white-black divergence be explained within a similar framework? We believe so. Recent cohorts of whites have judged their economic circumstances harshly in comparison with the recent past, the 1950s and 1960s. One response to this worsening climate has been delayed childbearing. Blacks, however, may perceive recent experience less harshly because of the substantial improvement in their socioeconomic position, especially for the most educated blacks. Part of this improvement results from increasing educational attainment. In table 14 we show the considerable convergence in the mean percentile educational scores of whites and blacks. Such convergence could be expected to produce greater similarity, net of other factors, in the aggregate trends for whites and blacks.

Our focus here, however, is on trends controlling for education. Featherman and Hauser (1978) show that blacks' improving socioeconomic status results also from greater returns to a given level of education. Such change is commonly interpreted as declining economic discrimination. The affirmative action programs of the 1970s may have increased

TABLE 15.
BLACK-WHITE EARNINGS RATIOS: MEN OUT OF SCHOOL ONE TO FIVE YEARS—
1967, 1973, 1978

	Annual earnings			Weekly earnings		
Schooling: Years completed	1967	1973	1978	1967	1973	1978
8–11	79	77	69	85	87	80
12	81	87	76	83	90	85
16 or more	74	92	98	75	92	96
All levels	69	76	74	73	82	81

NOTE: Numbers are average earnings of blacks as a percentage of average earnings of whites.
SOURCE: Welsh (1981); borrowed with permission. Data sources are 1967, 1973, and 1978 March
Current Population Surveys.

TABLE 16.
BLACK-WHITE HOURLY EARNINGS RATIOS: WOMEN AGED 25–34 IN
1960, 1970, AND 1980

Schooling completed	1960	1970	1980
2 years high school	70	99	99
4 years high school	70	104	104
2 years college	81	113	105
4 years college	93	122	105
All educational levels	66	88	98

NOTE: Numbers are average of black earnings as a percentage of average of white earnings.
SOURCE: Farley (1984:table 4.1).

further the value of a given level of schooling for blacks relative to whites
(Burstein 1979). To illustrate, table 15 presents black-white earnings
ratios for males out of school between one and five years. These ratios
show some overall black-white convergence, but there is a strong pattern
of differential change. College-educated blacks have increased their earnings from 74 or 75 percent of whites to 98 or 96 percent, depending on
the annual or weekly figures. Thus the recent economic gains by young
educated blacks may have allowed their family formations to have been
less influenced by worsening economic conditions of the late 1960s and
1970s than was the case for their white counterparts.

The economic explanation advanced here should be most applicable to husband-wife couples. Data in table 15 chart the economic progress of black men and are consistent with the fertility trends for black women. What of the earning trends for these black women? Table 16 provides information on hourly earnings by education for black women as a percentage of those of white women in 1960, 1970, and 1980. The data clearly demonstrate the trend toward racial parity in the 1960s. In fact, by 1970, black women with at least some college education were doing better in terms of hourly wages than similarly educated whites. By 1980, however, the relative *black* earnings advantage in the college categories had largely diminished. This pattern suggests that the relative opportunity costs of childbearing declined for well-educated black women at the same time that relative earnings of black males were rising. The juxtaposition of these circumstances could lead to the divergent fertility trends documented above.

One further piece of evidence follows from trends in family income. Farley (1984) reports that the ratio of black to white family income generally declined in the 1970s; but when considering only husband-wife families this ratio increased. Unfortunately it is not possible to examine the racial-educational trends in first-birth timing by family type using the CPS data.

ADDITIONAL EXPLANATIONS

Other explanations for the recent black-white divergence deserve consideration. Several complement our basic hypothesis since they relate to the socioeconomic progress experienced by blacks in recent years. Of course, no one explanation must account entirely for the divergent trends we report.

Perhaps the relevant comparison for potential parents is not with the recent past, as suggested above, but with their childhood years. If individuals assess their level of living compared to that experienced when growing up, as Easterlin has suggested, then blacks may judge current circumstances more favorably because of their lower origin status. A weakness of this argument is the failure of microlevel analysis to confirm that those with higher status relative to their parents form families earlier than those with lower relative status (see Crimmins-Gardner and Ewer 1978; MacDonald and Rindfuss 1981; Olneck and Wolfe 1978; Rindfuss and MacDonald 1980). But if one broadens the reference group from parent to one's racial group, then recent cohorts of blacks certainly have higher status (relative to origin) than do whites. Note, however, that this broader argument is only slightly different from the one we emphasize above.

Socialization with respect to fertility timing might also vary by origin status. As is well documented, origin status is a major determinant of current status (Blau and Duncan 1967). But there may be direct effects of origin status, net of current status, which influence fertility timing. These origin effects, excluded from the present analysis, would vary for the most educated whites and blacks because of sharper intercohort trends in education. If lower status socialization proves more pronatalist, then this difference could contribute to the divergence.

A different set of potential explanations hinges on the life course sequences followed by blacks and whites. The first birth is much more likely to be conditioned on marriage for whites (see Campbell 1980; K. Davis 1972; Freshnock and Cutright 1979; Hartley 1975; Ventura 1980). Thus conditions that might be a prerequisite to setting up a new household are more relevant to white first births. Specifically, among recent white cohorts childbearing may have been postponed because of the costs of setting up a new household (see chap. 4). Because blacks are less likely to marry or move to a separate residence following the first birth, they would be less affected by costs of establishing a household.

We noted earlier, however, that nonmarital fertility rates for the races have been converging. Moreover, the differential racial trends by education that we find for fertility behavior are not mirrored in marriage behavior. Cherlin (1981), for example, reports that racial differences in marital status changed considerably from 1940 to 1979. Black women are increasingly less likely to be married with husband present and conversely more likely to be never-married as compared with whites. But these changes were most pronounced for women with lower levels of education. Again, this finding suggests that racial patterns of marriage vis-à-vis childbearing do not primarily account for the divergent trends in first-birth timing. Of course, it is possible that factors that make marriage less critical for parenthood among blacks, in general, also lead to a quicker pace of first births among married blacks.

A final explanation also hinges on differences in life course sequences. We have argued that educational attainment affects fertility timing with little causal influence running in the opposite direction (Rindfuss, Bumpass, and St. John 1980). However, the measure of education used here is current education. This measure would attenuate the "real" effect of education if those who have children earlier are more likely to attend school after the first birth (but prior to the interview date). For several reasons blacks may be more likely to return to school following the first birth, thereby contributing to the weaker education effect observed for them. First, they are less likely to marry and set up new households, and they may rely heavily on parents for child care and economic support (e.g., Furstenberg, Brooks-Gunn, and Morgan 1987; Stack 1974). Second, social programs have targeted recent cohorts of black women perhaps making a return to school more feasible.

Using the National Longitudinal Study of the High School Class of 1972, table 17 shows the likelihood of being in school during 1977 and 1978 (when respondents were 22–24 years old) by parenthood status and race. All odds are substantially less than 1.0 showing that parenthood reduces the likelihood of being in school. Moreover, the ratio of white to black odds is also substantially less than 1.0 indicating that the negative effect of parenthood is greater for whites—indeed black parents in this high school cohort are much more likely to be in school than white parents. Unfortunately, we cannot examine trends in the likelihood of returning to school status since this is a sample of a single cohort.

SUMMARY AND CONCLUSION

To summarize, we find similar trends from the 1920s to the mid-1960s for whites and blacks. Since that time whites have delayed fertility sharply while blacks have been much less likely to do so.

Examination of these trends reveals quite different patterns by education and race. We showed that the more educated respond more sharply to the prevailing social and economic climate—not just by delaying childbearing in the seventies but by much earlier childbearing in the 1950s as well.

In terms of the racial differential, there have been similar patterns of declining childlessness for whites and blacks with little education. Less educated women may have benefited from improved health and health care which lowered involuntary childlessness. Or they may have benefited from the social programs of the 1960s which cushioned the impact of worsening economic conditions, or some combination of these explana-

TABLE 17.
EFFECT OF PARENTHOOD ON LIKELIHOOD OF BEING IN SCHOOL

Effect of being parent by year	In school in 1977			In school in 1978		
	White	Black	(W/B)	White	Black	(W/B)
1972	.398	.540	(.74)	.395	.603	(.66)
1973	.329	.528	(.62)	.341	.567	(.60)
1974	.274	.527	(.52)	.308	.599	(.51)
1975	.233	.484	(.48)	.284	.611	(.46)
1976	.215	.415	(.52)	.263	.531	(.50)
1977	.204	.390	(.52)	.236	.453	(.52)
1978	—	—		.215	.443	(.49)

tions. Among the more educated, whites show stronger recent trends toward fertility delay than do blacks. To explain these patterns we point to the divergent expectations and experience of these groups. Better educated blacks may have more easily met their expectations because of real gains in socioeconomic status compared with whites and, consequently, delayed fertility less than similarly educated whites. This may have been one of the consequences of the social programs of the 1970s and an indication that the programs had the most impact among the better educated blacks. We also discussed other explanations. It is quite possible that the mechanisms outlined may have been operating simultaneously and reinforcing one another.

These differing trends have important implications for whites and blacks. Of special interest are the effects on subsequent fertility, the roles women occupy, and socioeconomic achievement of parents and children. Recent divergence in black and white trends will produce a reversal in the historically higher childlessness among blacks—for women born in the 1950s, whites will have greater levels of childlessness. This declining childlessness for blacks and the connection between earlier and higher fertility (see Bumpass, Rindfuss, and Janosik 1978) suggest that the differentials in black-white completed fertility will widen net of other changes if the link between early and subsequent fertility is the same for both races.

Also, delayed childbearing and childlessness allow women to make greater commitments to long-term career goals. These women, therefore, may achieve positions of power and prestige which have hitherto been denied them—denied not only by overt sexual discrimination but also by traditional sex roles having assigned primary child care and housework responsibilities to women. These time- and energy-consuming roles are burdens that make career advancement more difficult. To the extent that this argument holds, the trends we document will affect the socioeconomic advancement of white and black women differently. Early parenthood could also affect the relative socioeconomic position of black and white males. Note, however, that the male differences may be offset if black women are more likely to rely on the extended family for child-rearing help.

The socioeconomic achievement of children can also be affected by their parents' age. Delayed childbearing results in older parents who have attained greater financial security. With age comes greater emotional maturity as well. Because whites show stronger delayed childbearing trends, white children will enjoy these benefits disproportionately. Again, this situation is conditioned on the parents' carrying out the primary child-rearing functions.

Finally, our results have implications for issues surrounding the minority group status and assimilationist perspectives, two prominent themes in the recent literature on differential racial and ethnic group fertility. The basic idea behind Goldscheider and Uhlenberg's (1969) original formulation is that certain aspects of minority group membership, such as being subject to discrimination, will be manifested in group fertility differentials net of compositional differences.

There have been a variety of interpretations as to what patterns of differential fertility would constitute evidence in support of minority group status effects, including the interaction between race or ethnicity and female education in their effects on fertility (Bean and Marcum 1978; Johnson 1979). Our results indicate such an interaction for the timing of the first birth and also suggest that the nature of this interaction has changed over time. However, our findings are not entirely consistent with either an assimilationist or a minority group status perspective.

The assimilationist position argues that as blacks become more integrated into American institutions then race will become a less salient factor in childbearing and particularly for the most educated blacks (Johnson 1979), but we find the very sharpest racial differences in the timing of the first birth among the most educated group of women when using the odds of childlessness at age 25 as a measure of delay. Similarly, the minority group status hypothesis first sought to explain the lower fertility of well-educated black women relative to whites, but our results point to racial differences in the timing of the first birth that imply the opposite pattern. Although both perspectives have usually been empirically addressed with cumulative fertility measures, the results presented in our analysis of delayed childbearing and in other work that examines components of cumulative fertility (e.g., St. John 1982) suggest a more complex picture of majority/minority group patterns than is apparent from examining differential completed fertility.

First, it would appear that racial factors remain and have perhaps increased in salience with respect to the timing of the first birth among recent cohorts of American women. Thus, any simple assimilation theory is unlikely to account for racial differences in patterns of childbearing. Also, the different racial patterns that emerge when comparing the timing of the first birth with children ever born measures suggest the link between the timing of the first birth and the pace and quantity of subsequent fertility may be quite different for blacks and whites (see St. John 1982 and St. John and Grasmick 1985 for supporting evidence). Furthermore, this linkage is likely to have varied across time for both races. In contrast to the minority group status hypothesis, our findings suggest that under certain circumstances, increased socioeconomic assimilation might raise rather than lower the relative fertility of the most educated minority group women.

As further research addresses these issues, we will be better informed about the likely consequences of the divergent patterns reported here. For example, among educated blacks the effects of earlier childbearing may be vitiated by lengthier subsequent birth intervals. The pursuit of such questions should provide a clearer picture of the complex and changing racial differences in family formation, along with a more precise and sophisticated statement about minority group status effects.

Finally, we would emphasize that even though recent cohorts of better educated black women are not delaying their first births as long as their white counterparts, education still plays an important role in the first-birth process for blacks. In chapter 5 we noted the effects of education on first-birth timing were substantial for the 1920–1934 birth cohorts of black women, and the material presented here confirms the persistent importance of these effects. Thus, the timing of first births for well-educated black women is late enough that it is unlikely to generate anywhere near the negative consequences that follow from the young parenthood characterizing poorly educated women of all races.

7

Contrasts Between
The United States and Japan

When asked, "Why do women have children later or not at all?" one immediately searches for a referent. Later than whom? More likely to be childless than whom? The referent is necessary because the answer depends on the contrast of interest. Variability across time in the United States is associated with the economic fortunes of potential parents, especially the expense of setting up a household (see chap. 4). Variability across individuals in the United States can be explained by differential resources and opportunities. Those who acquire more education, disproportionately those from higher socioeconomic backgrounds (Blau and Duncan 1967; Featherman and Hauser 1978), have children later in order to achieve their desired level of living (see chap. 5). While black-white differences in fertility timing can be explained in part by the traditionally disadvantaged position of blacks, recent differential changes also seem to reflect improved economic conditions for blacks, especially the more educated (see chap. 6). In sum, the distinctive patterns of parenthood across groups and time in the United States involve associated differentials in socioeconomic position and various aspects of the changing social context.

One way to understand the American experience better is through cross-national comparison. In this chapter we contrast parenthood timing in the United States and Japan. Both are highly modernized societies, but have dissimilar cultural heritages and have experienced substantially different histories. Further, while both are modern nations, sharp differences remain in the key societal institutions of family and work. Thus, the contrast between the United States and Japan allows us to assess the influence of the Western context on family formation. Most other comparisons we make take this Western context as a given, and examine variability within it. But much variability in parenthood timing can be traced to the social context that identifies normative behavior and determines the sanctions for noncomformity (see Cain 1977, 1985; Caldwell 1982; McNicoll 1980; Ryder 1980*b*, 1983, for discussions of the importance of social context for understanding fertility level and change).

Major supports for the mother and spouse roles in Japan include a dearth of alternative roles and strong ideological support for traditional roles. As preliminary evidence note that a recent Japan Institute of Population Problems (1983) study of *unmarried* Japanese finds an "almost universal intention to marry" and a preference for two or three children by over 90 percent of the respondents. Similar studies in the United States find that, while most still intend to marry and have children, the perceived costs of nonmarriage and childlessness have declined (see chap. 2). Watkins (1984:311) noted the East-West contrast in comparative study of historical levels of nonmarriage:

Asia would seem to be aptly described by a nineteenth-century Russian ethnographer . . . who said, "Only freaks and the morally depraved do not marry"—and there appear to have been precious few of those. . . . In Western Europe, in contrast, it could be said that spinsters were thick on the ground.

Cross-national fertility comparisons show that developed Western nations follow similar fertility trends, but fluctuations are much stronger in the United States (Campbell 1974). In chapter 4 we show that the same conclusion applies to the timing of parenthood, but we show a clear difference between developed Western nations and Japan. Fertility delayed in the West tends not to be made up at subsequent ages. Women in Japan delay the first birth but are very unlikely to remain permanently childless. The life course model we have adopted in this book posits that delay allows for competing alternatives that lead to further delay and eventual childlessness. A fundamentally different process appears to exist in Japan.

We now turn to a closer look at the contrasting features of parenthood in Japan and the United States. This chapter offers a unique perspective on American parenthood, and a quite different answer to why women have children later or not at all. This chapter also offers an opportunity to examine briefly the role of marriage. As argued in chapter 2, the role of marriage in the process of becoming a parent is extremely variable—indeed it is sometimes an effect rather than a cause. Further, for many couples, the marriage and fertility decision may be joint. But as we discuss below, the meaning of marriage is much more uniform in Japan. As we shall see, these differences in the meaning of marriage appear to have important implications for first-birth timing.

CONTRASTING MODERN FERTILITY PATTERNS AND SOCIETIES

In the United States, Ryder (1969, 1980a) documents the emergence of a modern fertility pattern—a pattern characterized by relatively early ages at childbearing, nearly universal parenthood, very small families, and the dominance of timing shifts (over number shifts) in affecting fertility rates. While small families are characteristic of both the United States and Japan, two other features of this modern pattern, first-birth timing and the proportion remaining permanently childless, vary considerably. Comparison of the American and Japanese 1950 birth cohort provides a good example of these contrasts. Figure 18 shows the proportions remaining childless by age (using vital registration data for the two countries).[1] The U.S. data are for whites only to produce a more homogeneous group to compare with the ethnically homogeneous Japanese. If we did not restrict the comparison to whites, the contrast between the two countries would be even more marked. Note that the Japanese cohort shows a much later pattern of childbearing. Few Japanese women become mothers until their early twenties. Conversely, teenage motherhood is relatively common in the United States. Despite getting a later start than the U.S. cohort, the Japanese cohort shows lower rates of permanent childlessness. Thus there are clear cross-national differences in two key features of the modern fertility pattern.

Historically, within Japan and regions of Western Europe, the timing of family formation varied sharply across time and space. Family formation for men was tied to the accumulation of capital assets, for women to levels of fecundity and infant mortality (see Mosk 1983). Overall though, age at family formation in the West and in Japan may have been more similar in the premodern period than today. With modernization and available wage labor, men and women in the West started families

---

[1]U.S. data are the same as those used in chapter 4. Japanese vital registration data were provided by Kiyosi Hirosima and his colleagues at the Japan Institute of Population Problems.

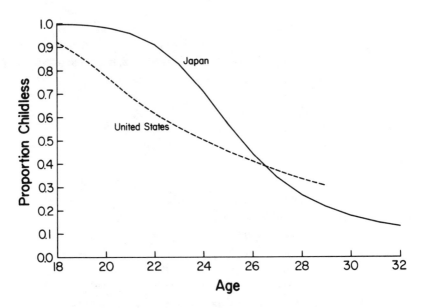

Fig. 18. Proportion of women childless by age—United States and Japan, 1950 birth cohort.

younger (see Levine 1977). Many assume that with the continued demise of the Japanese patrilineal family system, age at marriage and first birth will soon begin to decline in Japan for similar reasons (see Mosk 1983). Yet, no such decline is evident and, as Taeuber (1958:209) noted almost 30 years ago, "the major familial adjustment of the Japanese to industrialization and urbanization was the postponement of marriage." Moreover, Leonetti (1978) finds that second-generation Japanese-Americans show a later pattern of childbearing, and Rindfuss and Sweet (1977) find a much later pattern of childbearing among contemporary Japanese-Americans than among other American groups. Thus an explanation of this latter pattern must include the reasons for its persistence across time and space.

Blake (1972) documents the "coercive pronatalism" of American society. She argues that women's adult roles are closely tied to parenthood and that alternative routes to status are discouraged by existing institutional structures (see chap. 2). In Japan, pronatalism appears in even stronger forms and shows little indication of weakening. The scarcity of professional career paths for women in Japan is severe in comparison with the United States. Women workers are considered a temporary labor force; women tend to be concentrated in unskilled jobs with little opportunity for developing new skills or for career advancement (Coleman 1980, 1983; Osako 1978). Watkins (1984:323) uses much the same argument to explain historical differences in nonmarriage between East and West.

> In Asia, there were no goals, either familial or individual, that took precedence over female marriage. . . . In Western Europe there were justifications for remaining single. . . . What is, in the end, as remarkable as the proportions of spinsters is the plethora of explanations for remaining single. . . .

Similarly, in Japan today the relative lack of alternatives to motherhood and the influence of Confucianism which was embodied in marriage laws up until after World War II (Taeuber 1958) mean that Japanese women are very unlikely to remain voluntarily childless. In the United States, by contrast, women face "hard choices" regarding domesticity and motherhood versus work and career (see Gerson 1985).

A second difference is the sharp contrast in emphasis on emotional compatibility and companionship between marriage partners. Coleman (1980:3; 1983) argues that the Japanese couple "exhibits a deeper sex role division of labor" while "placing less stress on marital companionship and sexuality." In a study of couples living in Detroit and Tokyo, Blood (1967) comes to similar conclusions. In fact, an 11-country study ranked Japanese men last in time spent doing housework and first in hours spent at work (Keizaikikaku-Cho 1973:60). These differences in the marital relationship increase the relative importance of childbearing to the Japanese wife. The woman's emotional satisfaction from the family comes primarily from her children, not from her relationship with her spouse. This difference suggests a shorter time interval between marriage and first birth for Japanese couples and a greater reluctance to remain permanently childless. A related effect of these differences in marriage operates through marital disruption. The Western emphasis on compatibility and companionship produces a union that is inherently fragile—"emotionality alone is a quixotic foundation for an enduring arrangement" (Ryder 1974:86). As a result marital disruption is common in the United States, producing longer intervals between first marriage and first birth.[2] Such fertility delay can lead to intentional and unintentional childlessness. So

---

[2]Kumagai (1983) reports rising divorce rates in Japan. Yet she predicts they will remain far below levels seen in the West.

again, the nature of the marital bonds make permanent childlessness a greater possibility in the United States.

While Japanese society places less importance on the romantic love aspects of the conjugal relationship, intergenerational ties are given more importance. This emphasis again highlights the importance of eventually having children to preserve the linkage between past and future generations.

The arguments above help explain why childlessness is a less attractive option in Japan. But given the greater inherent pronatalism of Japanese society, why the late transition to parenthood? As mentioned before, the importance of children to marriage implies consistently short intervals between marriage and first birth. So the late age at childbearing is often explained in terms of delayed marriage; but given the very high correlation between age at marriage and at first birth, it is highly likely that these are joint rather than separate decisions. Coleman (1980, 1983) provides an explanation for this persistent pattern of late marriage. Part of the explanation lies in the sexual division of labor within marriage and the corresponding nature of the marriage market. Because emotional compatibility and companionship receive less emphasis within marriage, these attributes receive little attention in the marriage market. Few formalized mechanisms exist which promote contact with those of the opposite sex—especially in the teenage years. Preparation for marriage focuses instead on characteristics valued in the marriage market—career training for men and grooming for motherhood for women. This preparation, in turn, takes considerable time. Also note that the structure of education in Japan provides a far less efficient context for matchmaking than does American education because it sorts men and women into separate colleges and because recreational activities in lower schools are segregated (Coleman 1980:13).

A second important factor is the structure of the labor market and wage system. Japanese men in their early twenties receive low wages regardless of educational attainment (Keizaikikaku-Cho 1976:173–174). However, the greater Japanese emphasis on job security and seniority means that these earnings will grow in a predictable manner with age, leading many to put off marriage and childbearing until they can better afford them. Employers sometimes encourage this tendency because they want new employees to become adapted to their jobs before marrying (see, for example, Rohlen 1974).

Very expensive housing—primarily because of the cost of land—is another dominant feature of contemporary Japanese society. Thus, individuals often have to work several years before they can afford to marry and set up a household. (The cost of housing has affected the timing of marriage and parenthood in the Western context as well; see Frejka 1980, for instance.)

The societal differences above can explain the observed differences in figure 18. Most of these differences can be used to explain the distinct fertility pattern of Japanese-Americans too. Yanagisako (1975a, b) shows that many traditional family patterns and sex roles are well preserved in the American context. The occupational and wage structure, as well as the housing situation in Japan, are not relevant to Japanese-Americans. However, the late age at marriage pattern fits well with the value placed on advanced education in the United States. The educational successes of Japanese-Americans are well documented. So in both the Japanese and American context existing family structures and processes are successfully adapted to the modern era.

In looking at the family formation process, two events—marriage and first birth—as well as the interval between them could be examined. The biological basis of the first birth gives it a commonality of meaning across time and society (see chap. 2), and for this reason we examine it first. We do so knowing full well that for some individuals it is marriage delay that produces a later first birth.[3] We then examine alternative delay strategies and questions regarding the meaning of marriage by examining the length of time between first marriage and first birth. Thus, in this chapter we depart from our practice of not examining marriage, because the contrast between the two countries highlights differing definitions of marriage.

DETERMINANTS OF THE TRANSITION TO PARENTHOOD

We again use the same conceptual framework discussed in chapters 2 and 5. The decision to have a first birth and the actual event occur within three distinct dimensions: an aggregate time dimension, as indicated by period or cohort; an individual time dimension, as indicated by age or duration; and a social-structural dimension. Each of these dimensions,

[3]We do not include marriage age as a predictor of age at first birth because, for a substantial minority, the birth precedes the marriage, thus clearly violating the causality assumption. Further, differences in the level of premarital pregnancies and births across these two societies clearly indicate different social definitions of marriage.

in turn, has a number of components. The social-structural dimension includes ascribed characteristics such as race, achieved characteristics such as education, and the dimension of country or society on which this chapter focuses.

Note that our analysis includes variables measuring individual and social context characteristics. Emphasis on the social context does not deny individual reasoned choice or that these decisions might be systematically different depending on individual traits or characteristics. Instead, the social context determines the range of choices seriously considered and is thus a powerful determinant of individual behavior (see Ryder 1980b, 1983). As argued earlier in this chapter, the United States and Japan provide very different contexts. Likewise, different historical periods can represent changing contexts.

These conceptual distinctions are important because they focus attention on interactive effects. When one jointly considers variables from these different dimensions one can ask questions like these: Does education have similar effects across social contexts represented by different periods? Or of special interest here, how does the effect of education vary across cultural contexts? We anticipate that the effects of aggregate time can be quite different since period conditions can vary sharply from one country to another. Moreover, given earlier discussions, wife's education may have a stronger influence in the United States where nonfamilial roles are more accessible. The Japanese context makes nonfamilial roles less likely, even for better educated women.

The microdata we analyze come from nationally representative samples of ever-married women: the U.S. 1973 National Survey of Family Growth (see chap. 3 for description of these data), and the Japan 1974 National Fertility Survey (World Fertility Survey, 1979). From each survey we selected women in the 1929–1938 birth cohorts, thus avoiding an age-at-marriage bias. Only native-born white women are included in the U.S. sample to produce a more homogeneous comparison group.

Since the aggregate time, individual time, and social-structural dimensions have proven important in the United States (see chap. 5), we explicitly represent each in our analytic model. Aggregate time is represented by separating our sample into those born 1929–1933 and those born 1934–1938.[4] The social-structural dimension is measured by wife's years

___

[4]Since the Japanese fertility transition took place much later than in the West (e.g., completed in the 1950–1960 period; see Mosk 1983), can these Japanese cohorts be considered modern? Clearly many of the women in our sample were forming families during the

of schooling, farm or rural origin, and country. Definitions of these variables appear in table 18. Individual time is considered by explicitly recognizing that the first-birth process can take place over a period spanning two decades or more. Prior to the end of the reproductive period, a woman is eligible to have a first birth unless she has already had one. As age increases, the proportion who already have had a birth increases and the proportion still eligible declines. Again, we treat the first-birth process as a series of

TABLE 18.
MEASUREMENT OF AGGREGATE TIME AND SOCIAL-STRUCTURAL VARIABLES
IN THE MODELS

		Proportion Coded 1		
Variable	Description	Full sample	U.S. sample	Japan sample
Birth cohort	Coded 1 if born 1934–1938; 0 if 1929–1933	52.8	52.7	52.8
Education	Dummy variable coding. 0–11 is the omitted category			
0–11		45.0	30.7	71.5
12		38.6	46.8	23.4
13 +		16.4	22.5	5.1
Farm[a]	Farm background coded 1; others 0	40.3	31.0	57.7
Country	U.S. coded 1; Japan 0	65.0	—	—

[a]Farm is measured differently in the two surveys. U.S. women were asked if they lived on a farm while growing up. Japanese women were asked if they lived in a rural area while growing up. Clearly, this difference in measurement could cause differing effects for Japanese and American women.

middle to late 1950s. Thus, later cohorts would be preferable; however, they cannot be studied with available data without introducing considerable age-at-marriage bias. Regardless, these cohorts are clearly modern in the sense of reaching replacement-level fertility. Cumulative birth rates for birth cohort 1932 and later show that these cohorts will not exceed 2.1 children per woman. Whether these cohorts are "modern" in other respects is discussed later.

conditional first-birth probabilities, using the age boundaries in table 19. (See chap. 3 for a discussion of fertility measurement.)

Within each of these age segments, the proportion remaining childless and the proportion who have a first birth clearly varies by country. These differences reflect the same contrasts shown in figure 18, but for different cohorts. This series of conditional first-birth probabilities is analyzed as a series of dependent variables thus allowing all variables in the model to have effects that differ by age. Since the dependent variables are dichotomies, we used logistic regression.

Two final methodological issues remain and are resolved as in chapter 5. First is the question of whether there is a causal effect from the first-birth process on educational attainment. Among the variables we examine, this is the only one for which such a causality issue arises. Although there is some disagreement about this situation in the literature, recent research directly addressing the issue in the United States suggests there is no direct effect of the first birth on the amount of education a young woman receives (Rindfuss, Bumpass, and St. John 1980). Given the much later childbearing pattern of the Japanese, the same is also no doubt the case in Japan.

Our measure of aggregate time is labeled *birth cohort*. However, cohort also represents historical period. Thus for every age, the cohort variable could be relabeled *period*. Since our interpretations will often be in terms of period factors rather than cohort factors (see chaps. 4 and 5), keep this correspondence of cohorts and periods in mind.

Figure 19 shows the effects of aggregate time (birth cohort) and social-structural variables on the likelihood of a first birth at given ages (individual time). The effects shown are net of all other variables and represent additive changes in the log odds of a first birth. Given our focus on variation by country, we allowed country to interact with all the variables in the model. These interactions make the estimated coefficients difficult to interpret. So, in figure 19, we have plotted the estimated net effects by country (Stolzenberg 1979). If the effects are not statistically significant and if the pattern of effects by age is not substantively meaningful, we have not plotted the effect.

The first panel shows the net effect of aggregate time, measured here as birth cohort. The earlier cohort is used as a reference category and appears in the figure as a horizontal dashed line. The latter birth cohort (1934–1938) differs significantly from the earlier one only for Japan. The more recent Japanese cohort is less likely than the earlier one to have a

TABLE 19.
PROPORTION AT RISK AND PROPORTION OF THEM WHO HAVE A FIRST BIRTH
BY AGE (INDIVIDUAL TIME) AND COUNTRY (A SOCIAL-STRUCTURAL DIMENSION)

Age group	% Childless at beginning of interval			Of those childless at beginning, % having first birth in interval		
	Full sample	U.S.	Japan	Full sample	U.S.	Japan
<19	100.0	100.0	100.0	22.1	27.8	11.7
20–21	87.9	72.2	88.3	22.8	30.0	11.8
22–23	40.9	51.5	77.8	32.0	35.6	26.5
24–25	25.8	32.0	57.1	36.9	36.1	37.7
26–27	16.1	20.4	35.5	37.4	30.7	44.7
28–29	11.5	14.1	19.6	34.9	23.9	49.8
N	3086	2006	1080			

child at young ages. Since the cohorts examined here were bearing their first children in the 1950s and 1960s, we expect that this shift toward later ages at parenthood can be viewed as a continuation of the secular trend toward postponing family formation that took place during industrialization (Taeuber 1958).

Again, we found no consistent effect of birth cohort for the United States. This finding cannot be generalized. In chapter 4 we show strong aggregate cohort trends in fertility timing, and in chapter 5 we document strong cohort trends using individual-level data. Lack of an *aggregate time* effect for the United States results because the period socioeconomic conditions thought to be most crucial are very similar for these two five-year cohorts. More specifically, both cohorts reached age 20 during the Baby Boom.

The two social-structural variables in the model operate quite differently in the United States and Japan. Rural origin significantly increases the likelihood of births at ages 20–21, 22–23, and 24–25, for the Japanese. This effect in the United States is not significant (and thus does not differ from the dashed line shown). This difference could reflect measurement differences—in Japan the variable is *rural* origin and in the United States it is *farm* origin, but we think the difference is substantive.[5] Country

[5]In earlier work with other Asian countries (Rindfuss and Hirschman 1984; Rindfuss, Parnell, and Hirschman 1983), we had several data sets which included both measures of rural origin, and the substantive results were not dependent on type of measurement.

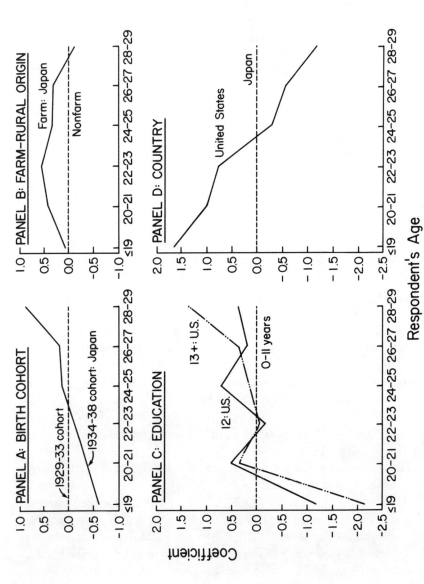

Fig. 19. Net effects of predictor variables on the timing of the first birth by respondent's age and country.

differences in rural effects probably involve changing patterns of first-birth timing in the United States. In chapter 5, we found farm background associated with greater likelihood of becoming a mother prior to age 20. Although this effect was quite modest, it was statistically significant. However, in that analysis we examined a much wider range of U.S. cohorts and sample sizes were larger. The cohorts (American) included here did much of their childbearing during the Baby Boom when socioeconomic fertility differentials of all types were reduced. Thus it seems reasonable to conclude that absence of a farm effect for the U.S. sample reflects period influences to which the Japanese sample was not subject. This interpretation is reinforced in the next chapter where we find that farm background has a statistically and substantive significant effect on first-birth timing of a more recent U.S. birth cohort.

Nevertheless, there are also reasons to believe that rural-urban differences should be sharper in Japan. The faster pace among rural Japanese women probably reflects the lower cost of establishing a household in rural areas. In urban Japan, housing costs are extremely high and tend to postpone family formation. The differential in housing costs is not nearly as sharp in the United States. Also, those growing up in rural areas are more likely to live with parents or parents-in-law, a strategy that drastically reduces housing costs (Morgan and Hirosima 1983). This living option is rarely exercised in the United States. Finally, those living in rural areas may often go to work in family enterprises, especially agricultural ones. Consequently, they do not begin with the very low entry-level salaries common in many larger urban firms.[6]

Education effects for Japanese women are weak and insignificant and, thus, do not depart from the dashed line. In contrast, education exerts a powerful influence on first-birth timing in the United States (see chap. 5). These U.S. effects can be seen in the third panel of figure 19 as well—especially at less than age 20. The effect of education in the United States, as expected, is to raise age at first birth.

Net of other variables in the model, country strongly influences the effect of the individual-time dimension. American women are far more likely to have a first birth at ages below 20, 20–21, and 22–23, while

---

[6]We should note that Japan is the first Asian country we have examined where rural origin has a significant effect on the first-birth process. No effect was found in less developed Asian countries (Rindfuss, Parnell, and Hirschman 1983).

Japanese women are more likely to have a first birth at older ages. This later pattern of childbearing in Japan is clearly not the result of differences in education or rural-urban origins since these factors are controlled.

Despite our having restricted the U.S. sample to native-born whites, it is still clear that the U.S. population being examined is considerably more ethnically and religiously heterogeneous than the Japanese population. We were concerned that our findings might be the result of differences in heterogeneity. To explore this possibility, we reran the analysis shown in figure 19 three times, restricting the sample in turn to (1) native-born, white Catholics living outside the South, (2) native-born, white, nonsouthern non-Catholics, and (3) native-born, white southerners. (Results are not shown here.) In all three cases results were similar to those shown in figure 19, and our substantive interpretations with respect to country differences remain unaltered.

For these cohorts then, aggregate-time and individual-time dimensions and the effects of other social-structural variables vary by country. Variable effects of aggregate time represent dissimilar period factors. As the world economy becomes increasingly integrated, such period changes, especially economic ones, may be similar for both countries. However, internal social movements or other factors affecting just one country, or one country disproportionately, may continue to produce disparities in the effect of period on the timing of the first birth.

Effects of the social-structural variables in the model depend on country. The rural effect in Japan may fade with continued economic development as the effects of modernization become pervasive. But such a change would widen, not narrow, the difference in the overall U.S.-Japan patterns because rural origin is a factor promoting earlier marriage and childbearing in Japan.

The strong effects of country on the individual-time dimension may be more stable. Japan has been successful at adapting industrialization to fit its existing social institutions. Western scholars sometimes expect that economic development will make Japanese institutions "more modern" when what is often implicitly meant is more Western. Differences in family structure and sex roles outlined earlier are not necessarily inconsistent with low fertility or industrial development. Japan and Japanese-Americans show that traditional institutions can be adapted to new exigencies.

The variable effects of education reflect the sharp social-structural differences in these countries. In Japan, sex is a more dominant factor affecting adult roles than in the United States. This is not to say that in the United States sex is unimportant in determining adult roles but rather that education affects the extent to which sex determines adult roles. As a result, education is important in sorting women into familial roles or career paths while in their late teens and early twenties. Education also operates as a major factor in the U.S. marriage-market structure.

DIFFERENCES IN THE MEANING OF MARRIAGE

We have argued that the Japanese couple places much less importance on the conjugal relationship and much more emphasis on parenthood. In the United States a variety of acceptable reasons are available for prospective couples to delay marriage and childbearing, or to marry and then delay childbearing. Japanese norms prescribe that marriage is for the purpose of procreation and, therefore, should not occur before the couple can afford children. Thus, while the U.S. norm seems to allow for widely variable first-birth interval lengths (e.g., variable by period and socioeconomic characteristics), Japanese norms do not promote such variability in the first-birth interval. Thus our argument implies shorter first-birth intervals (the interval between marriage and the first birth) among Japanese women and less variability.

To examine this phenomenon we selected Japanese and U.S. women who first married in the period 1961–1970 and prior to their thirty-fifth birthday. The age-at-marriage criterion ensures that all marriage cohorts are similarly truncated on this variable, and since few women first marry past age 35, our ability to generalize results to these marriage cohorts is not seriously compromised. Such a sample cannot be drawn from the 1973 NSFG alone, so we pooled this data with the 1970 National Fertility Survey. We then selected a stratified sample by marriage cohort including only white, native-born women for comparison with the Japanese data.

Following Hirschman and Rindfuss (1982), we identify three sequences of marriage and childbearing events:

A. Marital Conception:
    Marriage → Conception → First Birth
B. Premarital Conception/Premarital Birth:
    Conception → First Birth → Marriage
C. Premarital Conception/Marital Birth:
    Conception → Marriage → First Birth

Since date of conception is unknown, we infer these sequences from known dates of marriage and first birth. We compute the length of the

TABLE 20.
SEQUENCE OF MARRIAGE AND CHILDBEARING—UNITED STATES AND JAPAN

Country	Marital conception[a]		Premarital birth		Premarital conception		Total	
	N	%	N	%	N	%	N	%
United States	2018	83	78	3	338	14	2434	100
Japan	901	95	10	1	33	3	944	100

[a]Includes those who have not yet had a first birth but have been married for at least 24 months.

first birth interval, X, in months. If X is negative, then sequence B is assumed; if X is equal to 0 through 7, then sequence C is assumed; and if X is 8 or greater, then sequence A is assumed. Although these cutoff points are somewhat arbitrary, cross-national comparisons are not biased by choosing other cutoffs (Hirschman and Rindfuss 1982). We show the observed frequency and percentage distribution of these sequences by country in table 20. Sequence A is the normatively approved one in both countries. But as should be expected (see Coleman 1980), the deviant sequences are clearly more common in the United States. This finding points to more flexibility in the sequencing of these family formation events in the United States or less severe sanctions—reinforcing the arguments in chapter 2 that one cannot assume in the United States that marriage has causal priority. Here we will focus further on the length of time between marriage and first birth for those following sequence A. The greater number of couples following this sequence allows more detailed analysis, and the length of this interval lets us assess substantive differences in the meaning of marriage between these two countries.

Figure 20 shows the cumulative proportion having a first birth by month of marital duration. Only one line appears for the Japanese because both marriage cohorts show virtually identical patterns. In contrast, the more recent U.S. marriage cohort (1966–1970) shows a considerably later pattern of childbearing vis-à-vis marriage. This longer first-birth interval could be explained by the worsening socioeconomic conditions of the late 1960s, and perhaps by the uncertainty arising from the Vietnam War.

The rapid pace of childbearing in Japan suggests little or no contraceptive use in the interval between marriage and first birth. We can confirm this since the Japanese data contain information on contraceptive use in this interval.[7] Few Japanese women (28 percent) use contraception to prevent pregnancy in this interval. Those not using a birth control method knew about means of contraception but chose not to use any because they wanted children. Of those using contraception, most used it for only a short period and stopped in order to become pregnant. Quite a few (35 percent of users) became pregnant while practicing contraception. Such low use effectiveness is consistent with the lack of communication on such issues among Japanese couples, with a low level of motivation in the first interval, and with the contraceptive methods most often used, rhythm and the condom (see Coleman 1983). In short, contraceptive use is not a major determinant of the length of the first-birth interval in Japan.

In table 21 we show the results of a multivariate analysis of the likelihood of an early marital birth. As in figure 20, those following sequences B and C are excluded. In this analysis an early marital birth is one occurring within the first 15 months of marriage. But very similar results were obtained when we used fewer than 23 months as our definition of an early birth. Factors in this analysis include those in table 18 plus two additional variables: fetal death (equals 1 if the respondent had a stillbirth or miscarriage; 0 otherwise) and early marriage (equals 1 if the respondent married prior to her twentieth birthday; 0 otherwise).[8] Effects shown are additive changes in the log odds of having an early marital birth.

For the Japanese, only fetal death significantly affects the likelihood of an early marital birth—and the effect is strong. A beta of −2.538 means that a Japanese woman with a miscarriage prior to her first birth is over 12 times less likely to have a birth within the first 15 months of marriage. This strong effect is essentially guaranteed by the time required to conceive again and carry a birth to term. A strong negative effect of this variable appears for the United States too (−1.731), but its effect is significantly weaker (the difference is .807). This differential effect could

---

[7]The U.S. data only ask about contraceptive use prior to the first birth; thus we do not know whether it was used before or after marriage.

[8]One might question the inclusion of these additional variables. Fetal mortality is notoriously poorly measured in retrospective fertility surveys; and the decision about the *timing* of the first birth may have causally affected the decision of the timing of the first marriage. We have rerun the model excluding these two variables and the pattern of effects observed for the other variables that remain in the model does not change. Thus, given the substantive interest in these two variables, we have included them here.

TABLE 21.
EFFECTS OF SOCIAL-STRUCTURAL AND AGGREGATE TIME ON LIKELIHOOD OF AN
EARLY MARITAL BIRTH (WITHIN FIRST 15 MONTHS OF MARRIAGE)[a]

	Beta		Difference
Variable	Japan	U.S.	
Marriage cohort[b] (1966–1970)	.213	–0.503**	–0.716**
Education[c]	–0.099	–0.281*	–0.182
12	.219	–0.813**	–1.032**
13+			
Farm-rural[c]	.268	.203	–0.065
Fetal death[b]	–2.538**	–1.731**	.807*
Early marriage[b]	–0.497	.287*	.784**
Country (U.S.)[c]	—[d]	—[d]	–0.286

*Significant at .05 level.
**Significant at .01 level.
[a]Effects are additive changes in the log odds on having an early marital birth.
[b]See text for definition of variables.
[c]See table 18 for definition of variables.
[d]The intercepts for the Japan and U.S. equations are .231 and –.055, respectively.

be because of the widely known underreporting of fetal deaths. Perhaps the greater pressure to bear children in Japan makes a miscarriage prior to the first birth—and the consequent delay in motherhood—an event more likely to be remembered. If reported less accurately in the United States, then this systematic measurement error would attenuate the fetal death effect in the United States. Regardless, the more important point to note is that the aggregate-time and social-structural variables do not affect the first-birth interval for Japanese couples—none of the other variables is statistically significant. Japanese norms specify that couples have children as soon as possible following marriage, and their behavior appears to mirror these norms.

Family formation norms in America allow for a wider range of strategies. This greater individual choice regarding timing allows both cohort (aggregate-time) and social-structural variables to have effects. More specifically, the coefficients in column 2 of table 21 show strong effects of marriage cohort, early marriage, and college education in the United States. The reduced likelihood of an early marital birth in the United States (compared with the Japanese cohorts and the earlier U.S. cohort)

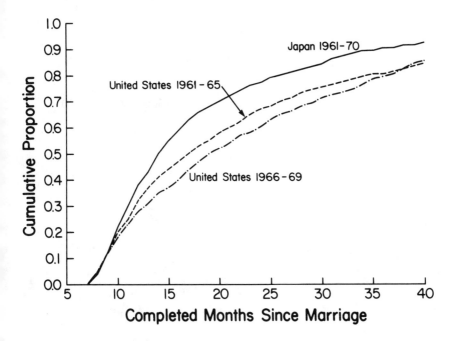

Fig. 20. Cumulative proportion of women having a first birth by country and marriage cohort.

may represent a strategy of delayed childbearing within marriage in the face of worsening socioeconomic conditions. Remember that there were substantial overall postponements in childbearing during this time (see chap. 4). The strong negative effect of college education for American women may reflect a strategy of fertility delay and labor force participation following marriage. Shorter first-birth intervals for those with an early marriage represent an overall strategy of early family formation.

Again, more important than these individual effects is the overall pattern—one indicating the centrality of procreation as a reason for marriage in Japan, and suggesting a set of norms in the United States which gives more importance to the conjugal relationship and views fertility delay and permanent childlessness somewhat more favorably.

We repeated the analysis for more homogeneous U.S. groups. Results for native, white southerners and native, white, nonsouthern non-Catholics again mirrored results for the full white sample. It is interesting that

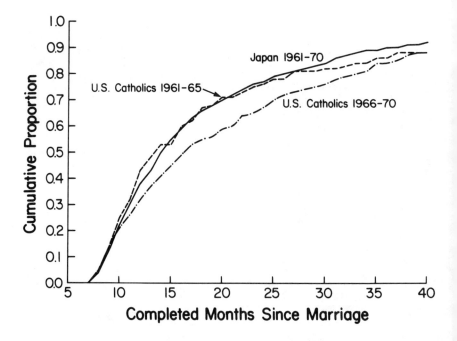

Fig. 21. Cumulative proportion of women having a first birth by marriage
cohort—United States Catholics and Japanese.

Catholics married in the early 1960s show first-birth interval lengths
similar to the Japanese (and clearly dissimilar from southern and non-
southern white Protestants), as figure 21 shows. This finding fits nicely
with the arguments presented above. Catholic ideology stresses the importance of parenthood. It prohibits abortion and most forms of contraception. Figure 21 also shows that Catholics married in the late 1960s
differ from the Japanese and more closely resemble the American pattern.
The worsening socioeconomic climate and the rejection of the church's
teachings on sexuality and birth control following the Papal Encyclical,
Humanae Vitae (see Greeley, McCready, and McCourt 1976) could
explain this changing Catholic pattern. We also note that strength of the
fetal loss variable is identical among Catholics and Japanese women (not
shown) supporting the argument that measurement error on this variable
is directly related to its saliency.

SUMMARY AND DISCUSSION

In a review of Taeuber (1958), Dore (1959:103) states:

Japan is a happy hunting ground for the demographer and for the comparative sociologist. Among other things it provides an opportunity, if not to answer, at least to add substantively to the evidence concerning one important question: how truly universal is the association of the "demographic revolution" with industrialization? Does the same configuration of trends as was observed in Western societies recur also in societies with entirely different cultural traditions?

At the more general level Japan, like Western nations, experienced a transition from high levels of mortality and fertility to low levels. Like Western nations, this transition accompanied economic development (see Mosk 1983). Japan has a modern fertility pattern, but as Taeuber (1958:52) warns, "the experience of one culture in transition cannot be used to predict the transition in another." Mechanisms by which societies reduce fertility depend on existing societal institutions (Davis and Blake 1956). While we do not focus on the demographic transition, per se, our results show that radically different patterns of family formation are possible in posttransition societies. Traditional family formation structures can adapt to changes in society in a variety of ways. Thus, an important lesson drawn from the U.S.-Japan comparison is that while change may be required, its content will be culturally based.

We have shown that three features of the modern fertility pattern vary considerably—age at initiation of childbearing, incidence of permanent childlessness, and the temporal relation between marriage and first birth. The United States shows great variability on all three features across time. Women of childbearing age during the Baby Boom had levels of permanent childlessness quite comparable to the Japanese levels discussed here. White women entering these ages in the 1960s and 1970s will differ considerably from their Japanese counterparts (see chap. 4; Bloom 1982). These period fluctuations make precise estimation of the "country" effect difficult. Yet, we feel certain that the differences we document are not confined to the birth and marriage cohorts examined. Extension of this analysis with more recent cohorts would answer this question and shed additional light on Japanese and U.S. differences. We would expect that the Japanese response to period factors will be much less. Further, while in the United States shifts to delayed childbearing are linked to increases in voluntary childlessness, this linkage does not appear to exist in Japan.

There are sound reasons to believe that these aspects of the modern fertility pattern will remain dissimilar in the two countries. This expectation rests on the remaining social-structural differences in these two nations. We have seen not only that fertility patterns are different in these two countries but that factors which affect fertility are also dissimilar. Education exerts a powerful influence on the first-birth process in the United States but not in Japan. Features of the Japanese economy, prevailing family structure, and sex roles help explain the contemporary Japanese fertility pattern. One need not view the contrasts with Western nations as illustrations of cultural lag. The Japanese patterns have persisted across time and space (see Leonetti 1978). Indeed a "structural fit" of economic development, family type, and fertility exists, but each element differs from its Western counterpart.

This prediction of lingering dissimilarities in family formation will be challenged. Some will claim that the structural features supporting the Japanese pattern cannot last. For instance, Christopher (1983) predicts substantial change in female roles in Japan. Davis and van den Oever (1982) provide some theoretical support for Christopher's claim by arguing that demographic change (especially declining mortality and fertility) provides the basis for new sex roles. Likewise, some predict changes in features of the economic system which promote delayed childbearing, such as the seniority system and wage scales for young workers (see Christopher 1983). We would not argue that these aspects of Japanese society are not under structural pressure to change. They clearly are, and we expect the social structural pattern that exists in Japan in the 1990s to differ from that which currently exists. But the process of change will take place within the context of Japanese culture and tradition, and the range of options seriously considered will be influenced by the existing context.

Our comparison with Japan provides a broader perspective on the process of becoming a parent in the United States. In chapter 2, figure 1, we identified a model where parenthood timing was dependent on background characteristics and the unfolding life course. As represented in the inner box in this figure, parenthood timing depends on a range of individual-level characteristics. But one should not expect a full understanding of the transition to parenthood from this individual- level approach alone. Broader contexts and institutions condition the form of the individual-level model. Thus in figure 1, we allow the model to vary across contexts. The Japanese-U.S. contrast demonstrates how the social context influences the individual-level model.

Once one acknowledges the importance of the social context, then one is led to questions of how and why contexts change. We are led to Ryder's (1983) claim that a theory of fertility change is just one aspect of a theory of social change. As such, the challenge is obviously a major one. We return to these broad issues of fertility change and social change in chapter 10.

8

Determinants in the Young Adult Years

Recent life course research repeatedly stresses the pivotal nature of events occurring during a person's late teens and early twenties (e.g., Elder forthcoming; Featherman, Hogan, and Sørenson 1978, 1983; Modell, Furstenberg, and Hershberg 1976; Sørenson 1984; Winsborough 1979). During this age range, Americans typically complete their education and begin to accumulate labor force experience. Establishment of a household independent of the parental household also generally occurs at these ages (Goldscheider and DaVanzo 1985). Military service also tends to begin and end during the late teens and early twenties. In short, many of the changes that mark the transition to adulthood are increasingly likely to take place during these ages, and the specifics of this transition are expected to have effects on subsequent stages of an individual's life.

The age group 18–25 is also critical with respect to fertility. A large share of childbearing in the United States is concentrated in this age range. For example, in 1976, 52 percent of all births were to women in this 8-year age span, despite its representing less than one-quarter of the 15–49 biological age span of childbearing. Analysis of cohort fertility trends (Namboodiri 1981) suggests not only the importance of fertility in the early twenties to a cohort's overall fertility level but also that fertility during a cohort's early twenties is particularly vulnerable to disruption by period factors. In addition, timing of the first birth exhibits great variability over time (Ryder 1980a) and across subgroups. The interval between the first and second birth shows remarkably little variation. Thus, timing of the first birth during an individual's late teens or early twenties is critical to understanding the fertility process. Finally, as we have shown in chapter 5, predictability of the transition to parenthood is greatest in a cohort's early twenties.

Despite the numerous and important life cycle changes occurring during the young adult years, relatively little is known about how these
various transitions (school, work, military service, and parenthood) are
interrelated. Although there are powerful theoretical reasons for linking
schooling, military service, or employment with the onset of parenthood
in the young adult years, this issue has received relatively little empirical
attention. This lack of attention reflects, in part, certain limitations in the
principal data sources used to examine first-birth timing. The national
fertility surveys conducted in the 1970s (e.g., 1970 NFS and the 1973 and
1976 NSFG) provide information on an array of potential determinants,
but are limited primarily to background factors temporally located in
early adolescence or before (see chap. 5). These factors include such variables as socioeconomic status of the family of orientation, farm origin,
religion, and number of siblings. The theoretical link between such variables and timing of the first birth rests, in part, on the alternative opportunities and roles to parenthood that background factors presumably
influence. In other words, they help set the early life course trajectory
and alter or constrain it at subsequent ages. For example, a child with a
large number of siblings probably will not be in a position to spend four
years in college earning an undergraduate degree. Instead the person
might begin working full-time or enter the military. These alternative
activity or career paths should powerfully influence when the transition
to parenthood occurs.

Recent research on childlessness and determinants of age at first birth
support this view. In each area, accumulated evidence indicates the importance of factors associated with late adolescence and early adulthood.
Studies of childlessness clearly document that voluntary childlessness
typically results from a series of postponements, and that these postponements themselves can generate the basis for further postponements (see
chap. 2). For example, a couple may decide to postpone childbearing
while completing their education. They may then decide to reap the
returns from those educational investments by both entering the labor
force. Having grown accustomed to two incomes, they may decide it is
necessary to purchase a house and other material goods before starting a
family. During this time they acquire a childless life-style which could
become a factor in its own right. Thus when young people move into
different career or life course paths, these paths or tracks have constraints
and effects associated with them which in turn influence timing of the
first birth.

Microlevel studies provide evidence of strong relationships between continued education and labor force participation and timing of the first birth (Bloom and Trussell 1984; Teachman and Polonko 1983). However, during this portion of the life cycle men and women pursue a variety of activities including school and work. The nature of education and work varies as do the sequences in which such activities are experienced. Much of this variation has been unexamined or was obscured by temporal ambiguities in available measures from demographic sources.

In this chapter we use longitudinal data to examine explicitly the effect of the activities of young men and women on the timing of entry into parenthood. We concentrate on the main activities a young man or woman is likely to engage in: work, school, military service, or house-work. As expected, these activity states have extremely powerful effects on the timing of parenthood. We also examine the extent to which these activity states mediate the effects of various background factors. Finally, we consider differences between blacks and whites in the effects of various activity states.

DATA AND METHODS

The data set used is the National Longitudinal Survey of the High School Class of 1972 (NLS). Chapter 3 includes a more complete description of these data. Here, we remind the reader that the NLS is a very large (over 20 thousand cases) and rich (over 3 thousand variables) longitudinal data set. Data for men and women, regardless of marital status, were collected. The data set includes detailed information on the respondents' activities from the fall following their senior year in high school until they were in their mid-twenties.

Approximately 75 percent of the members of this study were born in 1954 and 20 percent were born in 1953. These are the very cohorts that are delaying their fertility at rates matching the rates at which cohorts of 1910–1914 delayed their childbearing (see chap. 4). Thus, we have detailed data on the educational and early career experiences of a cohort which is clearly delaying its fertility to a substantial degree.

The NLS data, however, are not without some limitations. We cannot examine the entire age spectrum of delayed childbearing. At the time of the most recent follow-up, respondents were aged 25–26. We suspect that delay to this age is the most critical component of delayed childbearing; chapter 4 provides some evidence for this. More seriously, only persons enrolled for their senior year of high school were eligible to be included in the panel, thus limiting our analysis to an educational rather than a strict birth cohort. Since our focus is on the effect of activities and career lines subsequent to the senior year of high school, we must also exclude a small portion of the sample who became parents prior to the time when these early activities or career patterns could affect their parenthood status.

The NLS is a highly stratified sample, overrepresenting students in high schools in low-income areas and students in schools which have a high proportion of minority enrollment. Other stratification variables include region, size of high school, proximity to colleges, community size, and whether or not the high school was public. In our multivariate analyses we ran models including and excluding these stratification variables. Results for the variables of substantive interest were unaffected by inclusion or exclusion of the stratification variables, and so we present the simpler models here. It is important to remember that the tables showing distribution of the sample population are unweighted. Thus they represent the distribution of the *sample*, but not necessarily distribution for the United States. We present the unweighted distributions of the activity states because our primary concern is with effects of the various activities. The unweighted distributions provide a better indication of the data actually available.

Overall, our analytical strategy examines the effect of an individual's activity state at one time period on the probability of that individual's making the transition to parenthood in a subsequent time period. As such, temporal ordering is suggestive of causality. However, some caution needs to be exercised in interpreting the results because temporal ordering need not be equivalent to causal ordering. Individuals may anticipate becoming parents several years in the future and alter their sequence of activity states in preparation for parenthood. Under such circumstances, the causal flow would be from fertility to activity state. However, the design of our analysis is such that we expect that the principal, and perhaps the only, causal flow is from prior activity states to subsequent fertility behavior.

As in previous chapters, we employ a form of event history analysis or multivariate life table analysis. In this case, we examine a series of conditional first-birth probabilities for each single year following high school. The universe consists of those not yet parents, and the dependent variable is a dichotomy: whether or not the respondent becomes a parent

TABLE 22.
PERCENTAGE DISTRIBUTION OF WOMEN AND MEN BY ACTIVITY STATE FOR
THOSE NOT YET PARENTS IN INDICATED YEAR—OCTOBER 1972
THROUGH OCTOBER 1977

	Year					
Activity state	1972	1973	1974	1975	1976	1977
Women						
Homemaker	3	4	5	4	5	5
Working full-time	26	35	41	45	57	66
Working part-time	6	5	5	4	7	7
College student	31	30	33	34	18	13
Junior college student	14	12	6	5	4	3
Vocational school student	11	6	4	3	3	2
Military	0	1	1	1	1	1
Other[a]	9	7	5	4	5	3
Total	100	100	100	100	100	100
Men						
Working full-time	27	34	39	40	53	64
Working part-time	4	2	3	2	3	3
College student	34	32	35	37	25	18
Junior college student	15	14	7	5	4	3
Vocational school student	8	5	4	3	3	3
Military	4	6	7	7	5	5
Other[a]	8	7	5	6	7	4
Total	100	100	100	100	100	100

[a]Includes looking for work, hanging out, missing data.

during the year. Logistic regression techniques are used to estimate the models. Since yearly estimates are being produced, we can allow individuals to change activity states from year to year. Once estimates are made for each year, we can evaluate these equations for individuals with specific characteristics and link the resulting conditional probability estimates across years to provide convenient summary measures (e.g., Guilkey and Rindfuss 1987).

For October 1 of each year between 1972 and 1979, data were gathered on activities of the respondent. After some initial experimentation with alternative coding procedures, we classified each respondent for each year into one of the following eight activity states: homemaker, working full-time, working part-time, college student, junior college student, vocational school student, military, and other. "Other" includes looking for work, "hanging out", and missing data. So few males reported homemaker as their activity state that this category is maintained only for females. Respondents can hold more than one activity state simultaneously, such as an individual going to school part-time and working part-time. In the case of jointly held activity states, we gave greater weight to military, schooling, work, homemaker, and other, respectively. This hierarchy reflects our prior substantive impression of which role is most salient to the timing of parenthood.

The distribution of respondents not yet parents by activity state appears in table 22 for six Octobers from 1972 through 1977. In general, this distribution changes over time in an expected manner. The proportion in school declines as time since senior year in high school increases. The first year after high school, over half the male and female respondents are in school. By six years after high school, fewer than a quarter are still in school. The proportions working part-time, in the military, or in the "other" category are typically small, and show little annual variation. Finally, the proportion of the female sample in the homemaker role is consistently small. In interpreting this latter point, remember that the sample in each year is restricted to nonparents.

In addition to activity states, a series of background variables are included in the analysis. Because they are background characteristics, they do not change from year to year. For the most part these variables are measured as in the cross-sectional surveys analyzed in previous chapters. Thus it is possible to examine the extent to which their effects are attenuated by the inclusion of the activity state variables. The rationale for expecting these background characteristics to influence fertility was discussed earlier (see chaps. 2 and 5). Farm background is coded 1 if the respondent grew up on a farm. Catholic is coded 1 if the respondent was a Catholic during the senior year in high school. Southern origin is coded 1 if the respondent was living in the South as a senior in high school.

The final background variable measures parental socioeconomic status (SES). SES is based on a composite measure that included information on parents' education and income, father's occupation, and durable consumer items in the household (Riccobono et al. 1981; appendix K). This composite score was quartiled. We use the middle two quartiles as the reference category. Because of the composite nature of this variable, and because the information was collected while the respondent was a senior in high school (and thus has not had time to "forget" or "revise" parents' SES), we expect the quality of this measure to be superior to that of recall measures of parental SES usually obtained in cross-sectional surveys.

The most recent round of the NLS 72 study collected a complete birth history. Thus, unlike the case of the activity states, all respondents can be classified on a monthly basis as to whether or not they have become parents. This situation allows more flexibility in specification of the dependent variable than can occur with activity states measured only in October of each year. Fertility is examined in terms of parental status for a 12-month interval, but this could be any 12-month interval. The exact starting point is somewhat arbitrary. For example, a couple may decide on the basis of their activity state to have a child and deliberately stop using contraception. Assuming that they were not using the pill, the average waiting time to conception is about five months, and the average length of gestation is nine months. Thus, the couple might have a live birth 14 to 16 months after the decision was made. If the couple had been using the pill, the waiting time to conception might be several months longer. If, however, the couple did not deliberately stop using contraception but rather relaxed the vigilance with which they used it, then the expected waiting time to conception would be longer still.

Conversely, activity states are measured as of October of each year. However, the effect of that activity status may have begun many months prior to October. This is particularly problematic when there is a change in activity state from one year to the next. For example, a change from being a student to being a full-time worker will typically take place in June rather than October. Furthermore, such changes usually are anticipated. To continue with the student to worker example, a student might be able to predict accurately the change in activity status and plan accordingly. Thus, an October activity state might actually have influenced a decision to have a birth that occurred in the preceding month.

These situations obviously imply different lags between activity state and fertility interval. To balance these considerations, we examine the effects of activity states in October of a given year[1] on the probability of

---

[1]These are essentially time-varying covariates, to use the current event history analysis terminology. Respondents can and do change from one activity state to another from year to year. Also note that we are making the implicit assumption that the process forgets its past.

becoming a parent for the first time 6 to 17 months after that time period (e.g., the effect of activity state in October 1972 on the probability of having a first birth between April 1973 and March 1974). The measurement scheme is depicted graphically in table 23. This definition of our dependent variable allows for some continuity and anticipation effects for the activity states as well as sufficient time for conception and gestation following the October measurement. We experimented with alternative specifications of the parental status variable by moving the 12-month fertility interval several months closer to and several months farther from the activity state. In general, the results did not change as we shifted this fertility interval forward or backward.

We examine six intervals covering the time between April 1973 and March 1979. Again note that for each interval the universe is limited to those respondents not yet parents by the end of the preceding period. First births occurring prior to April 1973 are unanalyzed. These early first births are more likely to have affected early adult activity states than vice versa.

We show the transition process from nonparent to parent in table 24. By the end of the period of observation, approximately ages 25 or 26, one-quarter of the men and one-third of the women had become parents. The difference in the age pattern of the transition to parenthood for men and women is as expected, given the traditional pattern of women marrying[2] (or pairing with) men two to three years older than themselves. It may also reflect the greater tendency for men to enter occupations that require a long initial training period, which in turn postpones childbearing. Note that the proportion becoming a parent by ages 25 or 26 is somewhat lower than in the general population because we are using a sample that excludes those not reaching their senior year in high school.

The initial analysis is restricted to white, non–Hispanic-American respondents. The reason is that we expected the structure of the process to

[2]We have not included marriage in the analysis. Elsewhere (chap. 2) we have discussed the theoretical reasons for this decision. Furthermore, in the NLS data, a complete marital history was not obtained. Instead, in various years women were asked whether or not they were married, and when their present marriage began. For women who never married, or for women only married once and currently married, there is no ambiguity with respect to their marital status at any point during the study period. For those who are currently widowed, divorced, or separated, and for those who have had two or more marriages, we do not know unambiguously what their marital status is as of the various time points we are focusing our analysis on. Nor can we unambiguously relate their marital status to their fertility history.

TABLE 23.
Temporal Relationship Between Activity State Variables and Parental Status Variables (PS)

Year	Jan	Feb	Mar	Apr	May	Jun	Jul	Aug	Sep	Oct	Nov	Dec
										Activity State		
t												
t + 1				PS	PS	PS	PS	PS	PS	PS	PS	PS
t + 2	PS	PS	PS									

[a] PS = 1 if a live birth occurred in any of the indicated 12 PS months and = 0 otherwise.
[b] The universe for each interval analysis consists of all those who had not yet become a parent as of April, Year (t + 1).

TABLE 24.
CUMULATIVE PERCENTAGE HAVING BECOME PARENTS BY END OF
VARIOUS YEARS: WOMEN AND MEN

Parents	Year					
	1973	*1974*	*1975*	*1976*	*1977*	*1978*
Women	5	11	17	23	29	34
Men	3	6	11	15	20	25

be somewhat different for blacks (see chap. 6) and probably for Mexican-Americans (see Bean and Swicegood 1985) and other Hispanics as well. At the end of this chapter, we report on similar analyses for blacks, and contrast the results for the two racial groups. Unfortunately, there were not enough Hispanics to support a separate analysis.

All our analyses will be done separately for men and women for several reasons. First, as shown above, men and women have different age patterns of entering parenthood, partly as a result of traditional mate selection patterns. Second, relatively little is known about male fertility patterns and their determinants. The typical source of information about fertility is a survey that only interviews women regarding their childbearing. Third, and perhaps most important, differences in traditional sex roles suggest that some of the activity states would have different effects for men and women. For example, the traditional view of the male as the financial provider would argue that unemployment would have a strong negative effect on the probability of a male's making the transition to parenthood, but a weaker effect for females. In fact, unemployment lowers women's opportunity costs and may encourage childbearing (see Butz and Ward 1979). Although changes in sex roles have taken place within the United States, strong sex role differences still persist.

ACTIVITY STATES AND THEIR EFFECTS

The basic results of our analyses appear in tables 25 and 26, for women and men respectively. These tables show beta coefficients from logistic regressions. All the predictor variables are categorical and coefficients should be interpreted relative to the reference category.

TABLE 25.

EFFECTS (BETAS) OF ACTIVITY STATE AND BACKGROUND CHARACTERISTICS
ON CONDITIONAL PROBABILITY OF HAVING A FIRST CHILD IN
VARIOUS YEARS AFTER HIGH SCHOOL: WOMEN[a]

Variable	Having a Child in Year:					
	1973	1974	1975	1976	1977	1978
Activity State in Preceding Year						
Homemaker	1.69**	1.50**	1.20**	0.94**	1.09**	1.31**
Working part-time	−0.04	0.04	0.52	0.22	0.53**	0.23
College student	−1.90**	−2.38**	−2.11**	−1.58**	−0.94**	−1.24**
Junior college student	−1.04**	−1.53**	−1.56**	−0.86**	−0.45	−0.31
Vocational school student	−0.39*	−0.92**	−0.27	−0.97*	−0.43	−0.29
Military	0.60	−0.59	−1.13	0.60	0.30	−1.07
Looking for work or just hanging out	0.15	0.12	−0.28	−0.47	−0.38	−0.23
Parents' SES						
Top quarter	−0.55**	−0.06	−0.42	−0.46**	−0.43**	−0.22
Bottom quarter	0.23	0.24	0.19	0.29*	0.13	−0.22
Other Background Variables						
Farm	0.31*	0.22	0.26*	0.22	0.56**	−0.07
Catholic	0.01	0.06	−0.20	−0.05	0.04	−0.09
Southern	0.04	0.14	0.22*	0.31*	0.18	0.02
Model χ^2	330	386	375	279	143	99
N	6735	6378	5982	5568	5144	4771
Adjusted model χ2	294	363	376	301	167	125

*Significant at .05.
**Significant at .01.
[a]The universe for each year includes those who are not yet parents.

TABLE 26.
EFFECTS (BETAS) OF ACTIVITY STATE AND BACKGROUND CHARACTERISTICS
ON CONDITIONAL PROBABILITY OF HAVING A FIRST CHILD IN
VARIOUS YEARS AFTER HIGH SCHOOL: MEN[a]

| Variable | Having a Child in Year: | | | | | |
	1973	1974	1975	1976	1977	1978
Activity State in Preceding Year						
Working part-time	−0.47	−0.29	−0.70	−0.06	0.07	−0.71
College student	−1.63**	−1.69**	−2.06**	−1.67**	−0.72**	−0.64**
Junior college student	−1.21**	−1.24**	−1.39**	−0.88**	−0.32	0.10
Vocational school student	−0.86**	−0.35	−0.76**	−0.19	0.38	−0.06
Military	0.10	0.12	0.00	−0.05	0.15	0.13
Looking for work or just hanging out	−0.13	−0.34	−1.24	−1.40**	−0.67*	−0.77*
Parents' SES						
Top quarter	−0.86**	−0.28	−0.48*	−0.59**	−0.43**	−0.41**
Bottom quarter	0.29	0.28	0.34*	0.10	0.20	0.42**
Other Background Variables						
Farm	0.03	0.53**	0.44**	0.27*	0.31*	0.43**
Catholic	−0.29	−0.26	−0.36**	−0.31*	−0.32*	−0.10
Southern	0.16	0.24	0.25	0.32**	0.47**	−0.15
Model χ^2	132	156	247	198	98	74
N	6668	6479	6250	5960	5646	5332
Adjusted model χ^2	118	144	237	199	104	83

*Significant at .05.
**Significant at .01.
[a]The universe for each year includes those who are not yet parents.

As in earlier work with fertility survey data (chap. 5), the overall model fit and χ^2 adjusted for sample size[3] tend to decline with age. This phenomenon may simply be the result of unmeasured heterogeneity, or it may reflect diminishing pronatalist pressure at older ages in association with long duration of childlessness and the unique experiences in work and other nonfamilial areas that such a period allows.

In a subsequent section we examine effects of the background characteristics, and the extent to which they are mediated by activity states. For now we simply note that these effects are in the expected direction. Those with higher status backgrounds become parents later than those less advantaged. Those with a farm background and southerners tend to become parents at younger ages, and Catholics at older ages.

In tables 25 and 26, working full time is the omitted activity state category, and thus the other categories need to be interpreted relative to working full time. Although the descriptive information in table 22 included missing data in a combined "other" activity category, the multivariate models presented in the remainder of this chapter treat missing data as a separate category. Coefficients for the dummy variables representing missing data have no clear-cut interpretation and were not significantly different from the reference category in any of the estimated models. Consequently these coefficients are not shown.

Overall, the pattern of activity state coefficients is in the expected direction, and in many cases are quite large. It is not surprising that women homemakers are the most likely to become mothers in the subsequent year. However, a word of caution needs to be repeated with respect to interpreting the homemaker activity status effects. Despite the correct temporal ordering, this activity state has the greatest possibility for causality running in the opposite direction. Moreover, a larger portion of the homemakers as compared with other activities were married at each observation point. In general, married women will have higher conditional first-birth probabilities than unmarried women (Rindfuss and Parnell 1986). We discussed in detail why it is not feasible to include marriage in the empirical analysis (see chap. 2). Note that while marriage is a proxy (albeit a poor one) for routine exposure to the risk of birth,

---

[3]Modifying James Davis's (1982) procedure, we adjust for sample size as follows: adjusted $\chi^2 = (\chi^2 * 6000/N)$. The constant, 6,000, approximately represents our median sample size. The degrees of freedom do not change across ages and thus need no adjustment. The final row in tables 25 and 26 shows this adjusted model χ^2.

it is likely that the decidedly pronatalist nature of the homemaker role in conjunction with marriage underlies the large effects observed here.

For men and women, being in school tends consistently and substantially to suppress the probability of becoming a parent in the subsequent year. Furthermore, the type of postsecondary education program in which one is enrolled affects the timing of the transition to parenthood. We examine three different types of programs: four-year college or graduate school, junior college, and vocational school. With respect to immediate and long-term commitment, vocational school undoubtedly requires the least, and a four-year college program or a graduate school program the most. It would be far more difficult to combine parental status with being a four-year college student than to combine parenthood with vocational school. These differences in commitment and requirements are clearly reflected in the results shown in tables 25 and 26. For men and women, being a college student has the greatest effect on postponing parenthood, and being a student in a vocational school has the smallest effect.

The effect of working part-time is quite different for men and women. Men working part-time tend to be less likely to make the transition to parenthood than men working full-time—although the differences are not statistically significant.[4] In contrast, women working part-time are more likely to make the transition to parenthood than women working full-time. These differential effects undoubtedly reflect traditional sex role differences, with men expected to be the financial provider for children, and women expected to assume responsibility for a disproportionate share of child care. Thus part-time work would increase the woman's potential for assuming her traditional parental obligations and diminish the man's potential for assuming his. Moreover the opportunity costs associated with part-time jobs would on average be less than full-time jobs, even if we controlled for hours worked. Thus, women working part-time are likely to be more willing to give up that job. Finally, part-time work could be a deliberate strategy to maintain a low job commitment because the woman wants to become a parent in the near future—thus reversing the causal structure.

These traditional sex role differences are also reflected in the effects of

---

[4]The proportion of men working part-time is typically quite small, thus reducing the possibility of the part-time coefficient's being significant. In such a situation it is best to pay attention to the pattern of coefficients.

TABLE 27.
PERCENTAGE OF MEN AND WOMEN BECOMING PARENTS BY SEVENTH YEAR
AFTER HIGH SCHOOL BY ACTIVITY STATE IN WHICH THEY SPENT
THEIR FIRST SIX YEARS AFTER HIGH SCHOOL[a]

Activity state	Men	Women
Homemaking	—	81
Part-time job	22	48
College or graduate school	11	10
Junior college	19	19
Vocational school	27	26
Military	34	40
Looking for work or just hanging out	17	35
Full-time job	32	39

[a]All other variables are set to their mean.

looking for work or simply hanging out. Effects tend to be negative for all, but are substantially stronger for men than for women.

Finally, being in the military does not have an effect on the timing of parenthood that is significantly different from having a full-time job for men and women. Such a result was not expected. We had anticipated that being in the military would tend to postpone parenthood. The argument was that military duty was temporary, and young adults would want to complete it before becoming parents. Evidently, it is just another job—especially in the current era of the all-volunteer army. This finding probably also reflects subsidies that the military may provide to parents, such as medical services and housing. During wartime, this military effect presumably would be quite different.

To provide an indication of the magnitude of the effects of these activity states, we asked the following hypothetical question: If a group of individuals were to spend their first six years after high school in one of these activity states, what proportion would be parents by the seventh year?[5] To answer this question we set all the other variables in tables 25 or 26 at their mean, and used the procedures discussed in Guilkey and Rindfuss (1987) (see table 27).

[5]Strictly speaking, the question applies to the six-year fertility experience of respondents who were childless as of April 1973.

As expected, women who were homemakers the entire time are the most likely to have become parents by the end of the seven years, and those who stayed in college or graduate school the entire time are the least likely. The differences are enormous: 71 percentage points. While not as big, similar differences are found between working and being in college. Men who work are three times as likely to become a parent by age 25 or 26 as those who remain in college and graduate school. Among women, workers are four times as likely to become parents by age 25 or 26.

Comparing men and women, in general women are more likely to be mothers by the seventh year following high school than men are to be fathers. The differences are especially pronounced for part-time work and looking for work/hanging out, reflecting, as discussed above, differences in the traditional sex roles. For the three student categories, however, the proportion of men and women becoming parents by the end of seven years is virtually identical. The incompatibility of student and parent roles apparently is recognized and acted upon accordingly by both sexes.

Results in table 27 provide a convenient summary, but in certain instances they describe clearly artificial life courses. For example, few will spend six years in junior college. In table 28 we perform a similar exercise but present results for more realistic career paths. As before, all other variables are set to their mean. The powerful effect of homemaker status is still evident. Even among those who spend four years in college and only two years as homemakers, 40 percent are mothers by the seventh year following high school. With this exception, spending four years in college means that parenthood is unlikely by age 25 or 26, whether male or female. Spending just two years in junior college and then joining the military or working results in a substantial increase in the probability of being parents and produces the expected differential between men and women.

BACKGROUND CHARACTERISTICS
AND DIMINUTION OF THEIR EFFECTS

In examining overall fertility differentials and differences in the tempo of fertility, background characteristics (those of the family of orientation), have been a mainstay in social demography. Explanations for why such characteristics might affect behavior years after the individual has left the family of orientation generally fall into two categories. Perhaps the most

TABLE 28.
PERCENTAGE OF MEN AND WOMEN BECOMING PARENTS BY SEVENTH YEAR AFTER HIGH SCHOOL FOR VARIOUS ACTIVITY-STATE SEQUENCES FOR FIRST SIX YEARS AFTER HIGH SCHOOL[a]

\	\	\	Activity state in 1st 6 years after high school	\	\	% parents by 7th year after high school	
1	2	3	4	5	6	Men	Women
	college			work		16	18
	college			homemaking		—	40
	college			military		18	16
junior college			work			27	32
junior college		military		work		27	33
junior college		college		work		17	20
junior college			homemaking			—	64

[a]All other variables are set to their mean.

common one involves the opportunity structure facing young adults. It is argued that background characteristics condition the nature of the careers and opportunities individuals encounter. The more attractive the range of options, the less likely that a young man or woman will become a parent at an early age. Consider socioeconomic background. Those from wealthy, well-educated families are more likely to attend interesting and challenging schools, to receive outside support when needed, and have a variety of interesting career options. Under such circumstances, they are likely to postpone childbearing to allow themselves time to pursue some of these options. To the extent that this mediating role of opportunity structure exists, then the differences between groups that differ on background factors ought to diminish, and indeed approach zero, as activity states are controlled.

A second explanation for background effects on differential fertility stresses that different background characteristics imply differential socialization and, therefore, somewhat different sets of values and norms. While these acquired values and norms are continually refined and changed as the individual ages and comes to terms with the broader social structure, this process of change takes place from a base established in the family of orientation. Individuals do not initiate interaction with the broader social structure with tabula rasa. Consider Catholics versus non-Catholics. The Catholic Church teaches that sexual intercourse should not take place before marriage. To the extent that this norm is adhered to, we would expect Catholics to have fewer mistimed first births, thus resulting in a later age at entry into parenthood. Note that this should apply no matter what sequence of activity states young men and women enter. Thus the socialization explanation for the operation of background variables would argue that including the activity states would not mediate the role of background variables. For want of a better term, we shall label this second explanation *socialization effects*. Admittedly, socialization, in its traditional usage, would also include the effect of socialization on the choice of activity states. Thus, literally we will be looking at the effects of socialization after the indirect effects through activity states have been removed.

In this section we examine whether activity states do mediate the effect of background characteristics. (In chap. 9 we also include attitudes and values of these respondents.) The NLS contains most of the standard background characteristics used in the earlier fertility analyses (see especially chap. 5). Since information on these background variables was

TABLE 29.

GROSS AND NET EFFECTS (BETAS) OF BACKGROUND CHARACTERISTICS ON CONDITIONAL PROBABILITY OF HAVING A CHILD IN VARIOUS YEARS FOLLOWING HIGH SCHOOL: WOMEN

	Year & Model											
	1973		1974		1975		1976		1977		1978	
Variable	Gross[a]	Net[b]	Gross	Net	Gross	Net	Gross	Net	Gross	Net	Gross	Net
Parents' SES												
Top quarter	-1.16**	-0.55**	-0.69**	-0.06	-0.97**	-0.42*	-0.87**	-0.46**	-0.56**	-0.43**	-0.31*	-0.22
Bottom quarter	0.44**	0.23	0.49**	0.24	0.44**	0.19	0.48**	0.29*	0.22	0.13	-0.11	-0.22
Farm	0.33**	0.31*	0.22	0.22	0.27	0.26*	0.24**	0.22	0.58**	0.56	0.00	-0.07
Catholic	-0.06	0.01	0.02	0.06	-0.25*	-0.20	-0.08	-0.05	0.00	0.04	-0.13	-0.09
Southern	0.15	0.04	0.26	0.14	0.30**	0.22	0.34**	0.31**	0.18	0.18	0.00	0.02
Model χ^2	105	330	76	386	116	375	107	279	64	143	7	99
N	6,735	6,735	6,378	6,378	5,982	5,982	5,568	5,568	5,144	5,144	4,771	4,771
Adjusted Model χ^2	94	294	72	363	116	376	115	301	75	167	9	125

*Significant at .05.
**Significant at .01.
[a]Model only includes background factors shown here.
[b]Model includes background factors shown here as well as the various activity states.

TABLE 30.
GROSS AND NET EFFECTS (BETAS) OF BACKGROUND CHARACTERISTICS ON CONDITIONAL PROBABILITY OF HAVING A CHILD IN VARIOUS YEARS FOLLOWING HIGH SCHOOL: MEN

Year & Model

Variable	1973 Gross[a]	1973 Net[b]	1974 Gross	1974 Net	1975 Gross	1975 Net	1976 Gross	1976 Net	1977 Gross	1977 Net	1978 Gross	1978 Net
Parents' SES												
Top quarter	-1.29**	-0.86**	-0.07**	-0.28	-0.94**	-0.48**	-1.00**	-0.59**	-0.57**	-0.43**	-0.49**	-0.41*
Bottom quarter	0.50**	0.29	0.48**	0.28	0.51**	0.34*	0.23	0.10	0.25	0.20	0.43**	0.42*
Farm	0.11	0.03	0.60**	0.53**	0.52**	0.44	0.32**	0.27*	0.33**	0.31*	0.46**	0.43*
Catholic	-0.33	-0.29	-0.31	-0.26	-0.42**	-0.36**	-0.34**	-0.31*	-0.31*	-0.32*	-0.10	-0.10
Southern	0.14	0.16	0.23	0.24	0.24	0.25	0.32*	0.32**	0.47**	0.47**	-0.14	-0.15
Model χ²	68	132	79	156	117	247	90	198	67	98	54	74
N	6,668	6,668	6,479	6,479	6,249	6,250	5,956	5,960	5,643	5,646	5,330	5,332
Adjusted Model χ²	61	118	73	144	112	237	91	199	71	104	61	83

*Significant at .05.
**Significant at .01.
[a]Model only includes background factors shown here.
[b]Model includes background factors shown here as well as the various activity states.

TABLE 31.
GROSS AND NET PERCENTAGE POINT DIFFERENCES[a] BETWEEN SELECTED GROUPS
OF INDIVIDUALS IN PERCENTAGE HAVING FIRST BIRTH DURING
FIRST SEVEN YEARS AFTER HIGH SCHOOL: WOMEN AND MEN

	Women		Men	
Comparisons	Gross[b]	Net[c]	Gross	Net
Parents' SES				
Top quarter vs. center	−16	−6	−12	−7
Bottom quarter vs. center	10	3	10	6
Top quarter vs. bottom quarter	−26	−9	−22	−13
Farm vs. nonfarm	8	5	9	7
Catholic vs. non-Catholic	−2	−1	−5	−2
Southern vs. nonsouthern	5	3	4	3

[a]Differences are expressed using second named of paired comparisons as reference category. Other variables are set to the sample mean.
[b]Gross differences are estimated from models containing background characteristics only.
[c]Net differences are estimated from models containing background characteristics and activity states.

collected in the baseline survey, when panel members were seniors in high school, quality of the data should be higher than in the usual fertility survey.

We examined two models: one with and one without activity states (tables 29 and 30). As can clearly be seen in both tables, including the activity states substantially mediates the effect of the background characteristics, but it does not completely eliminate them. Adding the activity states has the greatest effect on parental SES variables and a more modest effect on the others.

Table 31 summarizes the mediating effect of the activity states in tables 29 and 30. For each category of the background variables, we estimated the proportion that would have had a birth by seven years following high school, assuming all other variables in the model were set to their mean. We did this for the models not including the activity states, and then subtracted selected pairs of estimates labeled "gross" differences because activity states are not controlled. Differences in terms of percentage points are reported in table 31, using the last mentioned category as the comparison. For example, other things being equal, women who grew up on a farm are 8 percentage points more likely to be mothers by seven years following high school than women who did not grow up on a farm. We then repeated this exercise for the models that contained the activity states labeled "net" in table 31. Comparison of the net and gross columns provides an overall view of the mediating effect of the activity states.

Comparing the top and bottom quarter on the parental SES scale, controlling on the activity states reduces the overall seven-year difference from 26 percentage points to 9 for women, and from 22 to 13 for men. Clearly these are substantial reductions and in the expected direction. Those from higher SES families are more likely to attend postsecondary schools, and thus are less likely to become parents at a young age. Note, however, that a substantial difference still exists among SES groups after controlling for activity states. This difference presumably reflects socialization differences, perhaps in emphasis on saving prior to starting a family, or perhaps in emphasis on investing in on-the-job training once full-time work commences.

For all other background variables, the initial differences (gross differences) were smaller, and the mediating effect of the activity states also seems to be smaller. For example, among men, the difference between those who grew up on a farm and those who did not is only slightly diminished by the introduction of activity states. Part of the reason, we expect, is that parental SES, more than any of these other background variables, has the strongest influence on late adolescent and early adult activity states.

BLACK–WHITE SIMILARITIES AND DIFFERENCES

So far the analysis has been restricted to white, non-Hispanic respondents because we expected that different structures may govern the process for different racial and ethnic groups. To address this issue, we conducted parallel analyses of first-birth timing among black NLS respondents. This procedure is the same one that we followed for the fertility surveys (see chap. 5). We summarize our results below, but first several qualifications need to be considered. The baseline NLS sample was restricted to high school seniors. Although the secondary school enrollment rates of black and white teens were similar in the early 1970s, black students were more likely to be in a lower grade than whites of the same age. Thus, on average, blacks eligible for inclusion in the study are slightly older than whites by having made less steady academic progress. Also the faster pace of first-birth timing for blacks means that relatively more blacks than whites are excluded from our analysis because they became parents prior to April 1973, the beginning of the first 12-month interval we investigate.

Using the same procedures as for whites, subsamples of 1,014 black women and 760 black men were delimited. These sample sizes are smaller than we would like for modeling annual first-birth probabilities. For example, on average fewer than 50 blacks report becoming a first-time father during each interval. Consequently, the standard errors for many of the coefficients in the black models are quite large. For this reason, we have chosen to discuss only the main features of these models rather than presenting them in full detail.

First, with respect to black women, we again find evidence that the structure of first-birth determinants for blacks is somewhat different from that of whites. In general, the delaying effects of the various activity states involving continued schooling (relative to full-time work) are much less pronounced for blacks. The logit coefficients for black college students are quite strong and statistically significant; yet they tend to be only about half the magnitude of the comparable estimates presented in table 25 for whites. A similar pattern occurs for junior college attendance. Moreover, there is evidence that black vocational school students are *more* likely than full-time workers to become mothers. We found no consistent effects of being a part-time worker in terms of direction or magnitude of the coefficients. Also, too few black women were in the military in any year to include this category in the models. As was the case for whites, the final activity state, looking for work or just hanging out, has no statistically significant effect on first-birth probabilities, but it is interesting that the pattern is similar for both races. That is, there is some hint that women in this activity state are less likely to become parents in the latter years of the survey than those in the reference category.

The patterns of background effects on black first-birth timing also show some similarities with and divergences from the white results. The estimated effects of parental socioeconomic status follow those for whites rather closely. Those from the bottom quartile generally have higher likelihoods of becoming mothers and those from the top quartile have lower ones. Although these contrasts with the middle quartiles are seldom statistically significant for blacks, the patterns are consistently in the expected direction. Farm background is positively related to white fertility, but not so for blacks. In contrast, southern black women, like their

white counterparts, tended to become mothers sooner than women residing elsewhere. In fact, this regional contrast appears more pronounced
for blacks than for whites. The remaining background variable, Catholic
religious identification, shows no consistent or interpretable pattern of
effects among black women; of course, the relatively few black Catholics
make stable estimates difficult to obtain.

Our results from the black male subsample must be regarded as even
more tentative than those for black women because of its small and
selected nature. Nevertheless, we report a few interesting aspects of these
analyses. First, the transition to parenthood appears to occur at a faster
pace for black as compared to white men. Thirty-eight percent of the
black men not yet a parent by April 1973 became fathers in the next
six-year period. The comparable figure for white males was only 25
percent (table 24). The racial differences in schooling effects observed for
women also are present for men. The childbearing delays associated with
being a college, junior college, or vocational school student observed in
table 26 for white males, in general, are not as pronounced for blacks.
Another difference between black and white men concerns the effect of
military service. For white men this appears to be just like full-time work
in other sectors, but our estimates for blacks suggest a rather consistent
delaying effect of military service. The pattern of effects for part-time
work and nonwork/nonschool activity states are, however, fairly similar
for black and white men. Finally, we found virtually no statistically
significant or consistent pattern of background effects in the models for
black men.

Given the paucity of significant background effects for black men and
to some extent for black women, the question of how such effects are
mediated by activity states becomes less compelling. It is interesting to
note, however, that the estimated coefficients for the background variables are virtually unchanged by including activity states. One possible
interpretation for this absence of mediating effect involves viewing the
background factors as reflecting differing cultural contexts within the
black community. In this sense, background factors like parental SES
may be less important for blacks than whites in shaping future activity
states but relatively more important in defining subcultural norms about
the initiation of childbearing.

Recently a number of researchers have discussed the bifurcation of the
black community into middle class and underclass spheres (see Farley
1984: chap. 6). Nicholas Lemann's (1986) popular account of this theme

argues that the underclass phenomena is deeply rooted in cultural rather than structural factors. Cherlin (1981) has discussed the ways in which marital and fertility behavior that presumably characterize the black underclass lead to racial divergence along these dimensions and to distinct alternative family networks. The results we present here do not directly assess the merits of a cultural versus structural/economic interpretation of these differences, but they are consistent with evidence presented in chapters 5 and 6 suggesting that the earlier first-birth pattern for blacks is not simply an underclass phenomenon. If this were the case, we would expect to find greater racial differentiation in first-birth timing among the less educated or poorer segments of each racial group. In general this is not what we find. In each of our analyses of education, for example, we find that schooling is less important in delaying parenthood for blacks than for whites.[6] In fact, we showed in chapter 6 that the racial differences in first-birth timing are probably greatest for women with college educations, hardly the constituency of the underclass. In short, while some of the racial differences in the process involve compositional differences, determinants of the process itself also vary across racial groups. One result is less heterogeneity in first-birth timing for blacks than whites.

SUMMARY AND CONCLUSION

As anticipated, the nonfamilial activities in which young men and women engage exert an extremely powerful influence on the timing of parenthood. For men, anything but being in the military or working postpones entry into parenthood. While college or graduate school has the largest effect, other types of schooling, part-time work, being unemployed, or simply hanging out also postpone parenthood.

Further specification of the influence of adolescent and early adulthood experiences and activities constitutes one important area for further research. As evidence of the importance of these life course stages, note the strong effects of early adulthood activity states documented here and the effects documented earlier in chapter 5 for age at menarche and teenage smoking. Our operationalization of activity states is, we argue,

[6]The relatively smaller coefficients observed here for blacks on the various schooling activity states suggest that the lesser effect of completed years of education among blacks in the fertility survey analysis (chap. 5) is not just a function of a greater tendency of blacks to return to school *after* becoming parents.

an important step in the right direction, but is a very crude approximation of the very complex, unfolding life course. Work currently under way (Rindfuss, Swicegood, and Rosenfeld 1987) shows that, as the life course perspective would suggest, earlier activity states have an influence net of current activity state. In other words, the life course, the progression or incumbency in various roles, has an effect net of current activity state. Richer treatment of this unfolding life course promises to bring substantial returns in terms of our understanding of the parenthood process.

Even though this chapter only examined the experience of one cohort, we expect that the same general process would be observed for other cohorts as well. Little evidence to date suggests strong interactions between structural effects and period (cf. chap. 5). Perhaps the most likely exception is that the effects of being in the military might change during a war.

Assuming that our findings for men hold for a wide range of cohorts, then they provide evidence for the micromechanism that is presumed in the explanations generally given for macrotrends (cf. chap. 4). For example, the Depression was a period when many young men were unemployed or working part time, and thus the transition to parenthood came later. During the 1970s, unemployment rates were not nearly as high as during the Depression, but a far greater proportion of men were in college and graduate school, and the combination again produced very late transitions to parenthood.

However, unless one is willing to assume that the female activity state distribution is irrelevant, an implicit assumption of the Easterlin (1966, 1973, 1978) hypothesis, the pattern and distribution of female activity states also need to be considered. The pattern of effects for women is quite different than for men. Looking for work is essentially the same as working full time. Having a part-time job makes a woman somewhat more likely to make the transition to parenthood than having a full-time job. Only education works the same for both males and females. Finally, an enormous difference exists between all the other activity states and being a homemaker. Women who identify themselves as homemakers have a very high probability of an early transition to parenthood.

Again comparing the Depression and the 1970s, during the 1970s women were far more likely to be in school or in the labor force. There were more educational and employment opportunities for women than during the 1930s. In conjunction with greater numbers of women pursuing these opportunities, we find that the delaying effect of female education is somewhat greater among more recent cohorts (chap. 5). Bloom and Trussell (1984) also report increasingly strong effects of education and female labor force participation among younger cohorts using Coale-McNeil models of first-birth timing. Thus, if only female activity states were relevant, women during the 1970s would have had a substantially later age at first birth than women during the 1930s. Yet we know (chap. 4) that they were similar, suggesting that male activity states had a more dominant influence during the 1930s and, perhaps, female activity states were more dominant during the 1970s. Of course, changes in employment, school enrollment, and military mobilization can have effects well beyond the individuals directly involved. The context in which all persons make decisions can be altered fundamentally. We discuss this point at some length in chapter 10.

Results in this chapter also help resolve the question of the mechanisms through which background factors affect the transition to parenthood. They partly do so by channeling young adults into activity states that lead to late or early childbearing. However, this is not the entire story. Even after controlling for the effects of activity states, some of the background factors still exert a significant effect on timing of the transition to parenthood. While this might simply be the result of our failing to capture fully the effects of the multitude of activity states, we expect that it also represents the effect of socialization for early or late parenthood.

9

Becoming a Parent: Intentions and Behavior

The conceptual model guiding our research (see chap. 2) assumes that individuals and couples make fertility-relevant decisions that, in turn, influence the transition to parenthood. But to this point we have not explicitly examined the decisions leading to parenthood. Our investigations of background characteristics, roles occupied in young adulthood, social-structural and historical context have not told us why people delay or do not delay parenthood, only that they have. However, the observed behavioral patterns can be judged as consistent or inconsistent with given hypotheses about motivations. For example, results in the previous chapter fit nicely with the hypothesis that individuals time parenthood so that the more time- and energy-demanding roles will not be held simultaneously.

In this chapter, we move toward a social-psychological approach by examining reports of timing intentions, inconsistency between these intentions and behavior, and correlates of intentions and inconsistency. We are concerned not only with a person's life cycle stage, historical period, and social position, but also with measures of attitudes and values. We wish to shed some light into the "black box" many of the earlier analyzed social-structural categories represent. As Jaccard and Davidson (1976: 330) note, understanding fertility-related behavior requires not only a description of differences by social and economic variables but also an understanding of the process by which these variables influence attitudes and values. After all, these attitudes and values provide the framework within which decisions are made.

Historically, and perhaps increasingly, the American context provides substantial latitude in individual choice. Moreover, there are competing ideologies that have quite different implications for parenthood timing.

Consider the divisiveness created by the divergent life-styles and interests of feminists and traditionalists. Luker (1984) argues that the conflict over the abortion issue is so intense because it hinges on whether the maternal role or some other one should take precedence in women's lives. Thus, one's view of appropriate sex roles or the importance of occupational success can potentially have powerful effects on parenthood timing. Those with a more traditional orientation might see parenthood as an appropriate transition for early adulthood. They might anticipate a division of labor where the man is the primary breadwinner and the woman the primary caretaker. Such an anticipated division of labor lowers perceived costs of childbearing and increases expected rewards.

As noted above, evidence of differential parenthood timing does not tell us why timing varies. Identifying attitudinal correlates, however, begs the question of the origin of these attitudes. In short, full understanding of the parenthood process requires consideration of structural and social-psychological variables.

Consistent with prior work and with results to be presented below, we argue that fertility decisions are reassessed continuously. Such decisions are couched in terms of "if things work out as I expect." But many individuals do not foresee how their life chances will develop (Gerson 1985) or how socioeconomic conditions will change. Unexpected developments can alter one's attitudes, beliefs, and values. Consequently, current attitudes can be seen as a result of an unfolding life history. For example, sex-role attitudes of women are associated with their years of schooling, labor force participation, and number of children (Mason, Gzajka, and Arber 1976; Smith-Lovin and Tickameyer 1978; Thornton and Freedman 1979). These elements of an individual's life history are apparently relevant to sex-role attitude formation.

Unfortunately, there are inherent difficulties in determining if attitudes affect behavior or vice versa. Thornton, Alwin, and Camburn (1983) locate part of the problem of establishing the causal direction between sex-role attitudes and work experience in the cross-sectional nature of most sex-role research. But they further note that longitudinal data seem to show effects that run in both directions. From a life cycle perspective such results appear neither contradictory nor surprising. Work status and attitudes at time 1 influence work status and attitudes at time 2. Work experience cumulates and attitudes form with passing time, and thus there could be considerable reciprocal influence.

Likewise for our study of the transition to parenthood, background variables and early life course experience could produce attitudes and values which influence the decision to postpone childbearing and engage in employment or enroll in school. These nonfamilial activities could bring experiences that alter attitudes and values in antinatalist directions. These more antinatalist worldviews then provide one with the rationale to delay parenthood further. Thus, the life course perspective can easily accommodate an explanation of parenthood timing which incorporates structural and social-psychological variables. In fact, our arguments throughout this monograph have included such variables and processes; in this chapter we extend the empirical analysis to incorporate them.

More specifically, we address four separate questions with distinct analyses. First, we assess the stability of childless intentions and find them to be unstable for both young men and women. In contrast, the intention to remain childless in the near future has clear predictive validity and more closely approaches, we argue, the kind of decisions individuals actually make. Nevertheless there is a substantial amount of inconsistency even between short-term intentions and behavior. The second set of analyses examines this inconsistency, the likelihood of an unanticipated birth and an unanticipated delay. Unanticipated delay is relatively common (compared to an unintended birth) at these ages and in this period, but anticipated births are better predicted by the socioeconomic variables we examine. Both these analyses support our characterization of parenthood decisions as a process accompanying the unfolding life course.

The third set of analyses estimates the association between intentions for a child in the near future and a set of attitude variables measuring sex-role orientation and the importance of career, family, and leisure pursuits. These variables are strongly associated with parenthood intentions. Finally, we incorporate these attitude items into a model including background and activity state variables (analyzed in chap. 8). This final analysis shows that these attitude items have strong effects that, generally speaking, do *not* have their origin in the life course experience included in our model. This result identifies a future research agenda.

THE DECISION TO REMAIN CHILDLESS

The decision-making framework has become an important perspective within which to examine fertility behavior. The basic tenet is that individuals and couples rationally weigh the costs and benefits of children.

The earlier formulations assumed that couples arrived at a fertility goal early in life and then worked toward this goal during their childbearing years (e.g., Becker 1960). Now the process is viewed as more sequential, allowing for reassessment at any time.

Since fertility decisions can be continuously reassessed they are necessarily built, either explicitly or implicitly, on the assumption that "things will remain the same" or "other things will work out as I expect" (Westoff and Ryder 1977b). The longer the time period under consideration, the less likely this assumption will hold. With the passage of time, social and economic conditions change. The importance of such change has been stressed in earlier chapters, without actually examining the fertility intention decision. In this section we now focus on this crucial decision: whether to become a parent. A central tenet examined is that people do not decide to become childless at a young age and then follow through on that intention. Rather, individuals (and couples) repeatedly postpone parenthood before making the decision to remain childless (e.g., Masnick 1980a; Veevers 1979). This is not to deny that a few voluntarily childless couples make the childless decision early and stick with it. However, the vast majority of the voluntarily childless arrive at that point through a series of postponing decisions.

Data from the National Longitudinal Study of the High School Class of 1972 allow examination of the stability of individuals' childless intentions. In each of three rounds (1973, 1976, 1979) respondents were asked their expected family size. Specifically, "How many children, altogether, do you eventually expect to have?" Because of our focus on the first child, we have dichotomized the responses into those who intend to remain childless and all others. Only those childless and not pregnant as of the 1973 survey are considered.[1] Also, we restrict our analysis to the non-Hispanic white population, because of evidence (see chap. 6) that the process may be different for blacks or Hispanics. Further, differences in traditional sex roles dictate that the analyses be done separately for males and females.

Table 32 shows childlessness expectations cross-classified by year. As expected there is considerable inconsistency across the three follow-up

---

[1]Those who already had had a child were asked about their intentions regarding the next birth. But given our focus on the transition to the first birth, this supplementary information is not examined here.

TABLE 32.
CHILDLESSNESS EXPECTATION BY SEX AND SURVEY ROUNDS—
1973, 1976, 1979

Childlessness expectation sequence				
1973	1976	1979	Women	Men
yes	yes	yes	131	142
yes	yes	no	63	111
yes	no	yes	51	68
yes	no	no	243	331
no	yes	yes	196	149
no	no	no	164	181
no	no	yes	359	337
no	no	no	5053	4189
Total			6260	5508

rounds. For instance, only 27 percent of the females who expected childlessness in 1973 gave this same answer in 1976 and 1979. Calculations from this table also show that more women intending childlessness changed their minds between 1973 and 1976 (while in their late teens and early twenties than between 1976 and 1979 (while in their early to mid-twenties).

Also note that the percentage of women expecting childlessness increases across the years despite some women having had children in the interim and thus no longer intending to be childless. Percentages expecting childlessness are 8, 9, and 12 in 1973, 1976, and 1979, respectively. This increasing level of expected childlessness is consistent with the argument that delay leads to childlessness by allowing women more time to develop interests that compete with motherhood. But even the 12 percent estimated level cannot be accepted as a reasonable estimate of those who will remain childless from this cohort. By projecting cohort trends in childlessness, Bloom (1982) estimates that 25 to 30 percent of women in these birth cohorts will remain childless. While this estimate is likely to be too high, we expect that for the cohort as a whole, at least 20 percent will remain childless (see chap. 4). Further, the NLS panel excludes women who did not reach the spring term of their senior year in high school—women who would have the lowest level of childlessness. Thus, it appears evident that for women in their late teens and early twenties, childless expectations are very unstable at the individual level and, for this cohort, seriously underestimate the aggregate level of eventual childlessness.

The point above is relevant to Sklar and Berkov's (1975) prediction that period fertility would increase during the latter half of the 1970s. Their prediction rested on the large proportion of women in their twenties and early thirties who were childless, coupled with the attitudinal evidence that few women wanted to remain childless. As we now know with the elapse of time, fertility did not increase. In short, individuals are poor predictors of their own likelihood of remaining voluntarily childless until quite late in their childbearing years. All this is consistent with the general findings cited earlier that the decision to remain voluntarily childless tends to be reached only after a series of postponement decisions.

Far less work has been done on male fertility expectations. Because women actually bear the children, only they are typically included in surveys concerned with fertility. When men's expectations have been considered it is usually in conjunction with their wives' response. The NLS survey asked men, regardless of marital status, how many children they expected to have. Results generally parallel those for women. Only slightly more men expect childlessness: 12, 11, and 13 percent respectively in 1973, 1976, and 1979. Thus, there is no clear trend, with increasing age, toward greater expected childlessness. Even more than for women, the expectation of childlessness is an unstable one. Of those expecting childlessness in 1973, only 22 percent maintained this expectation in the 1976 and 1979 survey waves. Since these estimates are the first of their kind, they should be accepted cautiously. But they suggest that men may be a little more ambivalent about parenthood—more expect childlessness, but these expectations are less firm than women's. Perhaps this is because parenthood generally places less severe constraints on men's roles than on women's. The occupational roles men assume are less likely to conflict with parenthood, given traditional child care arrangements.

In sum, childless expectations appear quite unstable. We suspect this occurs because the question forces the respondent to make an assessment that is not time bound. Asking if you will *ever* have a child forces a person to make assumptions about the distant future, 10–20 years in the future, which may not be correct.

THE DECISION TO REMAIN CHILDLESS, AT LEAST FOR NOW

Reasoning and evidence above suggests that as the time horizon grows shorter, the respondent's ability to predict behavior will increase. We now examine the predictive validity of expectations when respondents must make fewer assumptions about the distant future, using a question on parity-specific intentions with a time referent:

When do you expect to have your first (next) child?
1. No (more) children intended
2. Within the year
3. 1–2 years
4. 2–3 years
5. 3–5 years
6. 5+ years
7. Don't know
   (no answer)

This question was asked only in the 1976 and 1979 rounds. Since this information was not asked in earlier rounds, we must confine our analysis here to the 1976–1979 period. In table 33 we show the percentage having a first birth between 1976 and 1979 by 1976 timing intention and sex. To be included respondents had to be interviewed in both the 1976 and 1979 rounds of the NLS. Actual fertility information was collected retrospectively in 1979 and intentions prospectively in 1976. Only those childless and not pregnant in October 1976 are included.

There are a substantial number of inconsistencies, but timing intentions are clearly a powerful predictor of the likelihood of having a first birth soon. Of the women expecting a birth within a year, 66 percent actually had one by October 1979—presumably, many of these were already trying to have a birth in 1976. This percentage declines to 26 percent for women intending a child in two or three years and to 4 percent for those expecting no children.

Note that the intending-a-child-in-*five*-years and *no-child* responses have similarly low probabilities of a first birth between 1976–1979. In effect, these responses mean "I don't intend to have a child in the next few years." Further, the most popular response to this question is "I don't know." This response was offered to the respondents and is a legitimate answer (see Morgan 1981, 1982). The frequency of "don't

TABLE 33.
PERCENTAGE HAVING FIRST BIRTH BETWEEN 1976 AND 1979 BY 1976 INTENTION:
WOMEN AND MEN

	Women		Men	
	First birth between 1976 & 1979		First birth between 1976 & 1979	
Timing intention 1976	%	N	%	N
Within year	66	182	69	156
1–2 years	50	517	48	410
2–3 years	26	735	25	512
3–5 years	11	1024	11	891
5 + years	3	505	4	543
Don't know	9	1439	7	2299
No child expected	4	530	4	539
Total		4932		5350

know" responses in no way suggests that this question is inadequate for discriminating between those who intend a first child soon and those who do not. Instead, in this context, a "don't know" response means "not soon." This interpretation is supported by the low birth probability for those who did not know when they would have a first child.

While these results are presented separately by sex, the predictive validity of men's and women's expectations appear very similar—men's responses predict their behavior as well as women's responses predict their subsequent fertility. In fact, explicit tests (not shown here) reveal that the association between expectation and behavior does not vary by sex. Although men's long-term expectations are somewhat less stable than women's, in the short run, men predict their parenthood status as accurately as women.

To what extent do the same variables that predict behavior (see chap. 8) also predict short-term fertility intentions? This question is very important given the substantial inconsistency noted in table 33. Perhaps background variables and activity states influence parenthood timing by influencing contraceptive failure or infertility rather than by influencing timing intentions. As noted in chapter 2, parenthood need not result from explicit attempts, but can be an undesirable outcome of choosing an inefficient contraceptive technique or of having unprotected intercourse.

To examine this issue we drew the same sample as in table 33, and looked at the effects of background factors and 1975 activity states on parenthood intentions between 1976 and 1979 and actual fertility behavior in this same three-year period. Both dependent variables are dichotomies: intending a child in the next three years—yes (e.g., within a year, one to two years, or two to three years) or no (e.g., three to five years, five or more years, no children intended, don't know, and no answer); and becoming a parent in this three-year period, yes or no.

While not presented here, results of this analysis are easy to summarize. Overall effects estimated from intentions and behavior are remarkably similar. General substantive conclusions would not vary depending on the dependent variable chosen. Therefore as described in chapter 8, coming from a high-status background is associated with delayed parenthood, while farm origin is positively associated with parenthood at these ages. For men, southern origin increases the likelihood of parenthood, real and intended. For women, homemaking sharply increases the likelihood of parenthood in the near future (compared to working full time). Schooling has the opposite effect.

Some different effects on intention and behavior were observed and could be interpreted substantively. But we reserve speculation on these differences for the following section, and stress here the similarities between the processes affecting the two different dependent variables. Again this finding is very important because it suggests that timing intentions, conscious decisions about parenthood timing, play the primary mediating role between background variables and activity states and the transition to parenthood.

PREDICTING INCONSISTENCY

While conscious decisions to time parenthood explain a substantial portion of variability in first-birth timing, examining inconsistencies between expectations and behavior can shed further light on the parenthood process. To begin, what are the sources of the inconsistencies shown in table 33? One way to address this question is to look to the broader literature on the attitude-behavior relation. Ajzen and Fishbein (1977:889) argue that the correspondence between attitude and behavior will be greatest when there is congruence on four aspects of attitude and behavior: (1) when the relevant *action* is unambiguous, and when the (2) *target*, (3) *context*, and (4) *time* of the action are specified. The intention question includes a specific time referent. Further, in the case of fertility intentions and actual fertility, the action and target appear to be unambiguous, although they are unstated. One has unprotected intercourse (the action) in an attempt to become pregnant (the target). Conversely, one avoids intercourse or uses appropriate birth control methods to avoid having a child. But there is a source of inconsistency here, because the action does not guarantee the target will be achieved. In the present case, the target of having a birth requires the successful completion of a series of events— having intercourse, not using contraception, conceiving, and not having a spontaneous or induced abortion; and thus inconsistency is more likely (Davidson and Jaccard 1979:1365). Since conception and spontaneous abortions are beyond the direct control of the actors, they can be expected to produce substantial inconsistency.

Finally, the context has not been specified. A variety of unanticipated events might make respondents alter their expectations. Individuals and couples can adjust the timing of parenthood to fit other life course contingencies. For instance, an unanticipated change of marital status or job might lead to a postponement of parenthood. In fact, it was such anticipated contingencies that led us to place a time referent on expectations. As mentioned earlier, the unstated contextual referent is "if things do not change" or "if things unfold as I anticipate" (see Westoff and Ryder 1977b). Thus again there are strong theoretical reasons for expecting a considerable amount of inconsistency between intentions and behavior.

Inconsistency can be of two types: (1) respondents can intend to have no child but have one—an unanticipated birth, or (2) intend to have one and have none—an unanticipated delay. Errors of the second type appear to be far more common than the first. Findings in table 33 indicate that for men and women, unanticipated delay is approximately 18 times more likely than an unanticipated birth in the 1976–1979 period. Westoff and Ryder (1977b) reported this same pattern of inconsistency, although considerably weaker, for all births between 1970 and 1975.. Both sets of findings probably reflect, in part, the strong delaying effects of period factors present during this time. Presumably, if these longitudinal data sets had been collected during the early 1950s, when period factors had been producing younger ages at first birth, unanticipated births would not have outnumbered unanticipated delays to this extent.

In addition to period factors, there are, however, various individual factors that could lead to one or the other type of inconsistency. These include the array of variables examined throughout this monograph. The two types of inconsistency, an unanticipated birth and an unanticipated delay, may involve quite different processes. For example, in a society where fertility regulation is as effective as it is in the United States, one would expect biological factors to be much more prominent in unanticipated delays than in unanticipated births. Thus, instead of a single analysis, we examine each type of inconsistency separately, starting with the probability of an unanticipated birth.

In table 34 we show the effects of background variables and activity states on the probability of having a first birth during the period 1976–1979 for those who did not intend to have a first birth during this period[2] and who had not yet had a first birth by 1976. The model includes three dummy variables that indicate when the respondent intended to have a child: three to five years, more than five years, or no children are intended. The omitted category is "didn't know." Background and activity state variables are also included so that variation by SES, for instance, on expected timing would not influence the SES effect on consistency. As would be expected intuitively, those intending a child three to five years from the interview and those who "didn't know" (the omitted category) are much more likely to have a child between 1976 and 1979 than those who intend to wait five or more years or those never intending to have a child. Also, the effects of these last two categories are remarkably similar, further confirming that long-term postponement and the intent to remain childless are quite similar in the early adult years.

In general, the same factors that predict fertility behavior and intent also predict the probability of having an unanticipated birth. Nearly all coefficients in table 34 have the same sign as the corresponding effects estimated for yearly first-birth probabilities in chapter 8. Thus this type of inconsistency (having a child when none was intended) seems consistently to strengthen the behavioral effects relative to intentions. Put differently, the behavioral process described in the earlier chapters, including normative and structural factors, is operating in the short term (three years) even when at the beginning of that period the young men

---

[2]Again, because the intentions question was not asked in the earlier rounds, and because we have no behavioral information past 1979, the 1976–1979 period is the only one we can examine with this data set.

TABLE 34.
EFFECTS OF BACKGROUND VARIABLES AND ACTIVITY STATES ON LIKELIHOOD OF
FIRST BIRTH GIVEN THAT NO BIRTH WAS INTENDED: WOMEN AND MEN

Independent variables	Women	Men
Parents' SES		
Top quarter	−0.163	−0.270
Bottom quarter	.070	.476**
Other Background Variables		
Farm residence	.378*	.189
Catholic	−0.012	−0.017
Southern	.080	.191
Activity State		
Homemaker	.921**	—
Part-time worker	−0.180	−0.821
College student	−0.762**	−0.617*
Junior college student	−0.459	−0.509
Vocational school student	−0.087	1.010**
Military service	−0.467	−0.202
Looking for work or just hanging out	−0.089	−0.511
Intention Controls		
Intend child in 3–5 years	.209	.466**
Intend child in 5 + years	−0.921**	−0.617*
Intend no children	−1.132**	−0.675**
Intercept	−2.154	−2.376
Model χ^2	98.69	109.71
N	3238	3885

*Significant at .05.
**Significant at .01.

or women themselves do not intend to have a first birth in that period.
This may partly result from an unmeasured dimension of certainty of the
intentions. Fertility intentions are not as categorical as would be indicated
from the questions used here. Rather there is a range of certainty attached
to these intentions, and this degree of certainty has been shown to affect
fertility behavior (see Morgan 1981, 1982; Westoff and Ryder 1977*b*).
We expect that certainty is related to the same factors as intentions, thus
producing the systematic results we see here.

In addition to this overall pattern, several factors seem strongly associated with unanticipated parenthood. For women, having been raised on a farm sharply increases the likelihood of an unanticipated first birth. A weaker effect is observed for men. Perhaps in 1976, at age 22, those raised on farms did not anticipate the pronatalist pressure of their socialization experience.

For women, school (especially college) and the military decrease the probability of an unanticipated first birth. In contrast, homemakers in 1976 were over 2.5 times $(e^{.921})$ more likely to have an unanticipated first birth than women working full time (the omitted category). For women investing in schooling or training, parenthood may be especially costly. Therefore, they are more certain of their intent to remain childless in the near future. As mentioned above, certainty increases the predictive validity of reproductive intentions. Similarly, costs of parenthood for homemakers in terms of forgone opportunities are much less, thereby making it more likely that homemakers will "change their minds" or be less likely to terminate an unintended pregnancy. There may also be differences in the diligence with which contraception is used and the efficacy of methods used. For example, working women are more likely to be using the most effective methods (pill and IUD) than women not in the labor force (Rindfuss, Swicegood, and Bumpass 1986).

For men, this inconsistency (intending none, but having a child) is most common for those in vocational school. Further, vocational school has a very different effect than more general education—which, for men, like women, reduces the likelihood that they will change their minds, or if a pregnancy occurs by accident, allow the pregnancy to continue. The different effect for vocational schooling may occur because vocational training is usually of short duration. Thus those in vocational school in October 1976 will likely be moving into full-time work before October 1979. This transition makes men attractive as potential fathers. However, while in vocational school they may not fully internalize its short-term nature nor anticipate the effect of joining the labor force. In this same vein, being out of work reduces the probability of parenthood even among those not intending parenthood. Being unattractive as a potential breadwinner makes childlessness an easier status to maintain.

The second type of intention-behavior inconsistency is the nonoccurrence of a birth in a three-year time period even though one was intended —an unanticipated delay. Although we have no empirical measures of the biological factors involved in subfecundity and sterility, they probably

TABLE 35.
EFFECTS OF BACKGROUND VARIABLES AND ACTIVITY STATES ON LIKELIHOOD OF
FIRST BIRTH GIVEN THAT A BIRTH WAS INTENDED: WOMEN AND MEN

Independent variables	Women	Men
Parents' SES		
Top quarter	.139	−0.123
Bottom quarter	−.309*	.064
Other Background Variables		
Farm residence	.142	.265
Catholic	−0.203	−0.123
Southern	−0.172	−0.075
Activity State		
Homemaker	.021	—
Part-time worker	.162	−0.136
College student	.011	.081
Junior college student	−0.214	.087
Vocational school student	−0.131	.307
Military service	−0.677	−0.292
Looking for work or just hanging out	−0.607	−0.982*
Intention Controls		
Intend child within 1 year	2.092**	2.103**
Intend child in 1–2 years	1.076**	0.985**
Intercept	−0.912	−0.974
Model χ^2	192.01	148.92
N	1395	1018

*Significant at .05.
**Significant at .01.

play a substantial role in this type of inconsistency. Further, since this was a period when there were several pervasive forces producing delayed childbearing, these factors will not be visible when examining individual determinants of unanticipated delay. Our strategy here is similar to the one employed to examine the determinants of unanticipated births (see table 35). Again, a set of dummy variables is included to control for fertility intentions at the beginning of the time period, and as expected they have strong effects. Women intending a child in the next year are over eight times ($e^{.2.092}$) more likely to have a child in this 1976–1979 period than those intending one in two to three years (the omitted category). Those intending to have a child sooner should have higher birth probabilities because they are likely to start trying to conceive earlier.

Net of timing intentions, there is no clear pattern between the effects on behavior in chapter 8 and the effects on consistency shown in table 35. In fact, there are only two other significant effects in table 35. Women with lower parental socioeconomic status are less likely to have a child given that one was intended. This could reflect lower financial support from parents, but it is also possible that this reflects greater infertility among the lower SES group. Second, men not employed or "just hanging out" were less likely to realize parenthood. Parenthood may not have occurred because the man and the potential mother realized that resources were inadequate to provide for a child. Alternatively, these two variables could have been significant just by chance. The important point to remember is that, in general, the background and activity state variables have a negligible effect on unanticipated delay (the probability of not making the transition to parenthood, given that one had intended parenthood). This finding is in marked contrast to the pattern for unanticipated births, the first type of inconsistency examined.

Why the different *frequency* and *predictability* of the two types of inconsistency? The much greater *frequency* of "intending one, but having none," an unanticipated delay (compared with intending none, but having one—an unanticipated birth), has been reported in other studies focused on births of all orders (see Davidson and Beach 1981; Westoff and Ryder 1977*b*). Social psychologists claim that attitudes and associated behaviors may have different "thresholds"; a given factor may be enough to entice an individual to intend a birth soon, but not enough to entice the person actually to have one (see discussion in Davidson and Beach 1981:476). Consistent with this principle, Davidson and Beach suggest an "inertia" argument to explain why their model failed much more often when predicting a birth as opposed to fertility delay. Prediction errors are more common when a change in behavior or status is intended or predicted, they claim, perhaps because of fear of the unfamiliar. Parenthood is certainly a major status change with many inherent uncertainties.

Stated differently, given a low-fertility society that allows substantial flexibility in birth timing, unanticipated delay may always be more common. American norms specify that childbearing should occur when and if the couple can afford children, allowing great variability in fertility timing. A couple may realistically have a decade or more in which to initiate childbearing without wavering from the common intention of having children. The decision to have a child *now*, if realized, has serious and immediate implications. In contrast, delaying fertility for a few years, especially at the young ages we examine here (22–25), is a common and normatively acceptable life course strategy.

A second reason for the greater frequency of unanticipated fertility delay (versus unintended childbearing) could hinge on unfavorable social and economic conditions. Remember, pervasive fertility delay in the 1970s is a robust finding, and accompanying social and economic changes were unfavorable for family formation (see chap. 4). Given the normative context, fertility delay in the face of economic uncertainty and difficulty is appropriate. Replication of our analysis during a period of favorable social and economic conditions, when ages at parenthood were falling, would be needed to address this issue fully.

Finally, some inconsistency results because of low fecundity or low contraceptive effectiveness. As discussed earlier, waits to conception (averaging four to five months) and spontaneous abortions (approximately 20 percent of recognizable conceptions) introduce a sizable stochastic factor into first-birth timing (see Bongaarts and Potter 1983). Since childless women have little experience with conception waits or spontaneous abortions, they are unlikely to take these unpredictable events into account. Unanticipated delay is the result. Further, some research suggests that infertility is increasing among young women currently in their twenties—due to earlier IUD use or contraction of sexually transmitted diseases (see Menken 1985; Mosher 1986). If so, unanticipated delay may also increase. Effective contraceptives and access to legal abortion, however, make mistimed and unwanted births less likely. In sum, unanticipated delay may always be more common in the modern American context. But socioeconomic conditions and changing access to contraceptives and abortion will affect the balance of unanticipated delay versus unanticipated births.

Differences in the *predictability* of the two types of inconsistency are also observed. Unanticipated births are predicted well by the same general model developed for actual fertility and stated intentions. The general thrust of this model is that people time births to mesh with other aspects of their unfolding life course. Stated differently, they time fertility in conjunction with other roles; some of these early adult roles take precedence over or are incompatible with parenthood. With contraception and abortion, individuals have substantial control of their fertility. If those for whom childbearing is most costly resort to abortion when a mistimed or unwanted pregnancy occurs, as Leibowitz, Eisen, and Chow (1986) argue, then our general model should perform well.

Our social model does not predict unanticipated delay well. Perhaps this situation occurs because there is nothing comparable to abortion for those who want a child now but cannot conceive or carry a birth to term. Infertility treatment is available but one seeks such help only after a long conception wait. Further, infertility treatment is expensive, and the outcome uncertain. Stated differently, an unmeasured dimension of certainty accompanies a stated fertility intention. Moreover, this certainty is likely related to the same factors as stated intentions—where opportunity costs are greatest, certainty is greatest. In the case of an unanticipated pregnancy, this certainty about not wanting a child now increases the probability of choosing abortion. In contrast, no easily accessible method guarantees parenthood exactly when one intends it. In short, the stochastic aspects of conception and gestation are involved to a greater extent with the variability in unanticipated delay, weakening effects of our social model on this type of inconsistency. This effect is probably amplified because of the pervasive delaying effects of period factors for the time period examined. If this is the case, our social-structural and life course model would be more effective in the absence of such strong and pervasive period-delaying factors.

FERTILITY INTENTIONS AND ATTITUDINAL CORRELATES

The perspective adopted in our research argues that activities that compete with childbearing for the individual's time and attention (going to school, beginning a career, or time-demanding leisure activities) will postpone the timing of parenthood. This in turn implicitly suggests that respondents themselves view these activities as competing with one another—an assumption we now explicitly examine. The causal connections between attitudes toward career or leisure and fertility intentions are far from clear. Attitudes based on prior life course experience may influence expected parenthood timing. However, work or marital contingencies may cause parenthood delay that leads to attitude change, either because of the intervening experiences or a need to justify current behavior. At the current descriptive level, we are not trying to establish the exact causal mechanism but are simply asking whether the constellation of attitudes and intentions matches our theoretical expectations.

Given the time and energy demands of parenthood, and assuming respondents *recognize* these demands, parenthood will be timed so that these demands can be met. We expect that women who consider work roles as very important will be more likely to intend delay in order to pursue these work roles. In contrast, we expect no relationship between the importance of work for men and fertility-timing intentions since the importance of work and career is traditionally the man's major avenue to status regardless of parenthood status. In fact there is evidence that parenthood increases the salience of the breadwinner role (e.g., parenthood increases the number of hours worked; see Hofferth 1983; Lindert 1978; Waite, Haggstrom, and Kanouse 1985).

Those who value leisure activities will also be *more likely* to intend delay. Greater preference for leisure increases the cost of parenthood. Finally, those who give greater importance to marriage and family life will be *more likely* to intend a child in the next few years.

Next, those who anticipate jobs that require special training or long periods of training (e.g., professions) are more likely to delay fertility. This situation should be true for men and women: for women because motherhood often means women accept much of the child care responsibility—a difficult burden while involved in a second demanding role such as student or job trainee; for men, the breadwinner role may require the sacrifice of further investments in education or training for short-term gains in income.

Respondents' views of the appropriate roles for men and women could also influence intentions. Those with a traditional sex-role orientation might see parenthood as an appropriate transition for early adulthood. They anticipate a division of labor where the man is the primary breadwinner and the woman the primary caretaker. Such an anticipated division of labor lowers the perceived costs of childbearing and increases the expected rewards.

Especially among women, these life-style goals and preferences should be strongly associated with fertility intentions for several reasons. First, as the contrast with Japan indicated, the Western context historically allowed for individual choice regarding marriage and parenthood. Second, social-structural change in the past few years has greatly expanded the opportunities for nonfamilial roles for women, allowing a broader range of legitimate choices with very little change in familial roles for men.

Third, and very important, neither a domestic nor a nondomestic choice is likely to go unchallenged for women. As Gerson (1985:190) writes:

to justify their own embattled positions, domestic and nondomestic women denigrated each other's choices. . . . (F)ew, if any, unambiguously legitimate paths [exist] for women.

To justify these "hard choices," women are likely to express an ideology consistent with their expected behavior. Attitudes examined here are closely connected with ideologies that support domestic and nondomestic female life courses.

Using data from the NLS 72, analyses were completed separately for 1976 and 1979, and for men and women. To be included in the 1976 sample one had to be childless and not pregnant as of October 1976. Similarly, to be in the 1979 analysis, one had to be childless at the fourth follow-up survey (in October 1979). In both these follow-ups, a series of questions was asked about how important an item was "in your life" or how important a factor was "in determining the kind of work you plan to be doing for most of your life." Earlier work, especially chapter 8, showed that certain roles were incompatible: full-time student and motherhood, for instance. Here we are interested in the competition among various goals and preferences.

Five response items shown below measure the importance of career (SUCCESS, PROMOTION), family (MARRY, CLOSE), and leisure (LEISURE). These items are available in the 1974, 1976, and 1979 NLS rounds.

1. SUCCESS "Being successful in my line of work" (question 151A in 1976 and 197A in 1979)
2. PROMOTION "Advancement in the long run" (question 152I in 1976 and 198I in 1979)
3. MARRY "Finding the right person to marry and having a happy family life" (question 151B in 1976 and 197B in 1979)
4. CLOSE "Living close to parents and relatives" (question 151H in 1976 and 197H in 1979)
5. LEISURE "Having leisure time to enjoy my own interests" (question 151K in 1976 and 197K in 1979).

Responses were "very important," "somewhat important," and "not important." In each case except one, these variables were dichotomized into very important and other (somewhat important and not important).

TABLE 36.
Multivariate Analysis: Intent for Child in Next Three Years by Importance of Family, Career, and Leisure: Women and Men

Independent variables	Women (A)	Women (B)	Women (C)	Men (A)	Men (B)	Men (C)
1976						
Leisure–1976	−0.248*	−0.279*	−0.223*	−0.159*	−0.211*	−0.168*
Success–1976	−0.708*	−0.700*	−0.689*	−0.368*	0.134	−0.322*
Close–1976	0.450*	0.335*	0.359*	0.237	0.142*	0.219*
Marry–1976		1.670*			1.552*	
Promotion–1976		−0.132			−0.210*	
Leisure–1974			−0.166*			0.005
Success–1974			0.038			0.279*
Close–1974			0.298*			0.083
χ²	168.32	383.72	181.72	32.02	183.52	43.91
d.f.	3	5	6	3	5	6
constant	−0.506	−1.880	−0.645	−1.698	−2.957	−1.944
1979						
Leisure–1979	−0.171*	−0.251*	−0.196*	−0.051	−0.087	−0.169*
Success–1979	−0.525*	−0.542*	−0.452*	0.425*	0.208*	0.185*
Close–1979	0.552*	0.437*	0.478*	0.278*	0.184*	0.206*

Marry–1979	—	1.746*	—	—	1.870*	—
Promotion–1976	—	–0.135	—	—	0.061	—
Leisure–1976	—	—	0.116	—	—	0.014
Success–1976	—	—	–0.212*	—	—	0.341*
Close–1976	—	—	0.187*	—	—	0.202*
χ^2	111.71	377.10	121.18	48.88	312.59	62.20
d.f.	3	5	6	3	5	6
constant	–0.216	–1.512	–0.238	–1.104	–2.558	–1.181

*Significant at .05 level.

The exception is CLOSE which was dichotomized as important (very important and somewhat important) versus not important. These decisions were made because some response categories were rarely used making separate analysis difficult (for instance few said SUCCESS and MARRY were not important). In all cases those considering an item more important were coded 1; others are coded 0.

Estimated associations between these five attitudinal items and the intention to have a child in the next three years appear in table 36. No background or activity state variables are included in the models in table 36. Model A includes one variable from each domain (e.g., career, family, and leisure) measured at the same time as the fertility intention. Model B includes all items measured contemporaneously (e.g., two measures from the first two domains). Model C adds to model A the identical response items measured in the previous round of the survey. Overall, these items are strongly related to timing intentions. Assuming such preferences are jointly determined, it is clear that the decision to have children is imbedded in a set of life-style choices. Indeed women in their twenties who have no children see that childbearing competes with other roles.

An expected, but nevertheless interesting finding is the differing effect by sex of SUCCESS (the importance of being successful in your line of work). SUCCESS decreases sharply the odds of intending a child soon for women. The opposite effect is true for men. This reversed effect is strong and apparent in both years. The intent to become a parent is associated with less emphasis on success for women but more for men. If these expectations reflect investments in family and career areas, then it shows how the transition to parenthood presses individuals more firmly into traditional sex roles.

Adding MARRY and PROMOTION does not alter the story. In fact every coefficient in model A and B (regardless of sex or year) is in the predicted direction. The MARRY variable has a huge effect that attenuates the other family domain variable (CLOSE), but in all cases both are significant. The PROMOTION variable has weaker effects than the SUCCESS variable. Both always have the predicted sign but are not always statistically significant.

Model C adds variables from a previous round of the NLS 72. Some of these variables have effects net of the contemporaneously measured ones, but the effects are generally smaller.

We also expected that those with more traditional sex-role orientations would be less likely to postpone parenthood. Here we present the relationship for three sex-role items:

1. PRESCHOOL "A working mother of pre-school children can be just as good a mother as the woman who doesn't work" (question 150A in 1976 and 196A in 1979).
2. MANACHIEVE "It is usually better for everyone involved if the man is the achiever outside the home and the woman takes care of the home and the family" (question 150B in 1976 and 196B in 1979).
3. WIFEHELP "It is more important for a wife to help her husband than to have a career herself" (questions 150H in 1976 and 196H in 1979).

Again we chose these three items on the assumption that they reflected most clearly the respondents' opinion of whether career or family should take precedence in women's lives. Responses to each item were "strongly agree," "agree," "disagree," "strongly disagree." Strength of opinion was ignored in results presented here and variables were created where 1 equals the more traditional responses and 0 otherwise.

We show the relationship between these sex-role items and fertility intentions in the next three years in table 37. Regardless of year or sex, all estimated bivariate effects are positive and significant—traditional responses increase the likelihood of intending to have a child soon. When all effects are estimated simultaneously, each independent effect is attenuated as expected. Again the effects are stronger for women than men.

Finally, we examined the relationship between career plans and fertility intentions. In 1976 and 1979, respondents were asked about the kind of work they preferred to be doing when they were 30 years old. We do not show the results here, but they suggest that respondents adjust their fertility and occupational plans so that these demanding roles are not in direct competition. Those expecting to be professionals (doctors, lawyers, etc.) were least likely to intend having a child in the early and mid-twenties, for instance. Further, occupational plans are more strongly associated with fertility for women than for men, indicating the greater role incompatibility women face in trying to combine a career with parenthood.

To summarize, we have shown that respondents are more likely to delay the first birth intentionally if they consider leisure and career as very important and consider living close to family as not so important. One's occupational plans at age 30 and one's view of appropriate sex roles also are associated with timing intentions. All evidence suggests that respondents time parenthood in conjunction with other goals, plans, and preferences. This finding is not surprising, and reinforces our behavioral results from chapter 8.

TABLE 37.

INTENT FOR CHILD IN NEXT THREE YEARS BY SEX ROLE ATTITUDE ITEMS: WOMEN AND MEN

Independent variables	Women (A)	(B)	(C)	(D)	Men (A)	(B)	(C)	(D)
1976								
PRESCHOOL	0.351*	—	—	0.185*	0.311*	—	—	0.206
MANACHIEVE	—	0.537*	—	0.187	—	0.395*	—	0.170
WIFEHELP	—	—	0.786*	0.670*	—	—	0.548*	0.435*
χ^2	29.20	61.13	132.35	148.63	20.05	32.31	59.65	74.31
d.f.	1	1	1	3	1	1	1	3
Constant	0.351	-0.515	-0.352	-0.374	-1.527	-1.153	-1.029	-1.106
1979								
PRESCHOOL	0.240	—	—	0.019	0.174*	—	—	0.097*
MANACHIEVE	—	0.591*	—	0.478*	—	0.207*	—	0.141
WIFEHELP	—	—	0.546*	0.335*	—	—	0.222*	0.127
χ^2	10.81	60.74	45.64	78.90	7.50	9.94	10.18	16.50
d.f.	1	1	1	3	1	1	1	3
Constant	-0.383	0.129	0.114	0.311	-0.692	-0.491	-0.461	-0.475

*Significant at .05 level.

SOCIAL-STRUCTURAL VARIABLES, ATTITUDES, AND BEHAVIOR

In the introduction to this chapter, we described how background variables and early life course experience could influence early adult activities, attitudes, and values. Each, in turn, could influence parenthood timing. In addition, earlier results showed that conscious decisions by individuals (timing expectations) mediated much of the effect of background variables and early adult activity states. One way in which these background and life course variables could influence parenthood decisions is by influencing individuals' aspirations, attitudes, and values. The analysis to which we now turn incorporates each of these sets of variables.

Chapter 8 employed a model containing background variables and activity states:

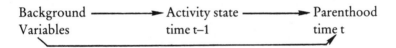

Some, but not all, of the influence of background factors is mediated by recent activity state. Thus background variables measure some aspects of socialization experiences and/or opportunity structure that are not fully accounted for by recent activity state. We now add to the model recent attitudes about appropriate sex roles and preferred life-styles. Determinants of these attitudes presumably can be found in that portion of the life history that has unfolded. The question of interest here is the effect of background variables, activity states, and attitude items on the transition to parenthood. The focus now is on net effects. Specifically, do sex-role attitudes and life-style preferences mediate most of the influence of background variables and recent activity state?

Since attitudes are measured approximately two years prior to fertility behavior, it would appear that they are also causally prior. Nevertheless this presumption needs to be tempered a bit and the results should be viewed with some caution. To see that causality might be operating in the opposite direction, one need only consider an individual (or couple) whose waiting time to conception was three or four years.

Our model builds on the basic one from chapter 8 by adding four of the attitudinal variables described earlier in this chapter, measured in

TABLE 38.
GROSS AND NET EFFECTS[a] (BETAS) OF BACKGROUND CHARACTERISTICS AND ON
CONDITIONAL PROBABILITY OF HAVING A CHILD: WOMEN

Independent variables	Parenthood 1976–1979		Intent 1976–1979	
	Gross effects	Net effects	Gross effects	Net effects
Parents' SES				
Top quarter	–0.200*	–0.123	–0.313**	–0.256**
Bottom quarter	–0.018	–0.058	0.174	0.137
Other Background Variables				
Farm residence	0.330**	0.348**	0.190*	0.196*
Catholic	–0.140	–0.101	–0.011	–0.013
Southern	0.002	0.019	0.115	0.121
Activity State				
Homemaker	0.808**	0.751**	0.753**	0.658**
Part-time worker	0.086	0.155	–0.097	–0.080
College student	–1.011**	–0.867**	–1.179**	–1.042**
Junior college student	–0.503*	–0.377	–0.458**	–0.316
Vocational school student	–0.378	–0.345	–0.554*	–0.498
Military service	–0.427	–0.246	–0.334	–0.135
Looking for work or just hanging out	–0.568**	–0.643**	–0.804**	–0.797[a]
Attitude Variables				
LEISURE		–0.224**		–0.157**
SUCCESS		–0.484**		–0.565**
CLOSE		0.335**		0.441**
MANACHIEVE		0.367**		0.334**
N	4633	4503	4633	4503
Model χ^2	172.63	258.83	297.78	421.11

*Significant at .05.
**Significant at .01.
[a]Columns labeled "gross effects" do not include attitude variables while those labeled "net effects" do.

TABLE 39.
GROSS AND NET EFFECTS[a] (BETAS) OF BACKGROUND CHARACTERISTICS AND ON
CONDITIONAL PROBABILITY OF HAVING A CHILD: MEN

	Parenthood 1976–1979		Intent 1976–1979	
Independent variables	Gross effects	Net effects	Gross effects	Net effects
Parents' SES				
Top quarter	-0.394**	-0.382**	-0.312**	-0.271**
Bottom quarter	0.276**	0.276**	0.066	0.074
Other Background Variables				
Farm residence	0.354**	0.342**	0.348**	0.304**
Catholic	-0.188	-0.201	-0.125	-0.138
Southern	0.183*	0.121	0.224**	0.169*
Activity State				
Homemaker	—	—	—	—
Part-time worker	-0.813**	-0.747*	-0.683**	-0.656**
College student	-0.630**	-0.635**	-0.725*	-0.710**
Junior college student	-0.414	-0.443	-0.318	-0.284
Vocational school student	0.616**	0.607**	-0.013	0.010
Military service	-0.253	-0.218	-0.086	-0.072
Looking for work or just hanging out	-1.029**	-1.142**	-0.863**	-0.814**
Attitude Variables				
LEISURE		-0.092		-0.118
SUCCESS		0.041		0.305**
CLOSE		0.003		0.148*
MANACHIEVE		0.241**		0.303**
N	4903	4708	4903	4708
Model χ^2	173.62	182.72	173.62	197.85

*Significant at .05.
**Significant at .01.
[a]Columns labeled "gross effects" do not include attitude variables while those labeled "net effects" do.

1976: LEISURE, SUCCESS, CLOSE, and MANACHIEVE.[3] The universe consisted of all those not yet parents in 1976. The dependent variable is the probability of becoming a parent between 1976 and 1979. We also repeated the analysis using birth expectations for 1976–1979. However, the reader should bear in mind that in this second analysis, the causality concerns become more severe.

Results appear in tables 38 and 39 for women and men respectively. Two types of models are shown: the gross model includes background and activity state variables; the net model adds attitudinal variables. The difference between these two models addresses the questions of whether background variables and recent activity states operate primarily through life-style preferences and attitudes.

Examining the female results first, surprisingly the net effects model (which includes preference and attitude items) does not consistently show weaker effects for all background characteristics and recent activity states. Among the background variables only high SES origin status tends to be consistently attenuated by these items. Effects of homemaking and being in school (college, junior college, and vocational school) are also slightly attenuated by including the attitudinal information. But overall the effects of the attitude items do not appear to have their origin in the life experience measured in our model (e.g., the background variables and recent activity states).

For men similar results can be seen in table 38. Although introducing the attitude items consistently attenuates the effects of high SES origin status, farm origin, and southern origin, these effects are only slightly weaker in the net effects model. Activity state effects do not show any clear differences in the two models.

These results indicate that other factors not included in these models affect life-style preferences and sex-role attitudes and, in turn, parenthood timing. Remember in chapter 8, we begin with a rather simple operationalization of early adult experience—we measure current activity state. The history of activity states across the young adult years may also be relevant (see Rindfuss, Swicegood, and Rosenfeld 1987). Additional variables measuring satisfaction with school or work (individuals' subjective evaluation of their activity state) may also be important. While we feel our model of the transition to parenthood is a promising framework for subsequent

---

[3]We experimented with other groups of attitudinal items and results were substantively unchanged.

analysis, it clearly needs to be elaborated. Roots of these life-style preferences and sex-role attitudes constitute an important example that we are
currently investigating in greater detail.

SUMMARY AND DISCUSSION

Analyses reported here shed considerable light on the parenthood process. Consistent with our theoretical arguments and previous work, few
young adults hold stable childless intentions. Instead, childlessness appears to result from a series of decisions to postpone childbearing. Those
for whom having a child now would prove most costly (along a variety
of dimensions) are most likely to intend delay; and even given that
intention, they are most likely to realize it. But there also is substantial
inconsistency. Many respondents change their minds and, in the period
and ages covered by the NLS High School Class of 1972 data, delaying
an intended birth is far more common than having one when none was
intended. Thus this high school cohort is not only delaying fertility
compared to previous cohorts and to those who dropped out of school
prior to twelfth grade but also are delayed childbearers by their own
expectations. This preponderance of unpredicted delays undoubtedly reflects the widespread period factors leading to delayed childbearing during
the 1970s (see chap. 4) which affected the entire cohort.

We also show that the same factors that predict behavior predict future
fertility intentions. In short, a consistent behavioral and attitudinal pattern exists. This pattern was further reinforced by our examination of
attitudes and expectations in nonfertility areas. Respondents are more
likely to delay the first birth if they consider leisure and career important
and living close to one's family unimportant. As the earlier behavioral
research suggested, young adults time parenthood in conjunction with
other goals, plans, and preferences in their unfolding life course.

Finally, we found that including preference and attitudinal items with
background and activity states in predicting the transition to parenthood
does not substantially attenuate the effects of either background variables
or activity states. These results were unanticipated. The attitude items
included operate largely independent of the model's background and
activity state variables. Where is the origin of these attitude effects? The
answer, obviously, is from other experience in the life history, but which
experience? Clearly the young adult years are far more complex than the

models we have been examining. Models that captured more of the life course experience would, no doubt, explain some variability in attitudes and, thus indirectly, some variability in fertility timing. Future work should move further in this direction.

More specifically, this future work should acknowledge the flexibility of the adult life course and the indeterminacy of childhood experience (Baltes and Brim 1979, 1980, 1982; Brim and Kagan 1980; Bronfenbrenner 1985). Much variability in parenthood timing lies in the recent work and family experience of adult women. As Gerson (1985) claims, boredom or dissatisfaction with work causes many women to choose parenthood, and their life course to veer toward domesticity. Likewise, Gerson's respondents often cited unanticipated rewards of working as reasons for delaying or forgoing parenthood, pushing the life course away from domesticity. Other of Gerson's subjects fell into a domestic or nondomestic life course trajectory at young ages, and the subsequent life course appeared to unfold by its own momentum. As mentioned in the previous chapter, work currently under way incorporates more of this early adult experience (earlier activity states). But future work should also consider the respondents' subjective evaluations of these roles, how such evaluations are formed, and their influence on parenthood timing.

Stable heterosexual relationships, or lack of them, also have important implications for the unfolding adult life course. In chapter 2 we presented a detailed explanation for why we have not included marriage in our analytic model. This argument does not deny that many see stable heterosexual relationships as a precondition for parenthood. Instead it stresses that the marriage date is a poor proxy for the initiation of such a relationship.

Such young adult experiences are excluded from the models we estimate in this monograph. As a result, more work must elaborate these models before we fully understand how the unfolding dynamics of the life course produce individual variability in parenthood timing. Clearly though, when attempting to link previous life course experience and subsequent choice, the mediating role played by attitudes, values, and life-style preferences constitutes an integral part of this work.

10

Conclusion

IMPORTANCE OF THE TRANSITION TO PARENTHOOD

In chapter 1 we justified our focus on parenthood timing by outlining its wide-ranging social and economic consequences. For individuals, parenthood can mark the most important role transition of adulthood. Because of the permanence and continual obligations characterizing parenthood, this transition impinges on other simultaneously held roles and shapes the subsequent life course. Aggregate changes in the timing of parenthood have equally profound influences at the institutional level. For example, the health care delivery system must alter the mix of services provided, depending on the mix of very young and very old mothers. Our economic institutions are affected by the reduced time women spend as mothers of small children and the increased work force attachment accompanying that change. Marriage and the family are certainly affected, as well. Childless marriages run higher risks of disruption, even though later parenthood and nonparenthood are associated with more egalitarian relations and reduced role differentiation between spouses. At the societal level, changes in the timing of parenthood have had a major impact on levels of period fertility. Period fertility determines new cohort sizes and, thus, has implications for a range of age-graded institutions. Political consequences are also possible because parents and nonparents may see a very different set of goals and policies as advantageous. Interest groups based on such distinctions could affect public policy and thereby alter the course of future social change.

This partial list of consequences demonstrates that the timing of parenthood is more than a key fertility variable. Parenthood is a functional requisite for societal survival, an important status in a range of institutions, and a status with a broad range of implications for individual behavior. Clearly it is important to understand as much as possible about its social, economic, and demographic determinants. Our work here has addressed a number of questions toward that end.

THE CONCEPTUAL AND ANALYTIC MODEL

In chapter 2 we introduced the conceptual model that guided our empirical analysis (see fig. 1). This model holds that individuals or couples make fertility-relevant decisions such as to try to have a child *now*, or to use contraception to delay a birth. Thus, the decision to become a parent is not a one-time decision, but a set of sequential decisions with a momentum of their own. In this important sense the transition to parenthood must be seen as a process. This conceptualization led us explicitly to investigate the differential effects of various social-structural factors by age, that is, by *the passage of time at the individual level.* Further, it is important to pay attention to all ages of the transition to parenthood, rather than just the extremes of adolescent fertility or becoming a parent for the first time past age 30. The importance of this broad focus is emphasized by the fact that for all cohorts passing through the childbearing years in the twentieth century, approximately half to two-thirds of their members became parents for the first time while they were in their twenties.

Decisions relevant to the parenthood transition are influenced by background variables that measure socialization experiences and available resources. Hence, these variables provide indicators of tastes for children relative to other goods as well as the opportunity to acquire more education and training. The parenthood decision is also influenced by more proximate measures of the unfolding life course. Background variables may set individuals on given trajectories but their individual experiences, abilities, and chance events will alter the directions of the subsequent life course. The conflict between familial and work roles is widely acknowledged by social scientists and young adults (see chap. 9). As a result, the decision about the beginning of parenthood is often made with a view toward minimizing such conflict. Thus, the life course is influenced by *individual-level characteristics* that comprise another focus of our study.

An individual-level model, like the one sketched above, can be elaborated for any given social context. But differences in individual behavior can also be traced to variation across social context and, therefore, adequate understanding must include consideration of social context, that is, the calculus of costs and benefits embedded in social norms and arising out of the social structure. Couples choose to become parents within such contexts, and their perception of the costs and benefits of becoming a parent at a given point in time is influenced by the social context. For example, an increase in nonfamilial roles for women may raise the perceived opportunity costs of parenthood. Alternatively, government provision of day-care services may reduce the costs of parenthood. This approach is consistent with Bronfenbrenner's (1979, 1985) call for a study of life course development in context. While this is not the usual analytical approach in the study of fertility, it is reflected in the increasing attention paid to cross-cultural fertility comparisons.

Our study examined parenthood timing across several relevant social contexts. The first of these involves differences between periods and/or cohorts. Historical events, economic booms and busts, and social movements can all alter the context in which decisions are made. Moreover, some of these events may affect life course development such that subsequent behavior is influenced. For example, Elder (1974) has demonstrated that the life course of the children of the Depression must be understood in terms of the social context in which they were raised. Thus, a second major dimension we analyzed is *aggregate time*, as indexed by either period or cohort.

Other contexts reflect an *aggregate social-structural dimension*. For example, our interpretation of black-white differences in chapter 6 hinges on the different and changing socioeconomic contexts confronted by whites and blacks. But the importance of context is most clearly demonstrated in the comparison of parenthood in Japan and the United States (see chap. 7). The process of becoming a parent is fundamentally different in these two economically advanced nations.

While our model includes a variety of factors from several different conceptual levels, it does not formally include marriage. We do not deny that marriage provides a normatively approved license for parenthood in the contexts we examine, but the extent to which these norms are followed and the stiffness of sanctions for nonconformity vary greatly. Consider, for instance differences in out-of-wedlock childbearing by race and historical period in the United States (Cutright and Smith 1986; J. A. Jones et al. 1985; Ventura 1980) or the differences documented in chapter 7 between U.S. whites and the Japanese. The meaning of marriage clearly varies across space and time. Moreover, the causal relation between marriage and parenthood is complex. Some individuals marry because they want to become parents; marriage and parenthood are joint decisions. Some marry and then decide they want children. For others, pregnancy determines the marriage timing. Further, recent work (Rindfuss and Parnell 1986) makes it clear that the actual empirical relationship between marriage and fertility varies across a number of socially defined groups, suggesting that the meaning of marriage is subgroup defined. Thus, at the individual and societal levels, marriage is a poor proxy for the complex of behaviors or norms surrounding the establishment of conjugal relationships. Finally, "new" institutions such as cohabitation are evolving. Whether it is really new or just a variant form of marriage is still the subject of conjecture. Either way, the data sources available to us do not explicitly measure cohabitation. We consider marital behaviors and norms in our substantive interpretations of results but do not introduce them into our empirical analyses.

MODEL, PROCESS, AND DATA

Careful consideration of our conceptual framework makes clear the potential complexity of the parenthood process. The intricacies of the unfolding life course have implications for the transition to parenthood, and this complexity is multiplied by the possibility that different individual characteristics and social contexts may fundamentally alter the process under study. The ideal data set would contain rich background and life course information on men and women, for a long series of cohorts and a number of countries. No such data set exists. Therefore we have used the data sources that best allow us to examine particular aspects of our model. For instance, vital registration data provided a long time series for examining intercohort variability in parenthood timing. This intercohort variability was best explained by period factors and was not dependent on the prior intracohort parenthood experience (see chap. 4). The temporal depth of the vital registration series made it clear that delayed childbearing is not of recent origin but rather is a strategy adopted by earlier cohorts. But these vital registration data are inadequate for testing for the factors underlying the significant shifts in first-birth timing that we observe. The data contain little information on racial or ethnic identification and no information on the nonfertility aspects of the life course. Consequently, these data cannot be used to determine if the similarity of the Depression pattern of fertility delay and the more recent one observed in the 1970s and 1980s have been produced by the same or distinct processes.

In sharp contrast to the time series data, the High School Class of 1972 data contain rich information on the unfolding life course of young adults. These data clearly showed that socioeconomic background affects parenthood timing directly, and also indirectly by influencing the life course. For example, being in school in the early adult years, which is partly dependent on socioeconomic background, is a powerful determinant of parenthood timing (see chap. 8). Obviously, the weakness of this data set is its focus on a single cohort in a single country. We do not know how the social contexts of other places and times might alter this process.

We examined several data sources lying between these first two examples, which covered a range of cohorts but also included data on individual characteristics. The best examples are the U.S. fertility surveys which we pooled to provide greater temporal depth. These data sets allowed us to examine whether the effects of some individual-level social-structural factors changed over time (see chap. 5). Somewhat surprisingly, our results suggest that the same general process has been occurring in all of the cohorts examined.

In short, there is no single data set that we could use to explore the complexity of the determinants of the parenthood process. Further, no single data set analyzed here stood out as being more important than the rest. Each had strengths and weaknesses. If future data collection efforts could produce a more appropriate data set, they should have fine-grained detail on the unfolding life course, cover as many cohorts as possible, include men and women, and be conducted in more than one country by coordinating major data collection projects. Repeating the large longitudinal surveys, such as the High School Class of 1972 survey, at regular intervals is one way to realize most of the desirable features. Large longitudinal surveys of this type are also being administered in other countries. Such a survey in Britain provides the basis for an excellent recent study of the timing of parenthood (e.g., Kiernan and Diamond 1983). International coordination is certainly possible and may prove to be useful in determining how social context shapes the entire process.

Resources required for such efforts are substantial. But the complexity of the process defies simple analytical strategies. We are attempting to understand the parenthood process within a species that can become parents over at least a 30-year period. Across this period individuals can adapt their fertility to exigencies of the unfolding life course. This unfolding life course is, itself, an adaptation to the exigencies of an existing or changing social context. In short, our results make it clear that the determinants of the fertility transition process are exceedingly complex, and our data sources have to mirror this complexity. The only justification for such a major research enterprise, and the only necessary one, is the broad array of consequences that flows from differences in the timing of the transition to parenthood (see Ryder 1983 for a similar argument regarding the importance, but complexity, of studying fertility in developing countries).

MAJOR FINDINGS AND IMPLICATIONS

Individual chapters in this book have focused on particular aspects of the overall process of the transition to parenthood. This section summarizes and integrates our findings. Figure 22 shows a revised version of our conceptual model (shown in fig. 1) based on results of the analyses reported in previous chapters.

TRENDS AND THEIR CAUSES.

In the United States, the broad changes that have occurred in parenthood timing can be described quite succinctly. Age at first birth increased during the Great Depression of the 1930s, as did the incidence of childlessness. Both decreased sharply following the Depression and during and immediately after World War II. The transition to parenthood remained relatively young throughout the 1950s and into the 1960s; childlessness reached very low levels (about 10 percent for whites). In contrast, delayed childbearing and childlessness are now prominent features of the contemporary demographic scene. Current trends suggest that women now in their thirties will surpass Depression levels of fertility delay and childlessness (see chap. 4).

As this summary indicates, our work documents sharp cohort differences in first-birth timing. The percentage of white women childless at age 25, for instance, has varied from a low of 25 percent during the Baby Boom to 50 percent for the most recent cohorts. How has this social

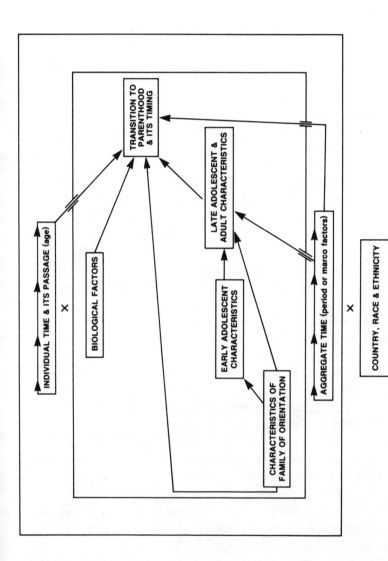

Fig. 22. Factors affecting the transition to parenthood.

change occurred? One possible process is cohort replacement. Cohort effects occur when new cohorts enter the childbearing ages with new parenthood-timing strategies. These new cohorts are less encumbered with the weight of past experience, and follow a different path.

A second pattern of social change is characterized by similar behavioral responses to period events by those of all ages regardless of content or quantity of their past experience. In this type of change all age groups, and hence all cohorts, respond similarly to the period factors. Our analyses show change in parenthood timing has occurred in this latter fashion. Specifically, women who are still not parents respond similarly to period factors regardless of their cohort membership. Thus, age and period effects appear to account for most of the variability in first-birth timing.

In short, cohorts have different fertility timing because they experience different sets of period experience. If there are "cohort effects," they are moderate at best. This result is consistent with prior research that focuses on births of all orders (see Namboodiri 1981; Pullum 1980; Rindfuss and Sweet 1977; D. P. Smith 1981; Sweet and Rindfuss 1983). Moreover, period effects also seem to predominate in other types of demographic change. This is perhaps most evident in recent studies of marriage and divorce (Morgan and Rindfuss 1985; Rodgers and Thornton 1985). Taken together the evidence for period effects on family formation is overwhelming. Yet, given the intuitive plausibility of cohort effects, we are surprised by their apparent absence. Ryder's (1965) seminal article provided a strong theoretical rationale for cohort effects and has spawned a generation of research. With respect to the sociology of fertility, it is time to ask why are recognizable cohort effects relatively rare and relatively small?

One possibility is that the relevant period effects in the recent past have altered the social context in a way that directly affects all age groups. Strong cohort effects would not be present in such a situation. In chapter 4 we showed that a set of period-specific factors can account for observed aggregate trends. Childless women in their teens, twenties, and thirties were responding similarly. Perhaps people past their early twenties are not as inflexible as is sometimes assumed. Indeed, it is the inability of individuals in their late twenties and thirties to change that is at the heart of many predicted cohort patterns of fertility behavior. Wrong (1961) has argued against an oversocialized conception of human action, and considerable research has demonstrated that change occurs across the life span, that developmental life courses are not entirely determined by childhood experiences, and that contextual features enhance and constrain the potential for change (see Baltes and Brim 1979, 1980, 1982; Brim and Kagan 1980). Socialization is an ongoing process which is never entirely completed. Increasing inflexibility with age has likely been overstated.

While we cannot extend our analysis back much before the 1930s, and in many cases have been restricted to more recent data, it is clear that the transition to parenthood is a *process* that continues to unfold until that transition has occurred or until parenthood is no longer a biological option (a sterilizing operation has taken place, menopause has occurred, or a long, unsuccessful attempt at conceiving and carrying a fetus to term has transpired). Not only do we find at the macrolevel that individuals who are still not yet parents respond similarly at every age to period factors but also at the microlevel our results repeatedly point out that men and women can, and do, change their minds about their fertility intentions.

Another plausible reason why cohort effects are so rare turns on the flexible timing and ordering of life course events in the United States. Over time a cohort's identity blurs as life chances work themselves out (Ryder 1965). But the speed with which they blur may be a function of the social context. If statuses are strictly age graded, then cohort identities may be clearly maintained across considerable periods of time. In contrast, where timing and ordering of life course events are more flexible, cohort distinctions may blur very quickly. For example, in a longitudinal study of mostly black, mostly economically disadvantaged, adolescent mothers, Furstenberg and his colleagues (1987) show a broad array of subsequent life courses. Seventeen years after their first birth, some of these mothers were firmly planted in the middle class, and others had a long history of being on public assistance. Likewise ongoing work (Rindfuss, Swicegood, and Rosenfeld 1987), using the High School Class of 1972 data, shows great variability in after high school life courses. These examples illustrate that even where the initial shared experience is great, there is much subsequent intracohort variability. Given heterogeneous experience, especially in adolescence and young adulthood, as an increasing amount of time passes birth cohorts or high school cohorts may represent very weak structural categories—incumbents have little in common that would predispose them to act similarly.

A third reason for the predominance of period effects, rather than cohort ones, stresses that the underlying changes could be structural and long term but the societal adjustment can be sudden and pervasive. For our problem here, the social context within which fertility decisions are made is comprised of norms and values, and structures which reward appropriate behavior. The change in norms and values need not coincide with structural changes. In fact, with respect to the fertility transition (i.e., from natural to controlled fertility), the pace and pattern of change seems more consistent with the diffusion of ideas and values than with change in structural conditions (see Cleland 1985; Coale and Watkins 1986). This notion does not imply that structural conditions are irrelevant. Quite the contrary, they can be the ultimate cause of the change. Structural change alters the underlying conditions of life (see Davis and van den Oever 1982) and the system that rewards appropriate behaviors. Norms and values can restrict new behaviors, but once innovative behavior is adopted by some it can change the landscape for all. Thus, especially in a modern society, many behavioral changes can appear as pervasive period phenomena even though the fundamental change bringing it about was gradual.

These issues are imbedded in several concepts Lieberson (1985) recently discussed: basic versus superficial causes and lags between cause and effect. Basic causes are the initial stimulus for change while superficial causes are the adjustments and readjustments of the component parts of the social system. Lieberson maintains that basic causes are relatively few but superficial causes are numerous and idiosyncratic. For example, consider economic development as a basic cause which represents a largely secular change. This development may slowly alter the underlying conditions of life, but people are typically slow to evaluate these changed conditions. Given such a scenario, the time gradually becomes ripe for a sudden change in the timing of parenthood. The most proximate cause, the spark, may be ideological because it makes previously unthinkable options acceptable.

Despite the extreme difficulty of linking long-term structural change to period change, several structural changes have occurred that are likely to have at least set the stage for trends in age at first birth. Perhaps the most obvious, and important, is the major change in women's roles, particularly in the workplace. For legal, economic, and social reasons, women's labor force participation has become easier, more necessary, and recently more rewarding. Although change has often been slow, formal and informal barriers to women's employment have been disappearing. In some cases, this situation has been aided by affirmative action programs. In contrast to being a homemaker, a woman's working post-pones the onset of parenthood (see chap. 8). Furthermore, the anticipation of work's being an important component in one's life implies the need for increased schooling, which also implies a postponement of childbearing.

Concomitant with the increase in female labor force participation has been change in its lifetime profile. At the turn of the century, the female labor force consisted primarily of young unmarried girls and older widows. Time out of the labor force to marry, bear, and rear children was a typical life cycle stage. The duration of this life cycle stage has been shrinking to the point where, for many women, it has all but disappeared. Maternity leaves are often very short.

In addition to this change in women's roles, the occupational structure of most Western societies has changed dramatically since the turn of the century. There has been a massive movement out of farming and manu-facturing into service and professional occupations. This move has been the case for men and women, although it has been most visible for men. The occupational transformation of the American economy has increased the educational demands on young individuals entering the labor force. Even within occupations, educational requirements have been increasing. Perhaps this phenomenon is nowhere more evident than in the case of the college-educated farmer.

Together this set of changes could be expected to produce a steady increase in age at first birth, but such a steady change has not occurred in twentieth-century America. Rather, a sharp increase occurred during the 1930s and 1970s, and an actual decrease in age at parenthood occurred during the 1940s and 1950s. These fluctuations argue against simply assigning all the movement to long-term secular trends. Our results suggest that the particular circumstances in which young nonparents find themselves have strong effects on whether they become parents in the near future (chap. 8). Ryder (1973b) has argued that young adults are urged to become parents as soon as they can afford to do so. Our results lend support to this argument. Unemployment (for males) and education postpone the transition to parenthood, as does female labor force partic-ipation. Thus, any period factors that increase male unemployment or the need for female employment will lead to increases in age at first birth.

Viewed in this light, the 1940s and 1950s were a time when a large number of period factors tended to reduce age at parenthood. The war itself probably encouraged some young men and women to try for a conception before it was "too late." After the war, there were numerous GI benefits that encouraged male employment opportunities, allowed young men simultaneously to be in school and start a family, and allowed couples to purchase affordable housing. The sustained postwar prosperity continued the early entry into parenthood during the 1950s.

Conversely, events during the 1930s and the late 1960s and 1970s tended to raise age at first birth over and above that which might have occurred if the long-term structural changes alone were operating. The 1930s saw high levels of unemployment for men of all ages. The late 1960s and early 1970s also had relatively high levels of unemployment, especially concentrated at the young adult ages. Wages decreased in the 1930s; in the 1970s wages increased, but housing prices tended to increase at an even faster rate. Thus, while conditions were quite different in the two periods, in both cases there were factors that made it difficult to start a family given the prevailing expectations for what was necessary to be able to start responsible childbearing.

The argument that the period circumstances facing young nonparents are important, indeed critical, to their parenthood decisions is further supported by the racial divergence in trends during the late 1960s and the 1970s (chap. 6). In general, this was a period when many young persons felt they could not afford to start a family. Unemployment rates among the young were increasing. Housing prices were increasing. The job skills required for entry-level jobs were increasing, thus placing a premium on increased education or "apprentice" type training and the large birth cohorts from the post–World War II era were entering the labor force. However, the various social policies aimed at ameliorating racial discrimination had some impact, especially for those better educated blacks who were positioned to take advantage of increased opportunities. Thus, while white first-birth ages were increasing, black first-birth ages were decreasing.

In short, the evidence suggests that period changes in the timing of the transition to parenthood are a function of long-term secular changes and short-term fluctuations in factors that make it easier or more difficult for young nonparents to be able to afford to start a family, recognizing that the definition of *affordability* changes through time and varies across groups. This, in turn, makes prediction of future trends difficult at best—a topic to which we return at the end of the chapter.

Many of our explanations for the underlying causes of period change in the timing of the transition to parenthood have involved economic-based reasons. This situation is partly because the prevailing normative proscription in the United States is that individuals ought to become parents as soon as they can afford to do so. But the use of economic explanations also reflects that economic conditions can be quantified and reasonable time-series data exist (e.g., see chap. 4). Nevertheless, we do not mean to imply that noneconomic factors have not been important. The development of modern contraceptive methods, changing views of the woman's role in society, and increasing rates of marital disruption are factors often mentioned.

We do not emphasize improvements in contraceptive techniques because earlier cohorts achieved late ages at childbearing with less effective methods. This historical precedent demonstrates that modern contraception is not necessary for fertility delay. Neither is it a sufficient condition, since couples must be motivated to control fertility. However, one cannot completely discount the role of improved contraception. Modern, coitus-independent methods have reduced the inconvenience and cost of fertility regulation. Thus, less motivation may be required to achieve low and late fertility. Indeed this is central to arguments Bumpass (1973) has proposed for continued low fertility in the United States.

The feminist movement has been among the most publicized changes of the past decade and, some claim, is a major cause of later childbearing and greater childlessness. According to this view, the greater justification for nonfamilial roles makes fertility delay and childlessness a more attractive option. Undoubtedly, these changes have had some effect; however, the relation between a woman's familial and nonfamilial roles is more complex than is often acknowledged. Davis and van den Oever (1982), for instance, claim that crucial demographic changes, including lower fertility and higher rates of marital disruption, have been the cause of changing sex roles. As a woman spends less time in the roles of wife and mother, she can invest more time and energy in nonfamilial roles. Thus, the feminist movement might be seen as an ideological affirmation of the acceptability of these nonfamilial roles.

The research reported in this book cannot distinguish which was cause and which was effect. And it is also likely that fertility changes and the broader nonfamilial changes interact with one another in a feedback system. This view suggests, then, that expanding roles for women in society and the concurrent feminist movement are, in fact, the result of economic and demographic change, with the trend to later childbearing and greater childlessness among women today being a case in point.

However, the importance of these changes on future trends needs to be emphasized. As feminist ideology becomes more firmly established, delayed childbearing and childlessness may be seen as viable preferred life course strategies by greater numbers of American women.

Finally, the greater frequency of marital disruption offers another potential explanation for the changes in childbearing patterns. This argument suggests that marital disruption reduces the proportion of the population at risk of conception. Also, the prevalence of divorce may serve to inhibit early childbearing, with couples choosing to delay parenthood to gain greater marital stability. It is interesting though that delayed childbearing within marriage has been seen to increase marital disruption (Morgan and Rindfuss 1985). As with changing sex roles, lessening normative disapproval of separation and divorce may influence future fertility by changing the context within which fertility decisions are made.

STRUCTURAL FACTORS AND INTRACOHORT VARIABILITY

Not only are there substantial cohort differences in age at parenthood but also there is considerable within-cohort variation. The comparison with Japan (chap. 7) shows far greater intracohort variance in first-birth timing in the United States than in Japan. This cross-national difference argues for the importance of cultural context to the process. The West's heritage stresses that the conjugal relationship should be postponed until the man and woman are in a position to support themselves. Thus, the independence of the conjugal pair was emphasized.[1] Consent of the couple has long been a basic tenet of Western marriage. This heritage is consistent with the characterization of the twentieth-century normative context that a couple should marry and have two children as soon as they can afford them. Thus, flexibility in the timing of family formation has such a long history in the West that it is indeed part of the common wisdom or folklore.

Historically, most Asian societies have been characterized by early and

---

[1]This notion is not meant to deny the role of extended family living or the inheritability of the family farm or trade. But even here the inheritance system of primogeniture insured intracohort variability because all but the oldest son needed to find other means of support—often through a very time-consuming apprenticeship. Further, the oldest son was sometimes encouraged to postpone marriage until the older generation was willing to relinquish control of the family farm or business.

nearly universal marriage. Industrialization, modernization, and age at marriage and parenthood have increased, but the normative pressure to marry and have children is still extremely strong. Variation in age at parenthood has remained small despite an increase in the mean of the distribution. Further, parenthood remains nearly universal (Rindfuss et al. 1983). Thus, responses of American and Japanese cohorts to the exigencies of modernization have been dissimilar (see chap. 7). Or as Hogan et al. (1985:17) report, "comparison of American and Japanese data on the demographic life course suggests that the responses of American cohorts to modernization and increased affluence were culturally based, and not simply an inevitable response to the forces of social history." Clearly, in the American context, a great deal of intracohort flexibility is permissible, and this is likely to be the situation for the foreseeable future.

Our study also examines how variation in parenthood timing is patterned by social-structural characteristics. Substantively, these structural characteristics have a far greater influence on *when* people have children than on *whether* they have them. Unlike our findings for aggregate time, if members of a given regional, religious, racial, or socioeconomic background have higher birth probabilities at young ages, then these tend to be matched by lower ones at older ages. In short, there is intracohort adjustment that results in most individuals becoming parents. Note that this pattern requires rather complex, time-dependent models and methods. For example, it is inappropriate to ask about *the* effect of religion; rather one has to ask about the effect of religion at age x for individuals who are not yet parents.

This complexity, of course, is consistent with the theoretical and empirical developments in the sociology of fertility. Early work in this area tended to examine the relationship between fixed socioeconomic characteristics and children ever born. Since then, it has been persuasively argued that certain factors operate differently at different parities. Our results show that the effects of important variables vary within parities as well—at least for the transition to the first birth.

These findings also fit well with the broader life course framework being developed in sociology. This perspective emphasizes that the resources a person brings to a situation (economic, social, and emotional) will influence one's behavior. Background (or structural) variables attempt to measure broad differences in these personal resources. Individuals also accumulate experiences and resources as they age. To capture this process fully, detailed longitudinal data are necessary.

Another connection of our work with the life course framework concerns how the process of becoming a parent is intertwined with the unfolding life course. Previous work on childlessness strongly suggests that childlessness is not an outcome of firm decisions made at a young age. Of those reporting an intent to remain childless in the High School Class of 1972 data, three-quarters changed their minds over the following six-year period (see chap. 9). Clearly, childlessness results from a series of decisions to postpone childbearing or the reaffirmation of earlier decisions about childlessness in some fewer cases. These decisions to postpone childbearing allow individuals and couples to invest in other activities and experience a childless life-style. These other activities and experiences, in turn, begin to exert an independent and unanticipated effect. Chapter 9 shows that individuals and couples adjust their childbearing timetable to fit with other considerations, such as career and leisure pursuits.

Actual activity states and their sequence are also critical to the timing of parenthood (chap. 8). Background factors operate through these activity states. They have an effect on the current activity state (whether an individual is in school, working, military, etc.) as well as a direct effect on the timing of parenthood. The life course perspective focuses attention on both kinds of effects. Our analysis of activity state effects made the simplifying assumption that only the most recent activity state need be considered. This strategy assumes that the process forgets its past, a Markovian-type assumption. The next logical step in this line of research is currently under way. It involves determining how much of this history and which parts of it have effects on the transition to parenthood. Work completed so far suggests that the Markovian-type assumption used in chapter 8 should be relaxed. While this work is still too preliminary for us to reach firm conclusions, the process governing the transition to parenthood appears more complex than assumed in this study. In short, prior activity states, not just the current one, influence the transition to parenthood.

One final point involves the interplay between the pattern of effects at the macro- and microlevels. Our results make it clear that there is no necessary relationship between the effect of some variable or constellation of variables at the microlevel and the effect of that same variable at the macrolevel. For example, at the microlevel, any measure we have of wealth or human capital (i.e., education) yields the same strong set of results: the more of it the individual has, the later that individual becomes a parent. At the macrolevel the effect of conceptually similar sets of variables is the opposite: the greater the level of prosperity in any given time period, the younger the age at parenthood. Further, this macroeffect is found to operate on individuals of all socioeconomic levels.

THE QUESTION OF PREDICTION

Our purpose in this book has been to understand the social-demographic foundations governing the process of the transition to parenthood. While we were doing the research, the question we were most often asked was: What will the future trends be? Indeed, there is an almost universal fascination with the future, whether it be the economy, weather, political events, or the timing of childbearing.

Those who desire a simple and straightforward prediction from us will be disappointed and perhaps frustrated. But, more than any other result, our research unequivocally argues against any single, simplistic prediction for the future course of age at the beginning of parenthood. First, the social process governing the transition to parenthood is complex. Indeed, as better data sets become available, we are likely to discover that the structure of the determinants is more complex than our results have indicated. Second, the pattern of changes we have documented in the twentieth century has been the result of period rather than cohort changes. By their very nature, period changes are inherently more unpredictable than cohort changes. Third, the changes that have occurred appear to be the combination of long-run secular changes and more short-term factors. Finally, when period changes have occurred, the better educated have responded slightly more sharply than those with less education (see chaps. 5 and 6). Thus, as the aggregate level of educational attainment continues to increase, the response to period events should also increase. For these reasons, the course of future trends in parenthood timing will be determined by the nature and direction of future social change. Hence, any prediction of trends in parenthood timing inherently contains predictions, implicitly or explicitly, about the broad spectrum of social change.

In a recent paper, Giddens (1985) argued that the direction of future social change was indeterminate. Such a noncommittal stance should not be taken as indicating that there has been no sociological progress in understanding social change but rather that a greater knowledge and appreciation of its complexity has led to a more cautious position. Past predictions often were based on simple, mechanistic notions of secular change and single causes.

A closely related flaw of sociological work of the past couple of decades is the assumption that current trends will persist (Giddens 1985). Our results clearly show that over the past 60 years trends in parenthood timing have fluctuated substantially rather than responding to a single powerful secular trend. Rather, there are long-term secular trends and shorter-term period factors. The change in female roles would be an example of the former, and World War II an example of the latter. Yet, despite the presences of short- and long-term factors, some predict continued and even greater fertility delay and childlessness based primarily on recent trends toward later parenthood, and what they see as the secular erosion of social support for the parenthood role.

Even though we run the risk of being dismissed as being entirely too wishy-washy, our results and our reading of possible future social change suggests that although the short-term indicators imply continued delayed childbearing, it is far too early to discard the possibility of a downward shift in parenthood-timing schedules. We discuss some alternative scenarios below, but our general guiding principle is that the timing of the transition to parenthood in the United States is affected by *anything* that influences the perception of young men and women of their ability to set up a household and take care of a child.

In chapter 2 and elsewhere we acknowledge that the imperative to marry and have children might have weakened. There has been a long-term shift toward viewing childbearing as an increasingly private act, one that does not have repercussions for broader society. Goode (1963) describes this change as a move toward the conjugal family's including greater freedom and independence for individuals. Carlson (1986) sees the unmarried, cohabiting couple as the ultimate form of this conjugal relationship, resting entirely on affective bonds. Yet the factors that have led to delayed and foregone parenthood may be balanced by pronatalist forces from a variety of sources. Concerns about the economic implications of low fertility may force society to reassess its view of parenthood. Also, the greater flexibility of adult roles has left a wake of introspection, soul searching, and role confusion that may be a source of renewed parenthood values (see Preston 1985). There may be a return to more traditional values as endorsed in *Habits of the Heart* (Bellah et al. 1985) or *The War Over the Family* (Berger and Berger 1983). As Preston (1986) points out, such endorsements may themselves be "an important social datum, perhaps the harbinger of a new social construction of parenthood and marriage."

Further, the influence of various exogenous changes on the family can be strongly influenced by governmental actions—the products of the perpetual struggles among interest groups. Such outcomes are typically uncertain. Michael Harrington,[2] also stressing the indeterminacy of social change, uses as an example the computer/communication revolution that may release many from the workplace, allowing for much more flexible work hours. Research in less-developed contexts has shown that women's employment per se does not necessarily raise age at first birth (Mason and Palan 1981). Rather, it is the extent to which the worker role and mother role are incompatible that determines the strength of the relationship between female labor force participation and the timing of parenthood. Perhaps computer technology and modern communication will allow many women and men to work in the home making parenthood and work less incompatible. If this happened, it might be that young individuals who are struggling with the beginning of a career might also be willing simultaneously to struggle with beginning parenthood.

Although there has been debate over the cause-and-effect relationship between the women's movement of the late 1960s and 1970s and the change in age at parenthood during the same time period, few, if any, would argue that the changes in women's roles will be reversed. It is a permanent revolution, still in progress, albeit now proceeding at a slower pace. Throughout the women's movement there has been considerable speculation and fear that childbearing would be abandoned in favor of careers. While this option has been taken by some, and while for many there still exists much conflict between motherhood and employment, the vast majority of contemporary American women now combine work and child rearing.

At present, however, it is unclear how flexible American society will be in coping with the existing conflict. If the answer is inflexible, then we may expect further increases in age at parenthood and in childlessness. But if mechanisms emerge that reduce these role incompatibilities, then a decrease in age at parenthood and in childlessness is likely. Unfortunately, from our study we know nothing about the perceptions of potential parents regarding child care problems—a topic that should be high

[2]In remarks during the Plenary Session on working and not working, 2 September 1985, during the annual meeting of the American Sociological Association in Washington, D.C.

on the future research agenda. Nevertheless, there are numerous signs of a growing institutional flexibility concerning child care. First, corporate America has begun to provide both for-profit day care centers for the public, and in a few instances, subsidized job-site day care for their employees' children. Shift-work and flextime have become popular options (Presser and Cain 1983) for those who have occupations which allow one of the spouses to work other than the "normal" eight-to-five shift. Also, a variety of traditional ad hoc day-care arrangements are expanding, including provision of services by immigrant women.

Thus, as a society, America is rapidly accumulating new experiences with child-care arrangements. While examples of logistical and other problems abound, numerous examples of satisfactory strategies also exist. To the extent the latter begin to outweigh the former, pressure from relatives and peers concerning use of child care facilities might move from negative to positive. Thus, since part of the present delay in childbearing may be related to difficulties in obtaining appropriate child care to allow the combination of worker and mother roles, increasing of child care availability would lead to earlier parenthood schedules.

That children should be cared for primarily by their mother is a recent, Western notion. The ideology and practice of child fostering in Africa provides a contemporary non-Western example (Page 1986). Historically, in the West, children were often sent from the home as apprentices at very young ages. Indeed, adolescence, as we now know it, is a relatively recent phenomena (e.g., Kett 1977).

If ongoing and future studies show that children are not adversely affected by care from nonparents and nonkin, the more acceptable alternative child care will become. Imagine the impact of compelling social science evidence that children mature better or more quickly (both socially and intellectually) if placed in "professional care" earlier.[3] Imagine further that society saw it in its collective interest to provide such care to the public or to give parents substantial tax credits to offset its cost. The principal point here is to show that even a long-term trend, such as women's increasing labor force participation, does not necessarily imply later parenthood. Societal responses could reduce the conflict between

---

[3]A study concluding that elementary school children of mothers working outside the home do better in school than children of women who are full-time homemakers was reported at the 1986 meetings of the American Psychological Association (Guidubaldi et al. 1986). These results were based on a national sample and held net of controls for family income.

work roles and motherhood, and thereby condition the influence of nearly universal female employment.

Closely related to this question of female roles and parenthood is the question of male roles and parenthood. Throughout the 20th century, the standard male role has been worker and provider. But when conditions made it difficult to find gainful employment, men have often left their home and families.[4] This was clearly common during the Depression years (e.g., Elder 1974). Indeed, it led to the initiation of one of the most central components of our present welfare program: Aid to Families with Dependent Children (AFDC). Thus, while female roles have evolved such that both work and parenthood are permissible, indeed encouraged, there has yet to be substantial evolution in male roles. In short, there is a greater variety of acceptable female roles than male roles. For men, there has been no evolution of anything comparable to the housewife role. Undoubtedly, this is why the unemployed male often withdraws from the family.

A logical possibility is a change in male roles involving a deemphasis on work and increased input into home and family. In many cases this change could accompany increased female labor force participation. Indeed, one could imagine that if the wife's career were proceeding well, the husband might decide to devote his energies to familial roles. Or alternatively, an unmarried, successful career woman might look for a "househusband." While such a change is a possibility, its occurrence would certainly be unprecedented in the Western historical context. Even though we are not in a position to argue whether such a revolution in male roles will occur, we can argue that if such a change were to occur it might lead to a younger transition to parenthood by lowering the psychic and perhaps economic costs of that parenthood.

Can we say anything more certain about future trends? First, despite the countervailing possibilities described above, the long-term change in female work roles, increased educational demands for men and women, ever-increasing costs of raising a child, and the high standard-of-living expectations of young Americans suggest continuation of delayed childbearing patterns. But we also expect continued intercohort variability. Changing social and economic conditions will lower or raise birth prob-

---

[4] The contemporary black family situation is particularly likely to be characterized by fathers' absence. The situation is almost certainly related to high levels of black male unemployment.

abilities. This situation is almost guaranteed by the normative injunction that people should have children when they can afford to do so. Thus, a steep rise in the cost of setting up a household will produce a temporary delay in the transition to parenthood. Conversely, a sudden and dramatic rise in the real income of young people should produce a younger age at parenthood. Thus, the prediction for continued delayed childbearing is a short-term one.

One can get more specific by examining how macrochanges might affect the activity states young men and women occupy. Any macro-change that would tend to pull young men and women out of the student role would tend to lower age at parenthood. Similarly, any change that would get men into full-time work and women in part-time work or look-ing for work would lower age at parenthood. The converse, men into part-time work or looking for work and women into full-time work, would tend to raise age at parenthood. Further, changes in activity states for a few may have broader consequences by influencing the context in which parenthood decisions are made. Fear of unemployment is felt by far more people than those who are actually unemployed. Many suspect that they may be next. In fact, this phenomenon is an important linkage between macro- and microfactors as they affect the transition to parent-hood.

In addition to intercohort variability, given our Western cultural heri-tage and the current norms surrounding the transition to parenthood, we feel confident that there will continue to be considerable intracohort variability in parenthood timing. Substantial proportions will bear their first child as a teenager while many women will be in their 30s before becoming mothers. This variability matches the variable life courses of men and women. Failure in school or in jobs leads people to search for happiness through other avenues—parenthood being an important one.[5] Success in school and jobs leads to the postponement of parenthood. Failure and success are endemic to modern social life—and perhaps more so in the American version of capitalism. As the time required for prepara-tion for various career choices increases and as some form of graduate

---

[5]Indeed, as noted in chapter 6, the growth of the so-called underclass among blacks may be why the less-educated black population did not delay their childbearing during the 1970s. Even though government programs provided some support, they were not sufficient to alter a context in which parenthood is seen as one of the few plausible options for establishing adulthood.

education becomes increasingly required, we expect increased intracohort variability in the ages at which men and women first become parents. Moreover, structural variables such as race and socioeconomic background strongly influence the likelihood of success and failure. Thus variability in fertility timing by structural characteristics is not a transitional feature of modern society.

In short, our best prediction is that there will be substantial intracohort and intercohort variability. The direction of intercohort variability will depend on whether it becomes easier or more difficult to set up a new household and on societal changes that affect the perceived cost of children. More concrete predictions will depend on correctly predicting change in other areas. Change in the future, whatever its direction, can be quite sudden since it seems to occur, not by cohort succession, but by pervasive period change. An important goal of future research is to understand better how these pervasive period effects operate.

Appendix A
Effect of Excluding Never-Married Women

As noted in chapter 3, excluding the never-married will have an effect on fertility estimates only if (1) ever- and never-married women do not behave similarly and (2) there are large proportions of the never-married. Examining rows 1 and 2 of table A.1 shows that estimates of delayed childbearing vary considerably by ever/never marital status. At age 25, for instance, fewer than 40 percent are childless among the ever-married, while over 85 percent of the never-married are childless. The first condition then is met: these groups do *not* behave similarly with respect to timing of the first birth. Specifically, the never-married are more likely to be childless.

Row 4 of table A.1 shows the proportion of respondents in each sample who are ever-married. This proportion is highest (94.43) for those childless at age 25 and declines to a low 76.98 percent for the birth probability at age 35–45. For some variables then, the second condition is also met.

Row 3 compared with rows 1 and 2 shows the degree of bias resulting from excluding the never-married. Each dichotomous variable is affected considerably—eliminating the never-married lowers the proportion childless at age 25 and increases the birth probabilities at ages 25–30, 30–35, and 35–45. However, these variables may accurately reflect a trend if the bias introduced by excluding the never-married is the same for all cohorts. We will now determine if estimates of this trend are similar for an all-women and ever-married sample.

Figure A.1 shows, by birth cohort, the proportion childless at age 25 for samples of all women and ever-married women. Note that trends are similar but childlessness is higher for the all-women sample. This reflects the childlessness of most of the never-married.

TABLE A.1.
ESTIMATES OF PARENTHOOD TIMING FOR EVER-MARRIED AND
NEVER-MARRIED SAMPLES

	Childless at age 25	Birth probabilities		
		25–30	30–35	35–45
Ever-married estimate	36.39	50.59	32.72	21.87
Never-married estimate	86.53	3.21	1.62	.81
All-women estimate	39.20	44.75	26.75	17.02
Percent ever-married	94.43	87.68	80.81	76.98
Ages included	30–69	30–69	35–69	45–69

Figure A.2 shows, by cohort, birth probabilities at ages 25–30. Note the clear mean shift because of the exclusion of the never-married (who are approximately 30 times more likely to remain childless). However, the trends are very similar whether estimated from an all-women or ever-married sample.

There is also a tendency for the difference between the two estimates to be greater among the more recent cohorts. This trend could indicate either the joint delay of marriage and parenthood that the ever-married sample excludes or an earlier age at marriage bias (see chap. 3) in the more recent cohorts.

Figures A.3 and A.4 show five-year moving averages of birth probabilities at ages 30–35 and 35–45, respectively. Again observable trends are quite similar. But the difference between the two estimates is larger for more recent cohorts. Because of an older age-at-marriage cutoff (ages 35 and 45, respectively), the young age at marriage bias discussed earlier cannot account for the observed increases in the differences. Instead, it represents an increasing proportion of never-married in these samples.

In summary, the levels of the four indicators of fertility timing are affected by the exclusion of the never-married. Specifically, because the never-married are much more likely to be childless, their exclusion from the sample reduces estimates of the proportion childless. However, cohort trends in the proportion childless or in birth probabilities are similar in both samples. In short, estimates of the *levels* of these variables are underestimated but general *trends* can be estimated from an ever-married sample.

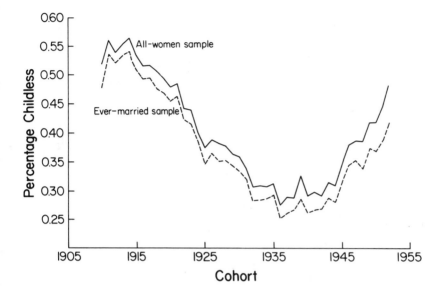

Fig. A.1. Percentage childless at age 25 by cohort for all-women and
ever-married samples—1980 Current Population Survey.

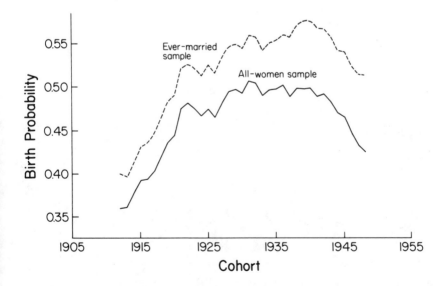

Fig. A.2. First birth probability at ages 25–30 by cohort for all-women and
ever-married samples—1980 Current Population Survey.

TABLE A.2.

EFFECTS OF EDUCATION, RACE, AND COHORT ON LIKELIHOOD OF BEING CHILDLESS AT AGE 25 IN AN ALL-WOMEN, EVER-MARRIED, AND NEVER-MARRIED SAMPLE (WOMEN OVER 30 FROM THE 1980 CPS)[a]

Independent variables	All-women sample		Ever-married sample		Never-married sample	
	Beta	SE	Beta	SE	Beta	SE
Education	-0.283*	.032	-0.247*	.034	-0.321*	.089
Education^2	0.012*	.0014	0.019*	.0015	0.026*	.005
Race	-0.059	.071	-0.014	.076	-2.595*	.173
Cohort						
1946–1950	-1.172*	.091	-1.244*	.095	-1.982*	.412
1941–1945	-1.401*	.092	-1.468*	.096	-1.405*	.425
1936–1940	-1.431*	.095	-1.453*	.098	-1.165*	.446
1931–1935	-1.286*	.096	-1.316*	.100	-1.202*	.454
1926–1930	-0.946*	.092	-0.973*	.095	-0.436	.482
1921–1925	-0.667*	.090	-0.637*	.093	-0.577	.480
1916–1920	-0.420*	.092	-0.418*	.095	.280	.554
Intercept	.907		.574		4.29	
Model χ^2 (d.f.)	855.50	(10)	813.91	(10)	501.44	(10)
N[b] (N childless)	9249	(3615)	8766	(3191)	1971	(1729)

*Significant at .05 level.
aStandard error.
bThe all-women and ever-married samples are 25 percent samples from the 1980 CPS. The never-married samples include 100 percent of the never-married women from the 1980 CPS.

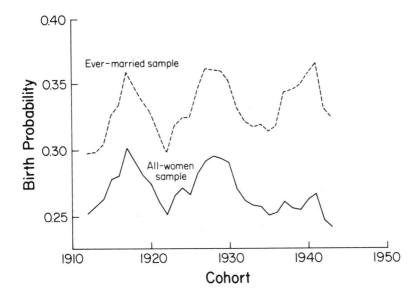

Fig. A.3. First birth probability at ages 30–35 by cohort for all-women and
ever-married samples—1980 Current Population Survey.

Within a multivariate framework, we now ask if potential determinants
of delayed childbearing have similar effects in an all-women sample and
an ever-married sample. Such an analysis allows us to assess the bias
introduced by excluding the never-married. Unfortunately, the CPS data
contain only three likely determinants of delayed childbearing: birth
cohort, education, and race. Consequently, we cannot determine if the
estimated effects of other factors are influenced by use of an ever-married
sample.

Table A.2 shows the effects of education in years (0–17 +), education
squared, race (1 = nonwhite; 0 = otherwise), and cohort on the likelihood of being a parent by age 25. The all-women and ever-married
samples produce very similar results. The never-married results, however,
are different, most notably with respect to race. The differences suggest
that blacks are more likely to become parents while never-married and
less likely to marry once they are never-married parents. Substantively,
these are both interesting points that we intend to pursue in future
research. However, with respect to the task at hand, that the all-women
and ever-married samples produce similar results suggests that no bias is
being introduced by using the ever-married fertility study samples.

TABLE A.3.
Effects of Education, Race, and Cohort on Likelihood of First Birth at Ages 25–30, 30–35, and 35–45 in an All-Women, Ever-Married, and Never-Married Sample

Independent variables	Dependent variables								
	Birth probability 25–30			Birth probability 30–35			Birth probability 35–45		
	All-women	Ever-married	Never-married	All-women	Ever-married	Never-married	All-women	Ever-married	Never-married
Education	.164*	.106*	.462*	.045	-.001	-.203	.023	-.040	-.104
(SE)[a]	(.034)	(.037)	(.185)	(.035)	(.039)	(.148)	(.051)	(.056)	(.266)
Education^2	-.006*	-.004*	-.032*	-.00002	.0027	.002	-.0005	.003	-.0007
(SE)	(.001)	(.002)	(.010)	(.002)	(.0017)	(.009)	(.002)	(.003)	(.015)
Race	-.423*	-.516*	2.262*	-.240*	-.365*	2.227*	-.032	-.222	2.950*
(SE)	(.078)	(.084)	(.308)	(.089)	(.094)	(.465)	(.129)	(.135)	(.869)
Cohort									
1946–1950	.218*	.365*	2.611*	—	—	—	—	—	—
(SE)	(.093)	(.098)	(1.060)						
1941–1945	.436*	.547*	1.464	-.155	-.007	.224	—	—	—
(SE)	(.097)	(.102)	(1.122)	(.112)	(.119)	(.950)			
1936–1940	.598*	.724*	2.404*	-.039	.115	.439	—	—	—
(SE)	(.101)	(.108)	(1.080)	(.108)	(.154)	(.952)			
1931–1935	.469*	.525*	2.311*	-.001	.071	.708	-.170	-.109	1.141
(SE)	(.101)	(.106)	(1.106)	(.107)	(.112)	(.950)	(.148)	(.154)	(1.267)

1926–1930	.500*	.537*	2.310	.175	.266*	1.225	-.078	0.31	.222
(SE)	(.094)	(.099)	(1.079)	(.097)	(.102)	(.873)	(.135)	(.141)	(1.452)
1921–1925	.470*	.495*	1.142	.032	.086	.187	.029	.099	-.609
(SE)	(.091)	(.095)	(1.178)	(.094)	(.099)	(1.027)	(.126)	(.130)	(22.32)
1916–1920	.230*	.233*	-.073	.177	.230*	.140	-.162	-.126	.832
(SE)	(.091)	(.094)	(1.431)	(.089)	(.093)	(.956)	(.126)	(.129)	(1.198)
Intercept	-1.506	-1.030	-6.692	-1.543	-1.186	-3.397	-1.703	-1.233	-5.103
Model χ²	126.30	130.52	111.63	48.25	77.78	59.92	4.44	13.32	21.36
(d.f.)	(10)	(10)	(10)	(9)	(9)	(9)	(7)	(7)	(7)
N	7197	6352	1729	6552	5308	1298	3754	2890	864
N childless	3971	3152	1677	4792	3568	1277	3115	2258	857

^aStandard error.

aStandard error.

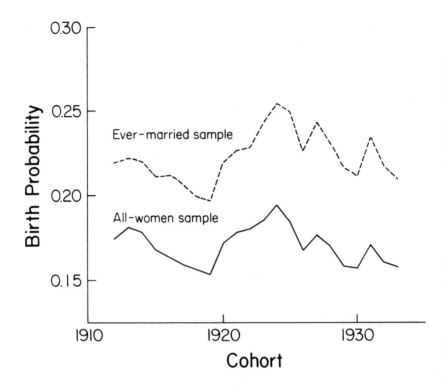

Fig. A.4. First birth probability at ages 35–45 for all-women and ever-married
samples—1980 Current Population Survey.

Table A.3 shows the effects of education, race, and cohort on the
likelihood of a first birth at ages 25–30, 30–35, and 35–45. Only those
childless at ages 25, 30, and 35, respectively, are included. The results
contrasting the all-women and ever-married samples are reasonably similar, giving us confidence in the results from chapter 5. Also, again, the
never-married results tend to differ from the other two suggesting interesting substantive work that needs to be pursued in the future.

Bibliography

Aird, John S. 1985. "Coercion in Family Planning: Causes, Methods, and Consequences." *Congressional Record* 131(75):S7776–7788.

Ajzen, Icek, and Martin Fishbein. 1977. "Attitude-Behavior Relations: A Theoretical Analysis and Review of Empirical Research." *Psychological Bulletin* 84:888–918.

Allison, Paul D. 1982. "Discrete-Time Methods for the Analysis of Event Histories." In *Sociological Methodology 1982*, edited by Samuel Leinhardt, 61–97. San Francisco: Jossey-Bass.

Anderson, Barbara A. 1975. "Male Age and Fertility: Results from Ireland Prior to 1911." *Population Index* 41:561–567.

Aral, Sevgi O., and Willard Cates, Jr. 1983. "The Increasing Concern with Infertility: Why Now?" *Journal of the American Medical Association* 250(17):2327–2331.

Baltes, Paul B., and Orville Gilbert Brim, Jr. 1979. *Life Span Development and Behavior*. Vol. 2. New York: Academic Press.

———. 1980. *Life Span Development and Behavior*. Vol. 3. New York: Academic Press.

———. 1982. *Life Span Development and Behavior*. Vol. 4. New York: Academic Press.

Banister, Judith. 1984. "Population Policy and Trends in China, 1978–1983." *The China Quarterly* (100):717–741.

Barnett, Larry D., and Richard H. MacDonald. 1976. "A Study of the Membership of the National Organization for Non-Parents." *Social Biology* 23:297–310.

Baum, Frances, and David R. Cope. 1980. "Some Characteristics of Intentionally Childless Wives in Britain." *Journal of Biosocial Science* 12:287–299.

Bean, Frank D., and John P. Marcum. 1978. "Differential Fertility and the Minority Group Status Hypothesis: An Assessment and Review." In *The Demography of Racial and Ethnic Groups*, edited by Frank D. Bean and William Parker Frisbie, 189–211. New York: Academic Press.

Bean, Frank D., and Gray Swicegood. 1985. *Mexican American Fertility Patterns*. Mexican American Monographs no. 10. Austin: University of Texas Press.

Becker, Gary S. 1960. "An Economic Analysis of Fertility: Demographic and Economic Change in Developed Countries." Universities-National Bureau Conference Series no. 11. New York: National Bureau of Economic Research.

Bellah, Robert N., Richard Madsen, William M. Sullivan, Ann Swidler, and Steven M. Tipton. 1985. *Habits of the Heart: Individualism and Commitment in American Life*. Berkeley, Los Angeles, London: University of California Press.

Berger, Brigitte, and Peter L. Berger. 1983. *The War Over the Family: Capturing the Middle Ground*. Garden City, N.Y.: Anchor Press/Doubleday.

Berkson, J. 1953. "A Statistically Precise and Relatively Simple Method of Estimating Bioassay with Quantal Response Based on the Logistic Function." *Journal of the American Statistical Association* 48:565–599.

Blake, Judith. 1972. "Coercive Pronatalism and American Population Policy." In *Aspects of Population Growth Policy*, edited by Robert Parke and Charles F. Westoff, 81–109. Vol. 6 of *The Commission on Population Growth and the American Future Research Reports*. Washington D.C.: U.S. Government Printing Office.

———. 1979. "Is Zero Preferred? American Attitudes Toward Childlessness in the 1970s." *Journal of Marriage and the Family* 41:245–257.

Blake, Judith, and Kingsley Davis. 1964. "Norms, Values and Sanctions." In *Handbook of Modern Sociology*, edited by Robert E. L. Faris, 456–484. Chicago: Rand McNally.

Blau, Peter M., and Otis Dudley Duncan with Andrea Tyree. 1967. *The American Occupational Structure*. New York: Wiley.

Blood, Robert O., Jr. 1967. *Love Match and Arranged Marriage. A Tokyo-Detroit Comparison*. New York: Free Press.

Bloom, David E. 1980. "Age Patterns of Women at First Birth; Essays in Labor Economics and Demography." Ph.D. dissertation, Princeton University.

———. 1982. "What's Happening to the Age at First Birth in the United

States? A Study of Recent Cohorts." *Demography* 19:351–370.

———. 1984. "Delayed Childbearing in the United States." *Population Research and Policy Review* 3:103–139.

Bloom, David E., and James Trussell. 1984. "What Are the Determinants of Delayed Childbearing and Permanent Childlessness in the United States?" *Demography* 21:591–611.

Bongaarts, John. 1975. "Why High Birth Rates Are So Low." *Population and Development Review* 1:289–296.

———. 1982. "Infertility After Age 30: A False Alarm." *Family Planning Perspectives* 14:75–78.

Bongaarts, John, and Robert G. Potter. 1983. *Fertility, Biology, and Behavior: An Analysis of the Proximate Determinants.* New York: Academic Press.

Brim, Orville Gilbert, Jr., and Jerome Kagan. 1980. *Constancy and Change in Human Development.* Cambridge, Mass.: Harvard University Press.

Bronfenbrenner, Urie. 1979. *The Ecology of Human Development.* Cambridge, Mass.: Harvard University Press.

———. 1985. "Interacting Systems in Human Development: Research Paradigm: Present and Future." Working paper prepared for the SRCD Study Group on Interacting Systems in Human Development conducted at Cornell University, Ithaca, N.Y., 15–17 May. Revised 1 October 1985.

Buck, Carol, and Kathleen Stavraky. 1967. "The Relationship between Age at Menarche and Age at Marriage among Childbearing Women." *Human Biology* 39:93–102.

Bullough, Vern L. 1981. "Age at Menarche: A Misunderstanding." *Science* 213(4505):365–366.

Bumpass, Larry L. 1973. "Is Low Fertility Here to Stay?" *Family Planning Perspectives* 5:67–69.

———. 1979. "The Changing Linkage of Nuptiality and Fertility in the United States." CDE Working Paper no. 79–6. Madison: Center for Demography and Ecology, University of Wisconsin-Madison.

Bumpass, Larry L., Ronald R. Rindfuss, and Richard B. Janosik. 1978. "Age and Marital Status at First Birth and the Pace of Subsequent Fertility." *Demography* 15:75–86.

Burstein, Paul. 1979. "Equal Employment Opportunity Legislation and the Income of Women and Nonwhites." *American Sociological Review* 44:367–391.

Butz, William P., and Michael P. Ward. 1977. "The Emergence of Countercyclical U.S. Fertility." Rand Report R–1605–NIH. Santa Monica, Calif.: Rand Corporation.

———. 1979. "Will U.S. Fertility Remain Low? A New Economic Interpretation." *Population and Development Review* 4:663–688.

Cain, Mead T. 1977. "The Economic Activities of Children in a Village in Bangladesh." *Population and Development Review* 3:201–227.

———. 1985. "On the Relationship between Landholding and Fertility." *Population Studies* 39:5–15.

Caldwell, John Charles. 1982. *Theory of Fertility Decline.* New York: Academic Press.

Caldwell, John Charles, P. H. Reddy, and Pat Caldwell. 1983. "The Causes of Marriage Change in South India." *Population Studies* 37: 343–361.

Campbell, Arthur A. 1968. "The Role of Family Planning in the Reduction of Poverty." *Journal of Marriage and the Family* 30:236–245.

———. 1974. "Beyond the Demographic Transition." *Demography* 11:549–561.

———. 1980. "Trends in Teenage Childbearing in the United States." In *Adolescent Pregnancy and Childbearing: Findings from Research,* edited by Catherine S. Chilman, 3–13. NIH Publication no. 81–2077. Washington, D.C.: U.S. National Institutes of Health.

Carlson, Elwood D. 1979. "Divorce Rate Fluctuation as a Cohort Phenomenon." *Population Studies* 33:523–536.

———. 1986. "Couples without Children: Premarital Cohabitation in France." In *Contemporary Marriage: Comparative Perspectives on a Changing Institution,* edited by Kingsley Davis with Amyra Grossbard Schechtman, 113–130. New York: Russell Sage Foundation.

Cates, Willard, Jr. 1984. "Sexually Transmitted Organisms and Infertility: The Proof of the Pudding." *Sexually Transmitted Diseases* 11: 113–116.

Chamratrithirong, Aphichat, S. Philip Morgan, and Ronald R. Rindfuss. 1988. "Living Arrangements and Family Formation in Thailand." *Social Forces.*

Cherlin, Andrew J. 1981. *Marriage, Divorce, Remarriage.* Social Trends in the United States. Cambridge, Mass.: Harvard University Press.

Chilman, Catherine S. 1983. *Adolescent Sexuality in a Changing American Society: Social and Psychological Perspectives for the Human Services Professions.* 2d ed. Wiley Series on Personality Processes. New York: Wiley.

Chowdhury, A. K. M. Alauddin, and Lincoln C. Chen. 1977. "The Interaction of Nutrition, Infection, and Mortality during Recent Food Crises in Bangladesh." *Food Research Institute Studies* 16(2):47–61.

Christopher, Robert C. 1983. "Changing Face of Japan." *New York Times Magazine* (27 Mar.):40–41 +.

Chudacoff, Howard P. 1980. "The Life Course of Women: Age and Age Consciousness, 1865–1915." *Journal of Family History* 5:274–292.

Clausen, John A. 1972. "The Life Course of Individuals." In *Aging and Society*. Vol. 3. *A Sociology of Age Stratification*, edited by Matilda White Riley, Marilyn Johnson, and Anne Foner, 457–514. New York: Russell Sage Foundation.

Cleland, John G. 1985. "Marital Fertility Decline in Developing Countries: Theories and the Evidence." In *Reproductive Change in Developing Countries: Insights from the World Fertility Survey*, edited by John G. Cleland and John Hobcraft in collaboration with Betzy Dinesen, 223–252. London: Oxford University Press.

Coale, Ansley J. 1971. "Age Patterns of Marriage." *Population Studies* 25:193–214.

———. 1984. *Rapid Population Change in China, 1952–1982.* Committee on Population and Demography, Report no. 27. Washington, D.C.: National Academy Press.

Coale, Ansley J., and Donald McNeil. 1972. "The Distribution by Age at First Marriage in a Female Cohort." *Journal of the American Statistical Association* 67:743–749.

Coale, Ansley J., and Susan Cotts Watkins (eds.). 1986. *The Decline of Fertility in Europe.* Princeton, N.J.: Princeton University Press.

Coale, Ansley J., and Melvin Zelnik. 1963. *New Estimates of Fertility and Population in the United States: A Study of Annual White Births from 1855 to 1960 and of Completeness of Enumeration from 1880 to 1960.* Princeton, N.J.: Princeton University Press.

Coleman, Samuel J. 1980. "Marriage and Childbirth Patterns in Present-day Japanese Society." Carolina Population Center Papers no. 12. Chapel Hill: Carolina Population Center, The University of North Carolina at Chapel Hill.

———. 1983. *Family Planning in Japanese Society: Traditional Birth Control in a Modern Urban Culture.* N.J.: Princeton University Press.

Comaroff, J. L., and S. Roberts. 1977. "Marriage and Extra-Marital Sexuality: The Dialectics of Legal Change among the Kgatla." *Journal of African Law* 21(1):97–123.

Cornell, Laurel L. 1984. "Why Are There No Spinsters in Japan?" *Journal of Family History* 9:326–339.

Crimmins-Gardner, Eileen, and Phyllis A. Ewer. 1978. "Relative Status and Fertility." In *Research in Population Economics. An Annual Compilation of Research*, Vol. 1, edited by Julian L. Simon, 247–259. Greenwich, Conn.: Jai Press.

Cutright, Phillips, and Karen Polonko. 1977. "Areal Structure and Rates of Childlessness among American Wives in 1970." *Social Biology* 24: 52–61.

Cutright, Phillips, and Herbert L. Smith. 1986. "Trends in Illegitimacy among Five English-Speaking Populations: 1940–1980." *Demography* 23:563–605.

Davidson, Andrew R., and Lee Roy Beach. 1981. "Error Patterns in the Prediction of Fertility Behavior." *Journal of Applied Social Psychology* 11:475–488.

Davidson, Andrew R., and James J. Jaccard. 1979. "Variables that Moderate the Attitude-Behavior Relation: Results from a Longitudinal Survey." *Journal of Personality and Social Psychology* 37:1364–1376.

Davis, James A. 1982. "Achievement Variables and Class Cultures: Family, Schooling, Job, and Forty-Nine Dependent Variables in the Cumulative GSS." *American Sociological Review* 47:569–586.

Davis, Kingsley. 1955. "Institutional Patterns Favoring High Fertility in Undeveloped Areas." *Eugenics Quarterly* 2:33–39.

———. 1972. "The American Family in Relation to Demographic Change." In *Demographic and Social Aspects of Population Growth*, edited by Charles F. Westoff and Robert Parke, Jr., 235–265. Vol. 1 of *The Commission on Population Growth and the American Future Research Reports*. Washington, D.C.: U.S. Government Printing Office.

———. 1976. "Sexual Behavior." In *Contemporary Social Problems*, edited by Robert K. Merton and Robert Nisbet, 219–261. New York: Harcourt Brace Jovanovich.

Davis, Kingsley, and Judith Blake. 1956. "Social Structure and Fertility: An Analytic Framework." *Economic Development and Cultural Change* 4:211–235.

Davis, Kingsley, and Pietronella van den Oever. 1982. "Demographic Foundations of New Sex Roles." *Population and Development Review* 8:495–511.

Davis, Nancy Jean. 1982. "Childless and Single-Childed Women in Early Twentieth Century America." *Journal of Family Issues* 3:431–458.

DeCherney, Alan H., and Gertrude S. Berkowitz. 1982. "Female Fecundity and Age." *The New England Journal of Medicine* 306:424–426.

Devaney, Barbara. 1983. "An Analysis of Variations in U.S. Fertility and Female Labor Force Participation Trends." *Demography* 20:147–161.

Donaldson, Peter J. Forthcoming. *Nature Against Us: American Foreign Assistance and the Problem of Rapid Population Growth.*

Dore, Ronald Philip. 1959. "Japan: Country of Accelerated Transition; A Review Article." *Population Studies* 13:103–111.

Driver, Edwin D. 1963. *Differential Fertility in Central India.* Princeton, N.J.: Princeton Unversity Press.

Duncan, Otis Dudley. 1943. "Rural-Urban Variations in the Age of Parents at the Birth of the First Child." *Rural Sociology* 8:62–67.

Duncan, Otis Dudley, and Albert J. Reiss, Jr. 1956. *Social Characteristics of Urban and Rural Communities, 1950.* New York: Wiley. Reprint. New York: Russell & Russell, 1976.

Easterlin, Richard Ainley. 1962. "The American Baby Boom in Historical Perspective." Occasional Paper no. 79. New York: National Bureau of Economic Research.

———. 1966. "On the Relation of Economic Factors to Recent and Projected Fertility Changes." *Demography* 3:131–153.

———. 1973. "Relative Economic Status and the American Fertility Swing." In *Family Economic Behavior: Problems and Prospects,* edited by Eleanor Bernert Sheldon, 170–223. Philadelphia: Lippincott.

———. 1978. "What Will 1984 Be Like? Socioeconomic Implications of Recent Twists in Age Structure." *Demography* 15:397–432.

———. 1980. *Birth and Fortune: The Impact of Numbers on Personal Welfare.* New York: Basic Books.

Edmonds, D. Keith, Kevin S. Lindsay, John F. Miller, Elsbeth Williamson, and Peter J. Wood. 1982. "Early Embryonic Mortality in Women." *Fertility and Sterility* 38:447–453.

Ehrenreich, Barbara. 1983. *The Hearts of Men: American Dreams and the Flight from Commitment.* Garden City, N.Y.: Anchor Press/Doubleday.

Elder, Glen H., Jr. 1974. *Children of the Great Depression: Social Change in Life Experience.* Chicago: University of Chicago Press.

———. 1975. "Age Differentiation and the Life Course." In *Annual Review of Sociology,* Vol. 1, edited by Alex Inkeles, James Coleman, and Neil Smelser, 165–190. Palo Alto, Calif.: Annual Reviews.

———. 1978. "Approaches to Social Change and the Family." *American Journal of Sociology* 84(Supplement):S1–S38.

———. 1985. "Perspectives on the Life Course." In *Life Course Dynam-*

ics: Trajectories and Transitions, 1968–1980s, edited by Glen H. Elder, Jr., 23–49. Ithaca, N.Y.: Cornell University Press.

Espenshade, Thomas J. 1985. "Marriage Trends in America: Estimates, Implications, and Underlying Causes." *Population and Development Review* 11:193–245.

Evans, M. D. R. 1986. "American Fertility Patterns: A Comparison of White and Nonwhite Cohorts Born 1903–1956." *Population and Development Review* 12:267–293.

Evans-Pritchard, Edward Evan. 1951. *Kinship and Marriage Among the Nuer.* Oxford, England: Clarendon Press.

Eveleth, Phyllis B. 1986. "Timing of Menarche: Secular Trend and Population Differences." In *School-Age Pregnancy and Parenthood,* edited by Jane Lancaster and Beatrix A. Hamburg, 39–52. New York: Aldine & DeGruyter.

Farley, Reynolds. 1970. *Growth of the Black Population: A Study of Demographic Trends.* Chicago: Rand McNally.

———. 1984. *Blacks and Whites: Narrowing the Gap?* Cambridge, Mass.: Harvard University Press.

Featherman, David L., and Robert M. Hauser. 1978. *Opportunity and Change.* Studies in Population. New York: Academic Press.

Featherman, David L., Dennis P. Hogan, and Aage B. Sørensen. 1983. "Entry into Adulthood: Profiles of Young Men in the 1950s." CDE Working Paper 83–38. Madison: Center for Demography and Ecology, University of Wisconsin-Madison.

Fienberg, Stephen E., and William M. Mason. 1978. "Identification and Estimation of Age-Period-Cohort Models in the Analysis of Discrete Archival Data." In *Sociological Methodology, 1979,* edited by Karl Schuessler, 1–67. San Francisco: Jossey-Bass.

Fracchia, John, Charles Sheppard, and Sidney Merlis. 1974. "Early Cigarette Smoking and Drug Use: Some Comments, Data and Thoughts." *Psychological Reports* 34:371–374.

Freedman, Ronald. 1962. "American Studies of Family Planning and Fertility: A Review of Major Trends and Issues." In *Research in Family Planning,* edited by Clyde Vernon Kiser, 211–227. Princeton, N.J.: Princeton University Press.

Freedman, Ronald, Pascal Kidder Whelpton, and Arthur A. Campbell. 1959. *Family Planning, Sterility, and Population Growth.* McGraw-Hill Series in Sociology. New York: McGraw-Hill.

Frejka, Tomas. 1980. "Fertility Trends and Policies: Czechoslovakia in the 1970s." Center for Policy Studies Working Paper no. 54. New York: Center for Policy Studies, Population Council.

French, Dwight K. 1978. "National Survey of Family Growth, Cycle I: Sample Design, Estimation Procedures, and Variance Estimation." *Vital and Health Statistics, Data Evaluation and Methods Research,* ser. 2, no. 76. Hyattsville, Md.: National Center for Health Statistics, Public Health Service, U.S. Department of Health, Education, and Welfare.

Freshnock, Larry, and Phillips Cutright. 1978. "Structural Determinants of Childlessness: A Nonrecursive Analysis of 1970 U.S. Rates." *Social Biology* 25:169–178.

Frisch, Rose E. 1978. "Population, Food Intake and Fertility." *Science* 199(4344):22–30.

Furstenberg, Frank F., Jr., Jeanne Brooks-Gunn, and S. Philip Morgan. 1987. *Adolescent Mothers in Later Life.* Cambridge, Mass.: Cambridge University Press.

Furstenberg, Frank F., Jr., S. Philip Morgan, Kristin A. Moore, and James L. Peterson. 1987. "Race Differences in the Timing of Adolescent Intercourse." *American Sociological Review* 52:511–518.

Furstenberg, Frank F., Jr., Christine Winquist Nord, James L. Peterson, and Nicholas Zill. 1983. "The Life Course of Children of Divorce: Marital Disruption and Parental Contact." *American Sociological Review* 48:656–668.

Gerson, Kathleen. 1985. *Hard Choices: How Women Decide about Work, Career, and Motherhood.* Berkeley, Los Angeles, London: University of California Press.

Giddens, Anthony. 1985. "Work Institutions and the Sociology of Everyday Life." Plenary presentation at the annual meeting of the American Sociological Association, Washington, D.C., 26–30 August.

Glenn, Norval D. 1976. "Cohort Analysts' Futile Quest: Statistical Attempts to Separate Age, Period and Cohort Effects." *American Sociological Review* 41(5):900–904.

Glick, Paul C. 1947. "The Family Cycle." *American Sociological Review* 12:164–174.

——. 1955. "The Life Cycle of the Family." *Marriage and Family Living* 17:3–9.

——. 1977. "Updating the Life Cycle of the Family." *Journal of Marriage and the Family* 39:5–13.

Glick, Paul C., and Arthur J. Norton. 1977. "Marrying, Divorcing, and

Living Together in the U.S. Today." *Population Bulletin* 32(5).

Glick, Paul C., and Robert Parke, Jr. 1965. "New Approaches in Studying the Life Cycle of the Family." *Demography* 2:187–202.

Glick, Paul C., and Graham B. Spanier. 1980. "Married and Unmarried Cohabitation in the United States." *Journal of Marriage and the Family* 42:19–30.

Goldscheider, Calvin, and Peter R. Uhlenberg. 1969. "Minority Group Status and Fertility." *American Journal of Sociology* 74:361–372.

Goldscheider, Frances Kobrin, and Julie DaVanzo. 1985. "Living Arrangements and the Transition to Adulthood." *Demography* 22: 545–563.

Goldstein, Sidney, Alice Goldstein, and Sauvaluck Piampiti. 1973. "The Effect of Broken Marriage on Fertility Levels in Thailand." Institute of Population Studies Paper no. 4. Bangkok: Institute of Population Studies, Chulalongkorn University.

Goode, William J. 1963. *World Revolution and Family Patterns*. Glencoe, Ill.: Free Press.

Goode, William J. 1982. *The Family*. 2d ed. Englewood Cliffs, N.J.: Prentice-Hall.

Gove, Walter, and Michael Hughes. 1979. "Possible Causes of the Apparent Sex Differences in Physical Health: An Empirical Investigation." *American Sociological Review* 44:126–146.

Greeley, Andrew M., William C. McCready, and Kathleen McCourt. 1976. *Catholic Schools in a Declining Church*. Kansas City, Kans.: Sheed & Ward.

Guidubaldi, John, Bonnie Nastasi, Helen Cheminshaw, and Joseph Perry. 1986. "Maternal Employment and Child Adjustment: Results of a National Study." Paper presented at the annual meeting of the American Psychological Association, Washington, D.C., August.

Guilkey, David K., and Ronald R. Rindfuss. 1987. "Logistic Regression Multivariate Life Tables: A Communicable Approach." *Sociological Methods and Research*.

Gustavus, Susan O., and James R. Henley, Jr. 1971. "Correlates of Voluntary Childlessness in a Select Population." *Social Biology* 18: 277–284.

Gustavus, Susan O., and Charles B. Nam. 1970. "The Formation and Stability of Ideal Family Size among Young People." *Demography* 7:43–51.

Haggstrom, Gus W., Thomas J. Blaschke, David E. Kanouse, William

Lisowski, and Peter A. Morrison. 1981. "Teenage Parents: Their Ambitions and Attainments." Rand Report R–2771–NICHD. Santa Monica, Calif.: Rand Corporation.

Haggstrom, Gus W., Linda J. Waite, David E. Kanouse, and Thomas J. Blaschke. 1984. *Changes in the Lifestyles of New Parents.* Rand Report R–3182–NICHD. Santa Monica, Calif.: Rand Corporation.

Harrell, Frank. 1980. "The Logist Procedure." In *SAS Supplemental Library User's Guide,* edited by P. S. Reinhardt, 83–102. N.C.: SAS Institute.

Hartley, Shirley F. 1975. *Illegitimacy.* Berkeley, Los Angeles, London: University of California Press.

Hastings, Donald W., and J. Gregory Robinson. 1974. "Incidence of Childlessness for United States Women, Cohorts Born 1891–1945." *Social Biology* 21:178–184.

Hendershot, Gerry E., William D. Mosher, and William F. Pratt. 1982. "Infertility and Age: An Unresolved Issue." *Family Planning Perspectives* 14:287–290.

Heuser, Robert L. 1976. *Fertility Tables for Birth Cohorts by Color: U.S. 1917–73.* DHEW Publication no. HRA 76–1152. Rockville, Md.: National Center for Health Statistics.

Hirschman, Charles, and Ronald R. Rindfuss. 1982. "The Sequence and Timing of Family Formation Events in Asia." *American Sociological Review* 47:660–680.

Hirschman, Charles, and Morrison G. Wong. 1981. "Trends in Socioeconomic Achievement among Immigrant and Native-Born Asian-Americans, 1960–1976." *The Sociological Quarterly* 22:495–513.

Hoem, Jan M., and Bo Rennermalm. 1985. "Modern Family Initiation in Sweden: Experience of Women Born between 1936 and 1960." *European Journal of Population* 1:81–112.

Hofferth, Sandra L. 1983. "Time Cost of a Baby: New Estimates from a Dynamic, Sequential Model." Paper presented at the annual meeting of the American Sociological Association, Detroit, 31 August–4 September.

———. 1984. "A Comment on 'Social Determinants of Age at First Birth.'" *Journal of Marriage and the Family* 46:7–8.

Hofferth, Sandra L., and Kristin A. Moore. 1979. "Early Childbearing and Later Economic Well-Being." *American Sociological Review* 44: 784–815.

Hogan, Dennis P. 1978. "The Variable Order of Events in the Life

Course." *American Sociological Review* 43:573–586.

———. 1980. "The Transition to Adulthood as a Career Contingency." *American Sociological Review* 45:261–276.

———. 1981. *Transitions and Social Change: The Early Lives of American Men.* Studies in Population. New York: Academic Press.

Hogan, Dennis P., Takashi Mochizuki, and Yoriko Meguro. 1985. "Demographic Transitions and the Life Course: Lessons from Japanese and American Comparisons." Paper presented at the annual meeting of the American Sociological Association, Washington, D.C., 26–30 August.

Houseknecht, Sharon K. 1979. "Female Employment and Reduced Family Size: Some Additional Insight on the Direction of the Relationship." Paper presented at the annual meeting of the American Sociological Association, Boston, 27–31 August.

Japan. Institute of Population Problems. 1983. *Japan. The Eighth National Fertility Survey, 1982: The Second Report. Views about Marriage and Children among Single Young People.* Tokyo: Institute of Population Problems.

Jencks, Christopher. 1979. *Who Gets Ahead. The Determinants of Economic Success.* New York: Basic Books.

Jencks, Christopher, Marshall Smith, Henry Acland, Mary Jo Bane, David Cohen, Herbert Gintis, Barbara Heyns, and Stephan Michelson. 1972. *Inequality: A Reassessment of Family and Schooling in America.* New York: Basic Books.

Jessor, Richard, and Shirley L. Jessor. 1977. *Problem Behavior and Psychosocial Development: A Longitudinal Study of Youth.* New York: Academic Press.

Johnson, Nan E. 1979. "Minority-Group Status and the Fertility of Black Americans, 1970: A New Look." *American Journal of Sociology* 84: 1386–1400.

———. 1982. "Religious Differentials in Reproduction: The Effects of Sectarian Education." *Demography* 19:495–509.

Johnston, John. 1972. *Econometric Methods.* 2d ed. New York: McGraw-Hill.

Jones, Elise F., Jacqueline Forrest, Noreen Goldman, Stanley Henshaw, Richard Lincoln, Jeannie Rosoff, Charles Westoff, and Deirdre Wulf. 1985. "Teenage Pregnancy in Developed Countries: Determinants and Policy Implications." *Family Planning Perspectives* 17:53–63.

Jones, Jo Ann, Joan R. Kahn, Allan M. Parnell, Ronald R. Rindfuss, and C. Gray Swicegood. 1985. "Non-Marital Childbearing: Diverging Legal and Social Concerns." *Population and Development Review* 11:677–693.

Kasarda, John D., John O. G. Billy, and Kirsten West. 1986. *Status Enhancement and Fertility. Reproductive Responses to Social Mobility and Educational Opportunity.* Orlando: Academic Press.

Keizaikikaku-Cho, ed. 1973. *Seikatsu Jikan no Kokusai Hikaku Chosa* [International comparative time allocation survey]. Tokyo: Printing Office, Ministry of Finance. (In Japanese.)

Kett, Joseph F. 1979. *Rites of Passage: Adolescence in America 1790 to the Present.* New York: Basic Books.

Keyfitz, Nathan. 1984. "The Population of China." *Scientific American* 250(2):38–47.

Kiernan, Kathleen E. 1977. "Age at Puberty in Relation to Age at Marriage and Parenthood: A National Longitudinal Study." *Annals of Human Biology* 4:301–308.

Kiernan, Kathleen E., and Ian R. Diamond. 1983. "The Age at Which Childbearing Starts—A Longitudinal Study." *Population Studies* 37: 363–380.

Kumagai, Fumie. 1983. "Changing Divorce in Japan." *Journal of Family History* 8:85–108.

Kuper, A. 1970. "The Kgalagari and the Jural Consequences of Marriage." *Man* 5:466–482.

Langsten, Raymond Lewis. 1980. "Causes of Changes in Vital Rates: The Case of Bangladesh." Ph.D. dissertation, University of Michigan.

Lee, Anne, and Everett Lee. 1959. "The Future Fertility of the American Negro." *Social Forces* 37:228–231.

Leibowitz, Arleen, Marvin Eisen, and Winston K. Chow. 1986. "An Economic Model of Teenage Pregnancy Decision-making." *Demography* 23:67–77.

Lemann, Nicholas. 1986. "The Origins of the Underclass." *Atlantic Monthly* 257(6):31–55.

Leonetti, Donna Lockwood. 1978. "The Biocultural Pattern of Japanese-American Fertility." *Social Biology* 25:38–51.

Leridon, Henri. 1977. *Human Fertility: The Basic Components*, translated by Judith F. Helzner. Chicago: University of Chicago Press.

Lesthaeghe, Ron. 1980. "On the Social Control of Human Reproduction." *Population and Development Review* 6:527–548.

Levine, David. 1977. *Family Formation in an Age of Nascent Capitalism*. New York: Academic Press.

Lieberson, Stanley. 1985. *Making It Count: The Improvement of Social Research and Theory*. Berkeley, Los Angeles, London: University of California Press.

Lindert, Peter H. 1978. *Fertility and Scarcity in America*. Princeton, N.J.: Princeton University Press.

Loomis, Charles P., and C. Horace Hamilton. 1936. "Family Life Cycle Analysis." *Social Forces* 15:225–231.

Luker, Kristen. 1984. *Abortion and the Politics of Motherhood*. California Series on Social Choice and Political Economy. Berkeley, Los Angeles, London: University of California Press.

MacDonald, Maurice M., and Ronald R. Rindfuss. 1981. "Earnings, Relative Income, and Family Formation." *Demography* 18:123–136.

Marini, Margaret Mooney. 1978. "The Transition to Adulthood: Sex Differences in Educational Attainment and Age at Marriage." *American Sociological Review* 43:483–507.

———. 1984a. "Age and Sequencing Norms in the Transition to Adulthood." *Social Forces* 63:229–244.

———. 1984b. "Women's Educational Attainment and the Timing of Entry into Parenthood." *American Sociological Review* 49:491–511.

Masnick, George S. 1980a. "The Continuity of Birth-Expectations Data with Historical Trends in Cohort Parity Distribution: Implications for Fertility in the 1980's." In *Predicting Fertility*, edited by Gerry Hendershot and Paul Placek, 169–183. Lexington, Mass.: Lexington Books.

———. 1980b. "Historical Trends in Cohort Parity Distributions: Implications for Fertility in the 1980s." Paper presented at the annual meeting of the Population Association of America, Denver, 10–12 April.

Masnick, George S., and Joseph A. McFalls, Jr. 1976. "A New Perspective on the Twentieth-Century American Fertility Swing." *Journal of Family History* 1:217–244.

Mason, Karen Oppenheim. 1974. *Women's Labor Force Participation and Fertility*. Research Triangle Park, N.C.: Research Triangle Institute.

———. 1983. "Norms Relating to the Desire for Children." In *Determinants of Fertility in Developing Countries*. Vol. 1, edited by Rodolfo A. Bulatao and Ronald D. Lee, 388–428. New York: Academic Press.

Mason, Karen Oppenheim, and V. T. Palan. 1981. "Female Employment and Fertility in Peninsular Malaysia: The Maternal Role Incompatibility Hypothesis Reconsidered." *Demography* 18:549–575.

Mason, Karen Oppenheim, John L. Gzajka, and Sara Arber. 1976. "Changes in U.S. Women's Sex Role Attitudes, 1964–1974." *American Sociological Review* 41:573–596.

Mason, Karen Oppenheim, William M. Mason, Halliman H. Winsborough, and William Kenneth Poole. 1973. "Some Methodological Issues in Cohort Analyses of Archival Data." *American Sociological Review* 38:242–258.

McFalls, Joseph A., Jr. 1973. "Impact of V.D. on the Fertility of the U.S. Black Population, 1880–1950." *Social Biology* 20:2–19.

McNicoll, Geoffrey. 1980. "Institutional Determinants of Fertility Change." *Population and Development Review* 6:441–462.

Menken, Jane L. 1985. "Age and Fertility: How Late Can You Wait?" *Demography* 22:469–483.

Michael, Robert T., and Nancy Brandon Tuma. 1985. "Entry into Marriage and Parenthood by Young Men and Women: The Influence of Family Background." *Demography* 22:515—544.

Miller, John F., J. Glue, and Elsbeth Williamson. 1980. "Fetal Loss After Implantation: A Prospective Study." *Lancet* 2(8194):554–556.

Modell, John. 1980. "Normative Aspects of American Marriage Timing Since World War II." *Journal of Family History* 5:210–234.

Modell, John, Frank F. Furstenberg, Jr., and Theodore Hershberg. 1976. "Social Change and Transitions to Adulthood in Historical Perspective." *Journal of Family History* 1:7–32.

Modell, John, Frank F. Furstenberg, Jr., and Douglas Strong. 1978. "The Timing of Marriage in the Transition to Adulthood: Continuity and Change, 1860–1975." In *Turning Points: Historical and Sociological Essays on the Family*, edited by John Demos and Sarane Spence Boocock, S120–150. Chicago: University of Chicago Press. Supplement to *American Journal of Sociology*, Vol. 84.

Morgan, S. Philip. 1981. "Intention and Uncertainty at Later States of Childbearing: The United States 1965 and 1970." *Demography* 18: 267–285.

———. 1982. "Parity-Specific Fertility Intentions and Uncertainty: The United States 1970 to 1976." *Demography* 19:315–334.

———. 1985. "Individual and Couple Intentions for More Children." *Demography* 22:125–132.

Morgan, S. Philip, and Kiyosi Hirosima. 1983. "The Persistence of Extended Family Residence in Japan: Anachronism or Alternative Strategy?" *American Sociological Review* 48:269–281.

Morgan, S. Philip, and Tim. F. Lio. 1985. "A Cautionary Note on the Analysis of Life Cycle Events: Comments on Smith and Meitz." *Journal of Marriage and the Family* 47:233–236.

Morgan, S. Philip, and Ronald R. Rindfuss. 1985. "Marital Disruption: Structural and Temporal Dimensions." *American Journal of Sociology* 90:1055–1077.

Mosher, William D. 1986. "Fecundity, Infertility and Reproductive Health in the United States: 1982." *Vital and Health Statistics, Data from the National Survey of Family Growth*, ser. 23, no. 14. Hyattsville, Md.: National Center for Health Statistics, Public Health Service, U.S. Department of Health, Education, and Welfare.

Mosk, Carl, ed. 1983. *Patriarchy and Fertility: The Evolution of Natality in Japan and Sweden, 1880–1960*. New York: Academic Press.

Muñoz-Perez, Francisco. 1979. "L'Évolution récente des premiers marriages dans quelques pays Européens." *Population* 34:649–694.

Namboodiri, N. Krishnan. 1974. "Which Couples at Given Parities Expect to Have Additional Births? An Exercise in Discriminant Analysis." *Demography* 11:45–56.

———. 1981. "On Factors Affecting Fertility at Different Stages in the Reproduction History: An Exercise in Cohort Analysis." *Social Forces* 59:1114–1129.

National Center for Health Statistics. 1979. *National Survey of Family Growth, Cycle 2: Tape Contents Manual, Respondent File*. Report no. NCHS/DF-79/012A. Hyattsville, Md.: National Center for Health Statistics.

Neugarten, Bernice L., and Nancy Datan. 1973. "Sociological Perspectives on the Life Cycle." In *Life-Span Developmental Psychology: Personality and Socialization*, edited by Paul B. Baltes and K. Warner Schaie. New York: Academic Press.

Neugarten, Bernice L., and Gunhild O. Hagestad. 1985. "Age and the Life Course." In *Handbook of Aging and the Social Sciences*, 2d ed., edited by Robert H. Binstock and Ethel Shanas, 35–61. New York: Van Nostrand.

Neugarten, Bernice L., Joan W. Moore, and John C. Lowe. 1965. "Age Norms, Age Constraints, and Adult Socialization." *American Journal of Sociology* 70:710–717.

O'Connell, Martin, and Carolyn C. Rogers. 1984. "Out-of-Wedlock Births, Premarital Pregnancies and Their Effect on Family Formation and Dissolution." *Family Planning Perspectives* 16:157–162.

Olneck, Michael R., and Barbara L. Wolfe. 1978. "A Note on Some Evidence on the Easterlin Hypothesis." *Journal of Political Economy* 86: 953–958.

Osako, Masako Murakami. 1978. "Dilemmas of Japanese Professional Women." *Social Problems* 26:15–25.

Page, Hilary J. 1986. "Childbearing and Childrearing: Co-Residence of Mothers and Children in Tropical Africa." Paper presented at the annual meeting of the Population Association of America, San Francisco, 2–5 April.

Parsons, Talcott. 1955. "Family Structure and the Socialization of the Child." In *Family, Socialization and Interaction Process*, edited by Talcott Parsons and Robert F. Bales, in collaboration with James Olds, Morris Zelditch, Jr., and Philip E. Slater, 35–131. New York: Free Press.

Pitcher, Brian L. 1980. "Cohort Variations in the Timing of Marriage and First Birth." Population Research Laboratory Working Paper Series no. 80–1. Logan: Utah State University.

Poston, Dudley L., Jr., and Erin Gotard. 1977. "Trends in Childlessness in the United States, 1910–1975." *Social Biology* 24:212–224.

Presser, Harriet B. 1978. "Age at Menarche, Socio-Sexual Behavior, and Fertility." *Social Biology* 25:94–101.

Presser, Harriet B., and Virginia S. Cain. 1983. "Shift Work among Dual-Earner Couples with Children." *Science* 219(4586):876–879.

Preston, Samuel H. 1986. "The Decline of Fertility in Non-European Industrialized Countries." In *Below-Replacement Fertility in Industrial Societies: Causes, Consequences, Policies*. New York: The Population Council.

Preston, Samuel H., and John McDonald. 1979. "The Incidence of Divorce within Cohorts of American Marriages Contracted Since the Civil War." *Demography* 16:1–26.

Pullum, Thomas W. 1980. "Separating Age, Period, and Cohort Effects in White U.S. Fertility, 1920–1970." *Social Science Research* 9:225–244.

Rainwater, Lee. 1965. *Family Design: Marital Sexuality, Family Size, and Contraception*. Chicago: Aldine.

―――. 1966. "Crucible of Identity: The Negro Lower-Class Family." *Daedalus* 95:172–216.

Reynolds, Carl, and Robert Nichols. 1976. "Personality and Behavioral Correlates of Cigarette Smoking: One-Year Follow-Up." *Psychological Reports* 38:251–258.

Riccobono, John, Louise B. Henderson, Graham J. Burkheimer, Carol Place, and Jay R. Levinsohn. 1981. *National Longitudinal Study: Base Year (1972) through Fourth Follow-Up (1979) Data File Users Manual.* 3 vols. National Longitudinal Study Sponsored Report Series. RTI/ 0884/73–18S. Prepared for National Center for Education Statistics, Office of the Assistant Secretary for Educational Research and Improvement, U.S. Department of Education. Research Triangle Park, N.C.: Research Triangle Institute.

Riley, Matilda White. 1985. "Age Strata in Social Systems." In *Handbook of Aging and the Social Sciences*, 2d ed., edited by Robert H. Binstock and Ethel Shanas, 369–411. New York: Van Nostrand.

Riley, Matilda White, Marilyn E. Johnson, and Anne Foner. 1972. *Aging and Society.* Vol. 3. *A Sociology of Age Stratification.* New York: Russell Sage Foundation.

Rindfuss, Ronald R. 1978. "Changing Patterns of Fertility in the South: A Social-Demographic Examination." *Social Forces* 57:621–635.

Rindfuss, Ronald R., and Larry L. Bumpass. 1977. "Fertility during Marital Disruption." *Journal of Marriage and the Family* 39:517–528.

―――. 1978. "Age and the Sociology of Fertility: How Old Is Too Old?" In *Social Demography*, edited by Karl E. Taeuber, Larry L. Bumpass, and James A. Sweet, 43–56. Studies in Population. New York: Academic Press.

Rindfuss, Ronald R., and Charles Hirschman. 1984. "Timing of Family Formation: Structural and Societal Factors in the Asian Context." *Journal of Marriage and the Family* 46:205–214.

Rindfuss, Ronald R., and Maurice M. MacDonald. 1980. "Earnings, Relative Income, and Family Formation, Part II: Fertility." Discussion Paper 616–680. Madison: Center for Demography and Ecology, University of Wisconsin-Madison.

Rindfuss, Ronald R., and S. Philip Morgan. 1983. "Marriage, Sex, and the First Birth Interval: The Quiet Revolution in Asia." *Population and Development Review* 9:259–278.

Rindfuss, Ronald R., and Allan M. Parnell. 1986. "How Much Does

Marriage Matter, Anyhow?" Paper presented at the annual meeting of the Population Association of America, San Francisco, 2–5 April.

Rindfuss, Ronald R., and Craig St. John. 1983. "Social Determinants of Age at First Birth." *Journal of Marriage and the Family* 45:553–565.

Rindfuss, Ronald R., and James A. Sweet. 1977. *Postwar Fertility Trends and Differentials in the United States.* Studies in Population Series. New York: Academic Press.

Rindfuss, Ronald R., and Charles F. Westoff. 1974. "The Initiation of Contraception." *Demography* 11:75–87.

Rindfuss, Ronald R., Larry L. Bumpass, and Craig St. John. 1980. "Education and Fertility: Implications for the Roles Women Occupy." *American Sociological Review* 45:431–447.

Rindfuss, Ronald R., S. Philip Morgan, and C. Gray Swicegood. 1984. "The Transition to Motherhood: The Intersection of Structural and Temporal Dimensions." *American Sociological Review* 49:359–372.

Rindfuss, Ronald R., James A. Palmore, Jr., and Larry L. Bumpass. 1982. "Selectivity and the Analysis of Birth Intervals from Survey Data." *Asian and Pacific Census Forum* 8(3):5–16.

Rindfuss, Ronald R., Allan M. Parnell, and Charles Hirschman. 1983. "The Timing of Entry into Motherhood in Asia: A Comparative Perspective." *Population Studies* 37:253–272.

Rindfuss, Ronald R., Craig St. John, and Larry L. Bumpass. 1984. "Education and the Timing of Motherhood: Disentangling Causation." *Journal of Marriage and the Family* 46:981–984.

Rindfuss, Ronald R., C. Gray Swicegood, and Larry L. Bumpass. 1986. "Contraceptive Choice in the United States: Process, Determinants and Change." Carolina Population Center, The University of North Carolina at Chapel Hill. Typescript.

Rindfuss, Ronald R., C. Gray Swicegood, and Rachel A. Rosenfeld. 1987. "Disorder in the Life Course: How Common and Does It Matter?" *American Sociological Review* 52 (December).

Rodgers, Willard L. 1982. "Estimable Functions of Age, Period, and Cohort Effects." *American Sociological Review* 47:774–787.

Rodgers, Willard L., and Arland Thornton. 1985. "Changing Patterns of First Marriage in the United States." *Demography* 22:265–279.

Rohlen, Thomas P. 1974. *For Harmony and Strength: Japanese White-Collar Organization in Anthropological Perspective.* Berkeley: University of California Press.

Rossi, Alice S. 1968. "Transition to Parenthood." *Journal of Marriage and the Family* 30:26–39.

Ryder, Norman B. 1956. "Problems of Trend Determination During a Transition in Fertility." *Milbank Memorial Fund Quarterly* 34:5–21.

———. 1965. "The Cohort as a Concept in the Study of Social Change." *American Sociological Review* 30:843–861.

———. 1969. "The Emergence of a Modern Fertility Pattern: United States, 1917–1966." In *Fertility and Family Planning: A World View*, edited by Samuel J. Behrman, Leslie Corsa, Jr., and Ronald Freedman, 99–123. Ann Arbor: University of Michigan Press.

———. 1973a. "A Critique of the National Fertility Study." *Demography* 10:495–506.

———. 1973b. "Recent Trends and Group Differences in Fertility." In *Toward the End of Growth. Population in America*, 57–68. A Spectrum Book. Englewood Cliffs, N.J.: Prentice-Hall.

———. 1974. "The Family in Developed Countries." *Scientific American* 23(1):122–132.

———. 1979. "The Future of American Fertility." *Social Problems* 26: 359–370.

———. 1980a. "Components of Temporal Variations in American Fertility." In *Demographic Patterns in Developed Societies*, Vol. 19, edited by Robert W. Hiorns, 15–54. Symposia of the Society for the Study of Human Biology. London: Taylor & Francis.

———. 1980b. "Where Do Babies Come From?" In *Sociological Theory and Research: A Critical Appraisal*, edited by Hubert M. Blalock, Jr., 189–202. A publication of the American Sociological Association. New York: Free Press.

———. 1983. "Fertility and Family Structure." *Population Bulletin of the United Nations* no. 15:15–34.

Ryder, Norman B., and Charles F. Westoff. 1971. *Reproduction in the United States, 1965*. Princeton, N.J.: Princeton University Press.

Santi, Lawrence. 1980. "Confidence in Selected Institutions in 1975: An Attempt at Replication Across Two National Surveys." *Social Indicators Research* 7:401–418.

Schwartz, Daniel, and M. J. Mayaux. 1982. "Female Fecundity as a Function of Age." *New England Journal of Medicine* 306:404–406.

Sheps, Mindel C., and Jane A. Menken. 1973. *Mathematical Models of Conception and Birth*. Chicago: University of Chicago Press.

Sherris, Jacqueline D., and Gordon Fox. 1983. "Infertility and Sexually

Transmitted Disease: A Public Health Challenge." *Population Reports,*
Series L: Issues in World Health, no. 4.

Shryock, Henry Soladay, Jr., Jacob S. Siegel, and Associates. 1971. *The*
Methods and Materials of Demography. 2 vols. Washington, D.C.:
Bureau of the Census, U.S. Department of Commerce.

Sklar, June, and Beth Berkov. 1975. "The American Birth Rate: Evi-
dences of a Coming Rise." *Science* 189(4204):693–700.

Sly, David F. 1970. "Minority Group Status and Fertility: An Extension
of Goldscheider and Uhlenberg." *American Journal of Sociology* 76:
443–459.

Smith, David P. 1981. "A Reconsideration of Easterlin Cycles." *Popula-*
tion Studies 35:247–264.

Smith, Tom W. 1982. "House Effects and the Reproducibility of Survey
Measurements: A Comparison of the 1980 GSS and the 1980 American National Election Study." *Public Opinion Quarterly* 46:54–68.

Smith-Lovin, Lynn, and Ann R. Tickameyer. 1978. "Nonrecursive
Models of Labor Force Participation, Fertility Behavior and Sex Role
Attitudes." *American Sociological Review* 43:541–557.

Sørenson, Annemette. 1984. "Role Transitions in Young Men's Lives:
Reversibility, Time between Events and Age Grading of Transitions."
CDE Working Paper 83–25. Madison: Center for Demography and
Ecology, University of Wisconsin-Madison.

Spanier, Graham B. 1983. "Married and Unmarried Cohabitation in the
United States: 1980." *Journal of Marriage and the Family* 45:277–288.

Spitze, Glenna D. 1978. "Role Experiences of Young Women: A Longitudinal Test of the Role Hiatus Hypothesis." *Journal of Marriage and*
the Family 40:471–479.

St. John, Craig. 1982. "Race Differences in Age at First Birth and the
Pace of Subsequent Fertility: Implications for the Minority Group
Status Hypothesis." *Demography* 19:301–314.

St. John, Craig, and Harold G. Grasmick. 1985. "Decomposing the
Black/White Fertility Differential." *Social Science Quarterly* 66:132–
146.

Stack, Carol B. 1974. *All Our Kin: Strategies for Survival in a Black*
Community. New York: Harper & Row.

Stolzenberg, Ross M. 1979. "The Measurement and Decomposition of
Causal Effects in Nonlinear and Nonadditive Models." In *Sociological*
Methodology 1980, edited by Karl F. Schuessler, 459–488. The Jossey-
Bass Social and Behavioral Science Series. San Francisco: Jossey-Bass.

Stolzenberg, Ross M., and Linda J. Waite. 1977. "Age, Fertility Expectations and Plans for Employment." *American Sociological Review* 42:769–783.

Swafford, Michael. 1978. "Sex Differences in Soviet Earnings." *American Sociological Review* 43:657–673.

Sweet, James A., and Ronald R. Rindfuss. 1983. "Those Ubiquitous Fertility Trends: United States, 1945–1979." *Social Biology* 30:127–139.

Swicegood, C. Gray, S. Philip Morgan, and Ronald R. Rindfuss. 1984. "Measurement and Replication: Evaluating the Consistency of Eight U.S. Fertility Surveys." *Demography* 21:19–23.

Swidler, Ann. 1983. "Love and Adulthood in American Culture." In *Family in Transition: Rethinking Marriage, Sexuality, Child Rearing and Family Organization*, compiled by Arlene S. Skolnick and Jerome H. Skolnick, 286–305. 4th ed. Boston: Little, Brown.

Taeuber, Irene B. 1958. *The Population of Japan*. Princeton, N.J.: Princeton University Press.

Tanner, James Mourilyan. 1981. *A History of the Study of Human Growth*. Cambridge: Cambridge University Press.

Teachman, Jay D., and Daniel Alex Heckert. 1985. "The Declining Significance of First-Birth Timing." *Demography* 22:185–198.

Teachman, Jay D., and Karen A. Polonko. 1983. "Delayed Childbearing Within Marriage: An Analysis Using Life Tables and Proportional Hazards Models." Final report, contract no. NO1–HD–12026. Washington, D.C. National Institute of Child Health and Human Development.

Theil, Henri. 1970. "On the Estimation of Relationships Involving Qualitative Variables." *American Journal of Sociology* 76:103–154.

Thoen, Gail Ann. 1977. "Commitment among Voluntary Childfree Couples to a Variant Lifestyle." Ph.D. dissertation, University of Minnesota.

Thornton, Arland, and Deborah Freedman. 1979. "Changes in the Sex Role Attitudes of Women, 1962–1977: Evidence from a Panel Study." *American Sociological Review* 44:831–842.

———. 1983. "The Changing American Family." *Population Bulletin* 38:1–43.

Thornton, Arland, Duane F. Alwin, and Donald Camburn. 1983. "Causes and Consequences of Sex Role Attitudes and Attitude Change." *American Sociological Review* 48:211–227.

Tolnay, Stewart E. 1985. "Black American Fertility Transition, 1880–1940." *Sociology and Social Research* 70:2–7.

Towman, Barbara. 1983. "Maternity Costs. Parenthood and Career Overtax Some Women Despite Best Intentions." *The Wall Street Journal* (7 Sept.):1, 23.

Treloar, Alan E., Ruth E. Boynton, and Donald W. Cowan. 1976. "Secular Trend in Age at Menarche, U.S.A.: 1893–1974." In *Biological and Clinical Aspects of Reproduction*, edited by Francis John Govier Ebling and I. W. Henderson, 25–28. Excerpta Medica International Congress Series no. 394. Amsterdam: Excerpta Medica.

Trost, Jan. 1975. "Married and Unmarried Cohabitation: The Case of Sweden with Some Comparisons." *Journal of Marriage and the Family* 37:677–682.

Trussell, James, and David E. Bloom. 1983. "Estimating the Co-variates of Age at Marriage and First Birth." *Population Studies* 37:403–416.

Tsui, Amy Ong. 1984. "Zero, One or Two Births: 1975 and 1980." Carolina Population Center Papers no. 31. Chapel Hill: Carolina Population Center, The University of North Carolina at Chapel Hill.

Turchi, Boone Alexander. 1975. *The Demand for Children: The Economics of Fertility in the United States.* Cambridge, Mass.: Ballinger.

U.S. Bureau of the Census. 1979. *Historical Statistics of the United States, Colonial Times to 1970.* Washington, D.C.: Bureau of the Census, U.S. Department of Commerce.

———. 1985. *Living Arrangements of Children and Adults.* 1980 Census of Population, Volume 2. Subject Reports, no. PC80–2–4B. Washington, D.C.: Bureau of the Census, U.S. Department of Commerce.

Udry, J. Richard. 1979. "Age at Menarche, at First Intercourse and at First Pregnancy." *Journal of Biosocial Science* 11:433–441.

Udry, J. Richard, and R. L. Cliquet. 1982. "A Cross-Cultural Examination of the Relationship between Ages at Menarche, Marriage, and First Birth." *Demography* 19:53–63.

Veevers, Jean E. 1973. "Voluntary Childless Wives: An Exploratory Study." *Sociology and Social Research* 57:356–366.

———. 1979. "Voluntary Childlessness: A Review of Issues and Evidence." *Marriage and Family Review* 2(2):3–26.

Ventura, Stephanie J. 1980. "Trends and Differentials in Births to Unmarried Women: United States 1970–76." *Vital and Health Statistics Series 21: Data from the National Vital Statistics System,* no. 36.

DHHS publication no. (PHS)80–1914. Hyattsville, Md.: U.S. National Center for Health Statistics.

Veroff, Joseph, Elizabeth Douvan, and Richard A. Kulka. 1981. *The Inner American: A Self-Portrait from 1957 to 1976.* New York: Basic Books.

Waite, Linda J. 1980. "Working Wives and the Family Life Cycle." *American Journal of Sociology* 86:272–294.

Waite, Linda J., Gus W. Haggstrom, and David E. Kanouse. 1985. "Changes in the Employment Activities of New Parents." *American Sociological Review* 50:263–272.

Walter, Carolyn Ambler. 1986. *The Timing of Motherhood.* Lexington, Mass.: Heath.

Watkins, Susan Cotts. 1981. "Regional Patterns of Nuptiality in Europe, 1870–1960." *Population Studies* 35:199–215.

———. 1984. "Spinsters." *Journal of Family History* 9:310–325.

———. 1986. "Conclusions." In *The Decline of Fertility in Europe; the Revised Proceedings of a Conference on the Princeton European Fertility Project,* edited by Ansley J. Coale and Susan Cotts Watkins, 420–449. Princeton, N.J.: Princeton University Press.

Weitzman, Lenore J. 1985. *The Divorce Revolution.* New York: Free Press.

Welsh, Finis. 1981. "Affirmative Action and Its Enforcement." *American Economic Review* 71:127–133.

Westoff, Charles F. 1978. "Some Speculations on the Future of Marriage and Fertility." *Family Planning Perspectives* 10:79–83.

Westoff, Charles F., and Elise F. Jones. 1977. "The Secularization of U.S. Catholic Birth Control Practices." *Family Planning Perspectives* 9:203–207.

———. 1979. "The End of 'Catholic' Fertility." *Demography* 16:209–217.

Westoff, Charles F., and Norman B. Ryder. 1977. *The Contraceptive Revolution.* Princeton, N.J.: Princeton University Press.

———. 1977. "The Predictive Validity of Reproductive Intentions." *Demography* 14:431–453.

Westoff, Charles F., Gerard Calot, and Andrew D. Foster. 1983. "Teenage Fertility in Developed Nations: 1971–1980." *Family Planning Perspectives* 15:105–110.

Whelpton, Pascal Kidder, Arthur A. Campbell, and John E. Patterson.

1966. *Fertility and Family Planning in the United States.* Princeton, N.J.: Princeton University Press.

Whittaker, P. G., A. Taylor, and T. Lind. 1983. "Unsuspected Pregnancy Loss in Healthy Women." *Lancet* 1(8334):1126–1127.

Wilkie, Jane Riblett. 1981. "The Trend Toward Delayed Parenthood." *Journal of Marriage and the Family* 43:583–591.

Willis, Robert J. 1973. "A New Approach to the Economic Theory of Fertility Behavior." *Journal of Political Economy* 81(2, part 2):514–564.

Winsborough, Halliman H. 1978. "Statistical Histories of the Life Cycle of Birth Cohorts: The Transition from Schoolboy to Adult Male." In *Social Demography*, edited by Karl E. Taeuber, Larry L. Bumpass, and James A. Sweet, 231–259. Studies in Population. New York: Academic Press.

———. 1979. "Changes in the Transition to Adulthood." In *Aging from Birth to Death: Interdisciplinary Perspectives*, edited by Matilda White Riley, 137–152. AAAS Selected Symposium 30. Boulder, Colo.: Westview Press.

World Fertility Survey. 1979. *The 1974 Japan National Fertility Survey: A Summary of Findings.* London: World Fertility Survey.

Wrong, Dennis H. 1961. "The Oversocialized Conception of Man in Modern Sociology." *American Sociological Review* 26:183–193.

Yanagisako, Sylvia Junko. 1975*a*. "Social and Cultural Change in Japanese-American Kinship." Ph.D. dissertation, University of Washington, Seattle.

———. 1975. "Two Processes of Change in Japanese-American Kinship." *Anthropological Research* 31:196–224.

Zelnik, Melvin et al. 1981. *Determinants of Fertility Behavior among U.S. Females Aged 15–19. 1971 and 1976. Final Report.* Contract NO1–HD–82848. Baltimore: Johns Hopkins University.

Zelnik, Melvin, and John F. Kantner. 1978. "First Pregnancies to Women Aged 15–19: 1976 and 1971." *Family Planning Perspectives* 10:11–20.

———. 1980. "Sexual Activity, Contraceptive Use and Pregnancy Among Metropolitan Area Teenagers: 1971–1979." *Family Planning Perspectives* 12:230–237.

Author Index

Subject Index

33, 115–116, 117, 120, 138, 183, 184–186; and role incompatibility, 237–238; role of marriage, 34–38, 39; as set of sequential decisions, 220; and social context, 146, 160–161; socialization differences, 179, 183; social-psychological approach, 189; social-structural factors, 32–34, 101–102, 116–117, 213, 216, 217–218, 233; and society, 219; and socioeconomic background, 179, 180, 183; structural factors, 118–119; as transition to adulthood, 19; trends since 1930, 224; in U.S., 22, 60–61, 63, 63–65; in U.S. vs. Japan, 139–140; variation by origin status, 234; and waits to conception, 204; and women's roles, 231–232; and working part time vs. full time, 175, 177. See also First birth

Unanticipated births, 191; factors associated with, 199, 201
U.S. fertility: declining, 60; origin of norms, 23; surveys, 48–55; understanding through cross-national comparison, 139–140

Vital registration data, 13–14, 46–47, 64, 121, 122, 124, 141, 141n, 222
Voluntary childlessness, 10–11; by activity state and sex, 167; aggregate trends by age and race, 122, 124; changes in perception of, 23; by cohort, race, and relative education, 129–130; decision for, 26, 191–194; decisions about permanent, 195–197; and delayed child-

bearing, 75; determinants, 25–26; difficulty in predicting, 28–29; and education, 129–130; effects of NLS sample on levels, 193–194; in England vs. U.S., 64; expectations by year, 192–193; importance of young adulthood in determining, 163; instability of expectations, 194; in Japan, 65; pattern, 61; and race, 129–130, 135–136; racial differences by education, 135–136; as repeated postponement of parenthood, 26, 46, 192, 194, 234; sanctions against, 20; sharp increase in, 69, 71; stability of intentions, 191; trends by age, 64–65; undesirability, 19

Wage system, effect on Japanese marriage pattern, 144
Waits to conception, and first-birth timing, 204
Women: age of and fertility, 8–9, 162; careers and delayed childbearing, 9–10, 65, 136–137; changes in number aged 30–44, 68–69; effect of excluding never-married in study, 243–244, 246, 250
Women's movement. See Women's roles
Women's roles, 81, 218; and delayed childbearing, 9–10, 65; in Japan, 140, 142–143; major changes in, 228–229; and parenthood, 26–27, 237, 238–239; as related to men's, 239; and transition to parenthood, 216, 231–232. See also Motherhood
Working. See Labor force participation

Designer: U.C. Press Staff
Compositor: Janet Sheila Brown
Text: Stempel Garamond 10/13
Display: Stempel Garamond
Printer: Edwards Bros., Inc.
Binder: Edwards Bros., Inc.